CRIME & INEQUALITY

CRIME & INEQUALITY
READINGS FOR INTRODUCTION TO CRIMINOLOGY

A CUSTOM TEXTBOOK FROM
FERNWOOD PUBLISHING

Edited by
Dawn Anderson, Gillian Balfour, Elizabeth Comack,
Sandra Rollings-Magnusson and Bernard Schissel

*Compiled for Walid Chahal
Department of Sociology, Lakehead University*

FERNWOOD PUBLISHING
HALIFAX & WINNIPEG

Copyright © 2017 authors

-All rights reserved. No part of this book may be reproduced or transmitted in any form by any means without permission in writing from the publisher, except by a reviewer, who may quote brief passages in a review.

Editing: Jessica Antony
Cover design: John van der Woude
Printed and bound in Canada

Published by Fernwood Publishing
32 Oceanvista Lane, Black Point, Nova Scotia, B0J 1B0
and 748 Broadway Avenue, Winnipeg, Manitoba, R3G 0X3

www.fernwoodpublishing.ca

Fernwood Publishing Company Limited gratefully acknowledges the financial support of the Government of Canada, the Manitoba Department of Culture, Heritage and Tourism under the Manitoba Publishers Marketing Assistance Program and the Province of Manitoba, through the Book Publishing Tax Credit, for our publishing program. We are pleased to work in partnership with the Province of Nova Scotia to develop and promote our creative industries for the benefit of all Nova Scotians. We acknowledge the support of the Canada Council for the Arts, which last year invested $153 million to bring the arts to Canadians throughout the country.

Library and Archives Canada Cataloguing in Publication

Crime and inequality: readings for introduction to criminology : a custom textbook from Fernwood / compiled by Walid Chahal.

Includes bibliographical references.
ISBN 978-1-77363-044-1 (softcover)

1. Criminology--Canada--Textbooks. 2. Crime--Canada--Textbooks. 3. Equality--Canada--Textbooks. 4. Textbooks. I. Chahal, Walid, 1955-, compiler

HV6807.C745 2017   364.971   C2017-905616-6

CONTENTS

About the Books / viii

About the Authors / ix

1. Measuring Crime by William O'Grady / 1
    Introduction / 1
    Official Statistics / 2
    Self-Report Surveys / 11
    Victimization Surveys / 15
    Observational Accounts / 18
    Is Crime in Canada on the Rise? / 21
    Trends and Correlates of Canadian Homicide / 24
    Conclusion / 29

2. Marginalization and Wrongful Convictions by Dawn Anderson / 32
    The Social Reality of Wrongful Conviction / 32
    How Many Are Wrongfully Convicted? / 33
    The Official Explanation / 34
    Bureaucratic and Professional Wrong-Doing / 36
    Social Inequality, Crime and Wrongful Conviction / 40

3. Crime, Justice and the Condemnation and Exploitation of the Young by Bernard Schissel / 52
    The Development of Youth Justice and the Erosion of Child Protection / 52
    The Youth Criminal Justice Act / 54
    The Repercussions of a More Punitive Form of Youth Justice / 55
    Still Blaming Children / 56
    Moral Panics and Power / 59
    The Media and the Politics of Morality / 63
    Conclusion / 66

4. Understanding Child-Hating by Bernard Schissel / 69
   The Sociology of Knowledge and the Deconstruction of Crime Myth / 70
   Feminist Theory and the Construction of Gendered Images / 73
   Ideology, Power and the Images of Youth / 75
   The Place of Children and Youth in the Global Economy / 80

5. The Power to Criminalize: An Introduction
   by Elizabeth Comack and Gillian Balfour / 85
   Focusing on Violent Crime / 87
   Studying Legal Practice / 89
   Our Analysis / 93

6. Law as a Discursive Practice by Elizabeth Comack and Gillian Balfour / 96
   The Socio-Political Context: Neo-Liberalism and Neo-Conservatism / 103
   The Agency of Lawyers / 107
   Theorizing Law / 110

7. The Feminist Engagement with Criminology by Elizabeth Comack / 114
   The Invisible Women of Mainstream Criminology / 115
   Women as "Other": Monsters, Misfits and Manipulators / 116
   Enter Feminism… / 119
   Feminist Empiricism: Countering Bad Science / 123
   Transgressing Criminology: The Issue of Male Violence against Women / 124
   Standpoint Feminism: Women in Trouble / 127
   Intersectionality / 130
   Blurred Boundaries: Challenging the Victim/Offender Dualism / 132
   Postmodern Feminism: Criminalized Women / 132
   The Shifting Socio-Political Context:
   Neo-Liberalism and Neo-Conservatism / 135
   Violent Women and Nasty Girls / 137
   Lombroso Revisited? Framing the P4W Incident / 139
   Feminist Criminologists Respond to the Backlash / 141
   The Power and the Challenge / 145

8. Crime in the Context of Organizations and Institutions by William O'Grady / 155
   Introduction / 155
   White-Collar and Corporate Crime / 156
   Limited Data on White-Collar and Corporate Crime / 159
   The Public as Victim / 159
   Crime Against Consumers / 161
   Workers as Victims / 163
   Causes of White-Collar Crime / 164

     Political Crime / 167
     Organized Transnational Crime / 171
     Police Misconduct / 172
     Crime in Trusted Social Organizations / 176
     Conclusion / 179

9. Racialization, Racial Profiling and Racialized Policing by Elizabeth Comack / 181
     Racialization and Policing / 181
     Racial Profiling versus Racialized Policing / 184
     Government Inquiries / 185
     Systemic Racism and Racialization / 186
     The Commission's Findings / 188
     From Racial Profiling to Racialized Policing / 191
     Moving Forward / 198
     Racialized Policing and Reproducing Order / 199
     The Denial of a Fundamental Problem / 200
     What Is to Be Done? / 203
     Reframing the Problem / 209
     Community Mobilization / 211

10. Towards a Theory of Terrorism by Gary Teeple / 217
     The Antilogies of the "War on Terrorism" / 218
     What is Terrorism? / 220
     Systemic Terror / 225
     The Age of Terrorism / 234
     Conclusions / 237

ABOUT THE BOOKS

Dawn Anderson, 2009, *Manufacturing Guilt: Wrongful Convictions in Canada*, Fernwood Publishing.

Gillian Balfour and Elizabeth Comack (eds), 2014, *Criminalizing Women: Gender and (In)Justice in Neo-liberal Times, 2nd edition*, Fernwood Publishing.

Elizabeth Comack, 2012, *Racialized Policing: Aboriginal People's Encounters with the Police*, Fernwood Publishing.

Elizabeth Comack and Gillian Balfour, 2004, *The Power to Criminalize: Violence, Inequality and the Law*, Fernwood Publishing.

Sandra Rollings-Magnusson, 2009, *Anti-Terrorism: Security and Insecurity after 9/11*, Fernwood Publishing.

William O'Grady, 2014, *Crime in Canadian Context: Debates and Controversies, 3rd edition*, Oxford University Press.

Bernard Schissel, 2006, *Still Blaming Children: Youth Conduct and the Politics of Child Hating, 2nd edition*, Fernwood Publishing.

ABOUT THE AUTHORS

Dawn Anderson teaches as a sessional instructor in both the Sociology and Justice Studies Departments at the University of Regina. She received a Ph.D. in sociology from York University where she wrote her dissertation on sentencing and Indigenous offenders. She is co-author (with Barrie Anderson) of two editions of *Manufacturing Guilt* (1998, 2009) and has co-authored an introductory text on conflict resolution.

Gillian Balfour is an associate professor in the Department of Sociology at Trent University. She is editor of *Understanding Society* (2012), co-editor (with Elizabeth Comack) of two editions of *Criminalizing Women* (2006, 2014) and co-author (with Elizabeth Comack) of *The Power to Criminalize: Violence, Inequality and the Law* (2004).

Elizabeth Comack is a professor in the Department of Sociology at the University of Manitoba. She is co-editor (with Gillian Balfour) of two editions of *Criminalizing Women, 2nd edition* (2006, 2014), editor of three editions of *Locating Law: Race/Class/Gender Connections, 3rd edition* (1999, 2006, 2014), co-author (with Larry Morrissette, Lawrence Deane and Jim Silver) of *"Indians Wear Red": Colonialism, Resistance and Aboriginal Street Gangs* (2013), and co-author (with Gillian Balfour) of *The Power to Criminalize: Violence, Inequality and the Law* (2004) and author of both *Racialized Policing: Aboriginal People's Encounters with The Police* (2012) and *Out There/In Here: Masculinity, Violence and Prisoning* (2008).

William O'Grady is a professor in the Department of Sociology and Anthropology at the University of Guelph. He is co-author (with Steve Gaetz, Sean Kidd and Kaitlin Schwan) of the reports *Without a Home: The National Youth Homelessness Survey* and *Homelessness and Hidden Homelessness in Rural and Northern Ontario*.

Bernard Schissel is a professor in and head of the Doctor of Social Sciences Program, Faculty of Applied and Social Sciences, Royal Roads University. He is co-editor (with Carolyn Brooks) of three editions of *Marginality and Condemnation* (2002, 2008, 2015). His most recent books are *Still Blaming Children* (2006) and *About Canada: Youth and Children* (2011).

Gary Teeple is a professor of Sociology in the Department of Sociology and Anthropology at Simon Fraser University. He is co-editor (with Stephen McBride) of *Relations of Global Power: Neoliberal Order and Disorder* (2011), editor of *Capitalism and the National Question in Canada* (1972) and author of *Globalization and the Decline of Social Reform* (2000) and *The Riddle of Human Rights* (2004).

Chapter 1
MEASURING CRIME

William O'Grady

From: *Crime in Canadian Context: Debates and Controversies*, 3rd edition, Chapter 7 (reprinted with permission).

INTRODUCTION
This chapter builds on the awareness of the complexities involved in defining crime within its social context while examining an issue that has claimed the attention of criminologists and policy-makers for some time: the measurement of crime. Even if there were complete agreement about the meaning or definition of crime (an unlikely scenario), measuring crime would not be a simple task. By no means do we have a completely satisfactory method even for counting crimes. By examining official police statistics, victimization surveys, self-report surveys and observational accounts this chapter will introduce the debates and controversies dealing with the measurement of crime, with a focus on the strengths and weaknesses of each technique. It also addresses such important questions as, "Is violent crime in Canada on the rise?" With an emphasis on homicide, this chapter considers the legal definition of homicide in Canada and reviews homicide statistics from the time in 1962 when they were first systematically collected. Finally, Canadian homicide rates will be compared to the rates of homicide in other industrialized countries.

Mass media are the principal resources Canadians rely on for their knowledge about the level and character of crime, and the ways in which crime is depicted by mass media often distort or even exaggerate what can be known about crime. Criminologists often point out that the images constructed by the media do not match "reality." But just what is empirical reality, and how is it measured?

Generally speaking, an empirical investigation refers to the systematic collection of observable data. For example, the criminologist may ask questions such as, "What forms of crime are the most common in Canada?" or "How many of these events are brought to the attention of the police?" Answers to factual questions such as these, however, are more thorny and difficult to answer than might be expected. If information used to measure crime is not accurate, then what are we to make of statements that purport to explain these data? Criminology is not just about collecting the "facts." The systematic study of crime also entails understanding criminal events. For example, if we are confident about data showing that homicide rates in Canada are lower than they are in the United States, the next logical step would be to explain *why* these differences exist. In short, criminology is not simply about describing the nature of crime in society, it must explain and *understand* the nature of crime using the most reliable and valid information possible. However, as the following discussion confirms, there is no one technique available that can successfully fulfill this need.

OFFICIAL STATISTICS

In attempting to understand the "real level of crime" the first place to turn is the Uniform Crime Reporting (UCR) system. While methods and resources vary, most countries around the world go to considerable lengths and expense to measure crime within their geo-political borders. By and large, all official crime-reporting systems rely on reports of crime by the police. For this reason, the way crime is measured falls under the objectivist-legalistic definition introduced in the previous chapter. In theory, whatever crime comes to the attention of the police is reported *by* the police to their government's statistical agencies. In the United States, the Federal Bureau of Investigation (FBI) is responsible for counting crime across the nation. In the United States, the origins of the Uniform Crime Reporting system can be traced to 1929, when the International Association of Chiefs of Police met and decided that a reliable, uniform crime statistics compilation was needed. In 1930, the FBI was commissioned with the task of collecting, publishing and archiving those statistics. Today, several annual statistical publications, such as the all-inclusive *Crime in the United States*, are produced from data provided by nearly 17,000 law enforcement agencies across the United States (FBI, n.d.). In the United Kingdom (England and Wales) the British Home Office is responsible for assembling and releasing crime statistics.

Crime data in Canada have been systematically collected on a national basis since 1962. While Canadian information about crime — especially homicide — was reported by the police and was available to the public prior to 1962, it was not until then that police forces in Canada were required by law to submit statistical crime reports to Canada's statistical agency, the Dominion Bureau of Statistics (now Statistics Canada). Today, the Canadian Centre for Justice Statistics (CCJS) in Ottawa is the division at Statistics Canada responsible for gathering and analyzing the reports submitted by police from across the country. On an annual basis, these reports are released to the public in the form of media releases, annual reports and website updates. In Canada about 1,200 separate police detachments, representing about 230 police forces, submit crime data to the CCJS.

UCR data are crimes *known by the police to have taken place*. This includes the following three general categories: violent crime, property crime and other Criminal Code violations. Within each of these categories several differing offences are accounted for. A detailed breakdown of these offences can be found in Table 1-1.

Since the inception of the national crime-reporting initiative in 1962, police detachments from across Canada have been required to submit a Uniform Crime Reporting Aggregate Survey to Ottawa, which is basically a tally sheet used to count offences within police jurisdictions. However, some Aboriginal police forces in Canada do not respond to the survey. According to Statistics Canada, these typically are very small communities and serve less than half a percent of the Canadian population. For these forces, obviously, estimates of reported crime cannot be produced. The UCR form collects summary data about more than one hundred Criminal Code offences.

More recently, in order to collect more detailed information on each incident, including data on victims and accused persons, the UCR2 Survey was developed. In this alternative method of data collection, a separate statistical record is created for each criminal incident and it is known as an "incident-based" reporting system. This system of respondent-reported, incident-based data began in 1988. According to Statistics Canada, this survey introduced certain efficiencies for police services and lowered response burden by removing or simplifying UCR2 (Sauvé 2005).

Crime data from police departments are submitted monthly on machine-readable forms, normally within two weeks after the end of each month's reporting. It is important to know how crime is actually counted in these reports. While UCR data represents "crime known to the police," this is not actually what is being counted. In fact, and this is clearly made known by Statistics Canada, there is at least some level of *alleged* law-breaking behaviour that does *not* appear on these records for the simple reason that the UCR Survey classifies incidents according to the most serious offence (MSO) occurring during the incident — generally interpreted as the offence that carries the longest maximum sentence under the Criminal Code. In categorizing incidents, violent offences always take precedence over non-violent

Table 1-1 Police-Reported Crime for Selected Offences, Canada, 2010–11

Type of offence	2010r number	2010r rate	2011 number	2011 rate	Per cent change in rate 2010 to 2011	Per cent change in rate 2001 to 2011
Total crime (excluding traffic) – "Crime Rate"	2,094,875	6,139	1,984,916	5,756	–6	–24
Violent crime						
Homicide	554	2	598	2	7	–3
Other violations causing death[1]	100	0	78	0	–23	–49
Attempted murder	668	2	655	2	–3	–19
Sexual assault – level 3 – aggravated	179	1	140	0	–23	–22
Sexual assault – level 2 – weapon or bodily harm	402	1	398	1	–2	12
Sexual assault – level 1	21,795	64	21,283	62	–3	–19
Sexual violations against children [2,3]	3,684	11	3,822	11	3	n/a
Assault – level 3 – aggravated	3,481	10	3,486	10	–1	15
Assault – level 2 – weapon or bodily harm	51,955	152	50,184	146	–4	5
Assault – level 1	175,289	514	172,770	501	–2	–19
Assault police officer [4]	15,913	47	11,943	35	–26	31
Other assaults	3,281	10	3,097	9	–7	–34
Firearms – use of, discharge, pointing	2,017	6	1,936	6	–5	–20
Robbery	30,478	89	29,746	86	–3	–13
Forcible confinement or kidnapping	4,301	13	3,774	11	–13	35
Abduction	449	1	402	1	–11	–46
Extortion	1,578	5	1,525	4	–4	–17
Criminal harassment	21,315	62	21,690	63	1	1
Uttering threats	76,347	224	71,945	209	–7	–28
Threatening or harassing phone calls	21,604	63	20,341	59	–7	–42
Other violent *Criminal Code* violations	3,830	11	4,597	13	19	9
Total	439,220	1,287	424,410	1,231	–4	–16
Property crime						
Breaking and entering	197,058	577	181,217	526	–9	–42
Possess stolen property [5,6]	30,275	89	21,496	62	–30	–28
Theft of motor vehicle	92,505	271	82,411	239	–12	–56
Theft over $5,000 (non-motor vehicle)	15,649	46	15,153	44	–4	–35
Theft under $5,000 (non-motor vehicle)	527,509	1,546	497,452	1,443	–7	–32
Fraud [7]	89,830	263	89,801	260	–1	–7
Mischief [8]	340,090	997	315,977	916	–8	–15
Arson	12,234	36	10,378	30	–16	–35
Total	1,305,150	3,824	1,213,885	3,520	–8	–31

Table 1-1 Police-Reported Crime for Selected Offences, Canada, 2010–11 (Continued)

Other *Criminal Code* offences						
Counterfeiting	815	2	620	2	−25	−68
Weapons violations	15,038	44	14,471	42	−5	0
Child pornography [9]	2,218	6	3,312	9	40	209
Prostitution	3,020	9	2,459	7	−19	−57
Disturb the peace	119,913	351	117,476	341	−3	17
Administration of justice violations	178,135	522	177,159	514	−2	2
Other violations	31,366	92	31,304	91	−1	−29
Total	**350,505**	**1,027**	**346,621**	**1,005**	**−2**	**2**
***Criminal Code* traffic violations**						
Impaired driving [10]	87,231	256	90,277	262	2	−2
Other *Criminal Code* traffic violations	55,615	163	55,938	162	0	29
Total	**142,846**	**419**	**146,215**	**424**	**1**	**8**
Drug offences						
Possession – cannabis	56,853	167	61,406	178	7	16
Possession – cocaine	7,325	21	7,392	21	0	23
Possession – other drugs [11]	9,761	29	10,352	30	5	97
Trafficking, production or distribution – cannabis	18,363	54	16,548	48	−11	−26
Trafficking, production or distribution – cocaine	9,873	29	10,251	30	3	37
Trafficking, production or distribution – other drugs	7,047	21	7,215	21	1	41
Total	**109,222**	**320**	**113,164**	**328**	**3**	**14**
Other federal statute violations						
Youth Criminal Justice Act	11,957	35	11,619	34	−4	−44
Other federal statutes	20,767	61	21,344	62	2	0
Total	**32,724**	**96**	**32,963**	**96**	**0**	**−22**
Total – all violations	**2,379,667**	**6,973**	**2,277,258**	**6,604**	**−5**	**−21**

r revised
1. Includes, for example, criminal negligence causing death.
2. Sexual offences against children is a relatively new crime category with only partial data available prior to 2010 therefore the per cent change from 2001 to 2011 is not shown.
3. Includes sexual interference, invitation to sexual touching, sexual exploitation, and luring a child via a computer. Excludes incidents of child pornography due to limited information on victim characteristics.
4. In 2010, a system anomaly resulted in some non-peace officer assaults being coded as peace officer assaults in 2010. Comparisons between 2010 and other years should be made with caution.
5. Includes trafficking and the intent to traffic stolen goods.
6. In 2011, the UCR survey was modified to create separate categories for possession of stolen property less than or equal to $5,000, and possession of stolen property over $5,000. As a result, incidents of possession under $5,000 may now be reported as secondary offences when occurring in conjunction with more serious offences, leading to a decrease in the number of possession of stolen property incidents reported in 2011.
7. Includes identity theft and identity fraud.
8. Includes altering, removing or destroying a vehicle identification number (VIN).
9. Due to incorrect reporting by a police service of incidents of child pornography from 2008 to 2011, the data originally contained in this report have been suppressed and revised data were made available on July 25, 2013 with the release of 2012 crime statistics.
10. Includes alcohol- and/or drug-impaired operation of a vehicle, alcohol- and/or drug-impaired operation of a vehicle causing death or bodily harm, failure or refusal to comply with testing for the presence of alcohol or drugs and failure or refusal to provide a breath or blood sample.
11. Includes precursors and equipment.

Note: Counts are based upon the most serious violation in the incident. One incident may involve multiple violations. Data for specific types of crime are available (in most cases) beginning in 1977. Rates are calculated on the basis of 100,000 population. Per cent change based on unrounded rates. Populations based upon July 1st estimates from Statistics Canada, Demography Division.

Source: Statistics Canada, Canadian Centre for Justice Statistics, Uniform Crimne Reporting Survey

offences. Take, for example, an incident involving both a breaking-and-entering offence and an assault. In this scenario the event would be recorded and counted as an incident of assault, not as a break and enter and not as both offences. As a result of the MSO-scoring rule, less serious offences are undercounted by the aggregate survey. While the incident-based survey allows the recording of up to four violations per incident, thus permitting the identification of lesser offences, not all police detachments in Canada submit these data because of its phased implementation. However, as of 2008 these data are based upon information reported by police services covering 98 percent of the population of Canada (Taylor-Butts 2010).

Yearly counts of crime in Canada are reported both as absolute numbers and as rates. Data produced by the Canadian Centre for Justice Statistics are standardized on the basis of differences in populations across Canada. For instance, because the total population in Canada has been increasing steadily since 1962, any meaningful understanding of relative change over time in levels of crime must standardize these absolute numbers by calculating crime rates. Furthermore, provincial populations vary considerably in Canada, and rates allow us to compare relative differences in crime levels among Canada's ten provinces and three territories. The way in which annual homicide rates are standardized is illustrated in the simple formula below:

Number of police-reported crimes × 100,000 ÷ population = Crime rate
Canada's population: 33,476,688

Using the homicide and population data above, the Canadian homicide rate for 2011 is:

598 homicides = 1.78 per 100,000 population

Not only does the UCR system illustrate the methods that government agencies, such as Statistics Canada, use to count behaviour that is defined as criminal, it is possible to examine levels of police-reported crime in Canada over time. Since all police departments across the nation are required to submit data to Ottawa, it is possible to compare crime rates between provinces, cities and smaller municipalities. Table 1-2 shows a selection of crime incidents and rates for Census Metropolitan Areas (CMAS) in 2011.

Even though the way in which crime is defined and measured varies from country to country, it is possible to compare some forms of crime — most notably homicide — between different nations. Since homicide is — and has been for some time — defined similarly in Canada, the United States and England and Wales, it is possible to compare homicide rates between these three countries over time. Homicide in Canada is considerably lower than in the United States, but rates in Canada are higher than they are in England and Wales.

Table 1-2 Police-Reported Crime Severity Index, Census Metropolitan Areas (CMAs), 2011

Census metropolitan area [1,2,3]	Population number	Total Crime Severity Index index	Total Crime Severity Index per cent change 2010 to 2011	Violent Crime Severity Index index	Violent Crime Severity Index per cent change 2010 to 2011	Non-violent Crime Severity Index index	Non-violent Crime Severity Index per cent change 2010 to 2011
Regina	222,125	124.5	−6	123.5	−18	124.9	0
Saskatoon	277,504	118.7	−8	134.5	−14	112.7	−5
Thunder Bay	119,999	107.3	−4	128.7	−8	99.1	−2
Winnipeg	767,277	107.2	−7	173.8	6	81.6	−16
Kelowna	182,239	97.4	−14	86.0	−11	101.8	−15
Vancouver	2,424,544	94.5	−7	98.3	−9	93.1	−6
St John's	188,653	93.3	−7	74.7	−16	100.5	−4
Brantford	140,267	92.2	−7	84.5	−10	95.2	−7
Edmonton	1,198,397	89.4	−13	105.9	−2	83.0	−18
Abbotsford–Mission	177,866	87.9	−11	72.4	−19	93.9	−9
Halifax	408,000	87.4	−9	111.7	6	78.1	−16
Montreal	3,924,554	80.9	−2	97.7	0	74.5	−3
Saint John	103,412	79.2	−14	91.3	−6	74.6	−17
London	499,637	79.0	−4	70.5	−5	82.3	−4
Greater Sudbury	162,892	78.9	−7	78.7	−8	79.0	−7
Victoria	362,264	71.3	−17	70.9	−15	71.4	−17
Saguenay	145,506	71.1	−3	55.2	−5	77.2	−2
Moncton	138,607	68.8	−5	68.2	−7	69.1	−4
Trois-Rivières	149,761	67.9	−3	46.2	4	76.3	−4
Calgary	1,270,927	65.8	−14	72.1	−11	63.4	−15
Hamilton	737,330	65.2	−8	75.8	−5	61.2	−9
Gatineau [4]	311,644	63.6	−8	68.1	14	61.8	−15
Kitchener–Cambridge–Waterloo	530,248	62.9	−7	69.5	0	60.4	−10
Windsor	331,284	62.5	−5	59.8	−7	63.5	−4
Peterborough	123,094	62.2	−8	60.2	−8	62.9	−8
Sherbrooke	190,154	60.7	−11	49.3	4	65.1	−14
St Catharines–Niagara	445,363	60.7	−13	48.0	−16	65.6	−13
Kingston	161,350	59.5	−5	48.1	−12	63.9	−3
Barrie	200,602	58.3	−3	49.2	−2	61.7	−3
Ottawa [5]	946,835	57.9	−5	63.9	−6	55.6	−4
Toronto	5,783,398	54.9	−5	84.7	−3	43.5	−6
Quebec	759,446	52.2	−6	46.8	−8	54.3	−6
Guelph	126,106	47.0	−7	48.2	8	46.5	−12
Canada	34,482,779	77.6	−6	85.3	−4	74.7	−7

1. A census metropolitan area (CMA) consists of one or more neighbouring municipalities situated around a major urban core. A CMA must have a total population of at least 100,000 of which 50,000 or more live in the urban core. To be included in the CMA, CMA adjacent municipalities must have a high degree of integration with the central urban area, as measured by commuting flows derived from census data. A CMA typically comprises more than one police service.
2. CMA populations have been adjusted to follow policing boundaries.
3. The Oshawa CMA is excluded from this table due to the incongruity between the police service jurisdictional boundaries and the CMA boundaries.
4. Gatineau refers to the Quebec part of the Ottawa–Gatineau CMA.
5. Ottawa refers to the Ontario part of the Ottawa–Gatineau CMA.

Note: Data on the crime severity indexes by census metropolitan area are available beginning in 1998.

Source: Statistics Canada, Canadian Centre for Justice Statistics, Uniform Crime Reporting Survey

Despite the fact that official police statistics are widely available and easily accessible, especially since these data are available online from Statistics Canada, this source of information about crime has long been recognized as problematic if they are taken to represent an accurate and true count of crime in Canada. There are a number of important reasons why official police statistics should be treated with caution. First, most crime that comes to the attention of the police is reported in the first instance by the public. There are many reasons why many criminal events may not be reported to the police. Data from victimization surveys — information collected over the phone from households sampled and asked to report experiences associated with being victims of crime — tell us that many victims feel intimidated by those who have offended them, particularly if they know the offender personally. In these cases, the victims feel that reporting the incident to the police could jeopardize their personal safety. Scenarios such as this are particularly evident and noteworthy in cases involving intimates. For a number of good reasons, women in intimate relationships may not call the police for fear of retaliation. In fact, a call to the police may trigger an immediate physical assault. Also, recent research has shown that women who have experienced violence in the home from their partner may wish that the perpetrator could be removed from the household, but do not necessarily want the offender to be arrested and perhaps face incarceration. This has been shown particularly to be the case in situations where women are economically dependent on their abusers (Dobash and Dobash 2003).

Other times crimes are not reported to the police because the public feels that very little, or perhaps nothing, would be accomplished by having the police involved. Take, for example, a hypothetical case of bicycle theft. Bicycle theft, according to the Criminal Code, is "theft under $5000." Consider the scenario where an individual finds that her bicycle has been stolen and contemplates reporting the theft to the police. However, upon realizing that her home insurance deductible is set at $500,

---

The Police-Reported Crime Severity Index

Unhappy with the use of the crime rates as the standard measure of crime and violence in Canada, in collaboration with a group of criminologists and policy workers from the community, the Canadian Centre for Justice Statistics has recently developed a measure that takes into account the severity of crime. The Police-Reported Crime Severity Index (PRCSI) was introduced in 2009 and tracks changes in the severity of police-reported crime. Data from this new measure are contained in Table 1-2. According to Canada's federal statistical agency: In the PRCSI, each type of offence is assigned a weight derived from actual sentences handed down by courts in all provinces and territories. More serious crimes are assigned higher weights, less serious offences lower weights. As a result, when all crimes are included, more serious offences have a greater impact on changes in the index.

Source: Statistics Canada 2009a

and the stolen bicycle is worth much less than this amount, there really is no point in making a claim and reporting the incident to the police — especially if there is little reason to hope that the bike would be recovered by the police.

Other reasons why the public fails to report illegalities to the police have to do with the fact that many people consider certain offences as trivial matters and would not likely report such behaviour to the police. Consider, for instance, a situation involving two young men who got into an argument and then started pushing and shoving each other. It would be unlikely that an event such as this would come to the attention of the police if neither individual was physically injured by the altercation. However, an incident like this one, according to the Criminal Code, would constitute a common assault.

It is also quite possible that many incidents that are defined as crimes occur but do not come to the attention of the police because a person may not realize that he or she has been a victim of a crime. For example, an individual may have given money at his or her home to a canvassing individual thought to be collecting for a legitimate charity. But, in actuality, the canvasser was an imposter and pocketed the donated money. Unless the activities of the dubious individual were brought to the victim's attention by the media, neighbours or the police, there is little likelihood that the victim would have realized that he or she was duped by such a fraud.

Even crimes of a more serious nature may not be reported to the police if citizens feel that reporting such activity would cost time and money, or that reporting would not lead to an arrest or conviction. For that matter, and this has been substantiated in victimology research, in some instances the public may not report crimes to the police because they may fear or distrust the police or even the judicial system (Jones et al. 1986). All of the above examples serve to illustrate why crime may or may not be reported to the police.

The volume of crime a police force tallies and reports to the Canadian Centre for Justice Statistics may also be a function of the size and resources of the force. This is particularly evident for offences pertaining to prostitution or drug dealing. Since these types of crime often require proactive policing, the resources that police departments commit to the enforcement of such activities can have a direct bearing on the amount of crime that makes its way into the record books. For example, a police department may be suspicious of certain activities taking place at so-called massage parlours located in the suburbs of a large metropolitan city. However, unless the police feel that there is a need to be proactive and rigorously enforce Canada's prostitution statutes — perhaps because of public complaints — there is a strong likelihood that these sorts of crime would not be subject to investigation or arrests. Similarly, since police exercise discretion while on the job, certain cases may be deemed less serious and may not be acted upon and, therefore, never make their way to Canada's annual statistical crime summaries.

The way in which crime is defined can also affect the official crime rate. Legal definitions of crime vary over time. Legislative changes in the wording of laws may cause new behaviours to be classified as "illegal," while at other times changes in legislation can eliminate behaviours from crime statistics. The rise during the mid-1980s in sexual offences provides an example. In 1983 Canadian rape laws were broadened to sexual assault laws. As a result of these legal changes, sexual assault referred to any form of sexual contact without voluntary consent. Beginning in 1983, the evidentiary requirement for penetration was also abolished and a wider array of sexually assaultive behaviours fell under the purview of criminal law. Acts such as kissing, fondling, vaginal intercourse, anal intercourse and oral sex were defined as sexual assault if voluntary consent is not involved. Since the previous rape laws were not defined as broadly as the new sexual assault laws, and since levels of other forms of sexual assault were generally greater than levels of rape had been, the statistics showed that sexual crimes in Canada spiked dramatically over a one-year period from 1982–3. One needs to understand that because of these legislative changes the definition of the crime had changed, and the statistics from prior years were not strictly comparable with statistics following the legislation.

A more recent example of legislative changes leading to a reduction in official measures of crime can be seen with the repeal of the Young Offenders Act and the implementation of the Youth Criminal Justice Act (YCJA) in 2003. According to the Canadian Centre for Justice Statistics, there was a 20 percent reduction in youth court cases over the period 2002–4. Between 1999 and 2002 there were 86,300 youth court cases on average annually in Canada, while in 2003 the number had declined to 70,465 (Carrington and Schulenberg 2005). The substantial dip in numbers of youth going to court is not indicative of a change in behaviour among Canadians aged 12–17. In fact, there is good reason to believe that the substantial fall in the number of young Canadians appearing in court was caused by the 20 percent of YCJA cases that received one of the new sentences (reprimand, intensive support and supervision, attendance centre order, or a deferred custody and supervision order) that were designed to keep first-time offenders away from the traditional court system (Moyer 2005). In this situation, the law appears to be achieving its intentions of reducing crime. According to research by Bala et al. (2009) the YCJA has succeeded in significantly reducing the rates of use of court and custody without increasing police-recorded youth crime. These authors also note that there continues to be some regional variation in rates of use of youth courts and custody, as rates of youth court cases dropped the most in Ontario and Atlantic Canada but no change occurred in the Prairie provinces.

Even though police-reported crime statistics have been collected systematically in Canada since 1962, for the reasons mentioned above this information must be treated with extreme caution if this source is used as a barometer for measuring the incidence of crime in Canada.

SELF-REPORT SURVEYS

Prior to the late 1950s, most empirical research in criminology relied on official records of the police, courts, or correctional institutions. Due in part to the described limitations imposed by these measures of crime, additional techniques have been developed. The best-known of these are self-report surveys. Self-report surveys are questionnaires that seek anonymous reports from respondents about offences they have committed over a selected period of time. The obvious intention of this technique is to capture information about crimes that may not have come to the attention of the police. In addition, these surveys normally seek information about the demographic characteristics of participants, such as age and gender profiles. Additional questions to these surveys are included so that explanations about the causes of crime can be tested or developed. The information gathered from crime surveys, therefore, is meant not only to describe the nature and extent of crime, but also to explain it.

Prior to the modern self-report survey, most information about crime relied on police or correctional institution statistics. Most of these data concluded that crime was primarily a lower-class phenomenon, engaged in mainly by young males. In fact, many well-known social psychological and sociological theories that attempt to explain crime are grounded in data that were obtained by these types of official records. However, because we know that a considerable amount of behaviour defined as crime does not come to the attention of the police and, therefore, is excluded from the official statistics, one must ask about the extent to which these explanations are based on suitable information.

The use of self-report surveys can be traced to about the middle of the twentieth century. Porterfield (1943) conducted one of the first self-report surveys to appear in the criminological literature. This survey compared official juvenile court records of 2,049 delinquents in Texas, with nearly 350 self-reports from a sample of college students in the same state. Porterfield discovered that every college student admitted to having engaged in the same sorts of illegal activities as the delinquent group, yet few of the students had ever been charged by police. While researchers may have suspected that these disparities were taking place in America, it became evident not only that people were quite willing to report their indiscretions to researchers, but also that the idea of low socioeconomic status being tied to delinquency was disputable (Thornberry and Krohn 2000).

The popularity of self-report surveys was further inspired by the work of Short and Nye (1958). In what is often taken to be a landmark study in this area, Short and Nye paid considerable attention to the methodological issues involved in the empirical study of juvenile delinquency, such as sampling, scale construction, reliability and validity. Continuing Porterfield's focus on the relationship between delinquent behaviour and social status, Short and Nye failed to find any statistically significant relationship between crime and social class. These findings were important because, like Porterfield's, they challenged the conventional wisdom of the day that crime was somehow connected to low socioeconomic status. In fact, Short and Nye found relatively few differences between crime and the socioeconomic status of the adolescents' parents they surveyed. These results posed a significant challenge to the validity of police-reported crime and the statistics that they generated. Findings from this research on self-reporting also gave reason to question many of the causal theories of crime, particularly those that linked crime with poverty and material disadvantage. This new method of measuring crime gave reason to believe that the juvenile justice system, for example, may be using what criminologists refer to as "extralegal factors" in making decisions concerning youth who are targeted by police. In other words, these findings raised the possibility that the reason why lower-class individuals are overrepresented in police-reported crime had less to do with actual levels of criminality among them and more to do with issues pertaining to policing practices, including possibly discrimination as to who was policed.

To construct a valid and reliable self-report survey is no simple task and involves a number of important steps. One of the first considerations concerns the issue of sampling. Sampling is a process of systematically selecting units (that is, people) from a population so that generalizations can be made about the larger population by studying the characteristics of a smaller group. A probability sample is most desirable in survey research. While there are several different types of probability samples, the simple random sample is the easiest to understand and is the one used as a model for other techniques. In simple random sampling, a researcher has a list of an entire population (for example, all cases investigated by the Alberta Securities Commission from 1990–2005) and randomly selects elements from this group using a mathematical random procedure. This means that a researcher is able to study this smaller group and is able to make inferences to a larger one. A common question often asked in survey research is how large a sample should be. While statisticians have developed techniques and formulas to determine an appropriate sample size for a given population, a general rule is the larger the sample the better. A good example of a large self-report survey is the Canadian General Social Survey (GSS). This is a large population survey that has been ongoing in Canada since 1985. Over this time the GSS has surveyed Canadians on a wide number of issues, including family and work life, education, use of information technology and criminal victimization. More than 19,000 Canadians were interviewed in the 2009 GSS.

It should be pointed out that, given the nature of the populations criminologists are interested in examining, it is not always possible to have a complete and accurate list of an entire group of people. For instance, researchers who work with homeless populations find it virtually impossible to draw simple random samples (see, for example, Hagan and McCarthy 1997). There are two fundamental reasons why this is the case. The first is a definitional matter: Who are homeless youth, for example? Definitions range from "those who sleep outside in places such as transit shelters and under bridges" to "persons residing in homeless shelters" to "those who move from place to place staying with relatives and friends" (a group sometimes referred to as "couch surfers"). While the circumstances and living conditions of these three groups vary considerably, different research has recognized each as constituting a homeless population. In short, since there is no simple, straightforward definition of "homelessness," the concept is difficult to measure.

Second, even if there were an agreed-on definition of homelessness, putting together a complete list of such a population would not be possible because homeless individuals do not have permanent addresses, nor do their names regularly appear on voter lists or in telephone directories — the sorts of lists that researchers often rely on to draw random samples of "conventional populations." For these reasons, researchers rely on other sampling techniques, such as snowball and quota samples, where no claims are made about statistical randomness.

For some time, self-report surveys have been the subject of some criticism, most of which pertain to issues of reliability — the extent to which a measurement procedure produces the same results on repeated trials — and of validity — the accuracy of a measure in relation to the concept that one is attempting to measure. The most obvious problem with these surveys is the fact that participants are not obliged or forced or coerced to tell the truth. Since it is standard practice in self-report research to guarantee subjects anonymity, there is no way a person's identity can be linked to their responses. Hence, there is also no way of safeguarding the truth. Consequently, it is possible that those who have committed a crime may not divulge such information on a self-survey. On the other hand, there is also the possibility of exaggeration, or of embellishing the amount of criminal activity in which one actually may have been involved.

Besides bald-faced deception, other forms of invalid data may be given unintentionally on self-report surveys. For instance, self-report crime surveys normally ask respondents to report criminal involvement (such as illegal drug use) over a specified period of time (such as one year). Because of memory loss or other reasons, respondents may offer inaccurate reports of their behaviour.

Some have been critical of self-report surveys because they neither ask questions about the more serious forms of crime (Hindelang et al. 1979) nor include many high-risk offenders among their respondents (Elliott and Ageton 1980). This point is particularly evident in self-report research on youth and delinquency where data are collected only from samples of school-aged youth. As was mentioned earlier, much of this research has failed to reveal social class differences in levels of criminal behaviour. Instead, explanations for youthful offending have tended to rely on the personal bonds and attachments that these youth have with parents and other adult authority figures. The limitation of this research and of the theory that has been generated from it is its basis on samples that often exclude youth who were absent from class on the day when a survey was administered. Besides missing information from youth who are inclined to skip school, these classroom surveys also omit students who either have been expelled or have left school altogether. In fact, in Canada, 18 percent of youth drop out of school — even though many return to school by the age of 24 (Bowlby and McMullen 2002). In response to the problem of not having representative samples of youth in school-based surveys, researchers have gone to "the streets" to collect self-report data from samples of youth who do not attend school. This task has been undertaken mainly by studies that have focused on street-involved and homeless youth. Unlike their high school counterparts, street-involved youth are more likely to commit crimes, in addition to being involved in more serious offences (Hagan and McCarthy 1997). Interestingly, this research has also shown that the reasons for this offending are not adequately explained by the sorts of factors that account for the more mundane deviant activities that are engaged in by youth who are captured in classroom surveys (Hagan and McCarthy 1997; Gaetz and O'Grady 2002; Tanner and Wortley 2002). Factors related to economic, physical and psychological deprivation must be included in explanations of why these marginal youth are involved in crime.

Even though self-report research has made concerted efforts to deal with sampling issues, another factor that must be attended to is that of deception. Ensuring that respondents tell the truth is difficult to safeguard, regardless of the composition of a sample. However, depending on how a survey is designed, it is possible to select responses of participants who may not be telling the truth. For example, a self-report study that examined the use of sexually explicit material among a sample of Canadian university students found that a small number of respondents reported accessing sexually explicit material in excess of the total hours that they claimed to spend online per week. Nineteen students from a total of 526 were dropped from the study because this discrepancy gave the researchers reason to believe that they had not taken the survey seriously or had not paid careful attention to the questions or to their answers (Byers et al. 2004). Researchers may take precautionary measures against deception by crafting their questionnaires to detect dishonesty and by engaging in careful analyses.

Because of the kinds of improvements that have been made to self-report research designs over the years, many analysts now rely on the self-report method as a tool to collect information about crime and other sorts of behaviour in the population. While critics are correct in pointing out the inherent problems with self-report surveys, research has shown that despite these limitations the tool can produce valid and reliable findings if careful consideration is given to issues of sampling and to the challenges inherent in deception (Thornberry and Krohn 2000).

A good deal of self-report research has been undertaken in Canada. One of the best-respected and longest-standing studies in the self-report field is the biannual study carried out in Ontario by the Centre for Addiction and Mental Health (CAMH). Every two years since 1977, CAMH has carried out drug surveys using large samples of elementary and high school students in Ontario. The Ontario Student Drug Use Survey (OSDUS) is a population-based survey of Ontario students in Grades 7 to 12 and is the longest ongoing school survey in Canada. This self-report survey is conducted with the intention of identifying trends in student drug use. In more recent years, the survey has also asked questions about mental health (such as depression), physical activity and such high-risk behaviours as violence and gambling. Normally, the OSDUS surveys about six thousand students in more than one hundred elementary and secondary schools across Ontario.

VICTIMIZATION SURVEYS

The most recent technique for measuring crime is the victimization survey. These instruments were developed first in the United States in the 1960s and were initially implemented in Canada in 1981 with the Canadian Urban Victimization Survey (CUVS). Since that time Statistics Canada has conducted national victimization surveys as part of the General Social Survey (GSS). These surveys differ from UCR data and self-report surveys in that they collect information on the victimization experiences of individuals, usually sampled at the household level. Over the years, crime victimization surveys have consistently revealed that a large number of crimes do take place that for various reasons do not come to the attention of the police. In fact, for many types of crime, these tools provide a much more accurate measure of criminal activities than do ucr data.

In 1981, the Canadian Urban Victimization Survey randomly sampled sixty thousand Canadians over the age of 16 in seven major cities. Over the telephone, respondents were asked to recall any criminal victimization experiences they had experienced during the past calendar year. Participants were asked to report victimization experiences in the following areas: assault, sexual assault, break and enter, car theft, theft of personal property, theft of household property, robbery and vandalism. The survey revealed that less than 42 percent of personal and household criminal victimizations had come to the attention of the police in 1981. One of the most revealing findings of that early survey was that 62 percent of sexual assaults go unreported in Canada. More recent Canadian victimization surveys have revealed similar results. For instance, the 2009 General Social Survey revealed that 31 percent of criminal incidents came to the attention of the police, down from 34 percent recorded in the previous 2004 survey (Statistics Canada 2010).

Not only are respondents in victimization surveys asked to report their experiences of victimization and whether or not they reported it to the police but they are also asked to provide information about each incident, including why they may or may not have reported the incident to police, and how they were affected by the event. Demographic information, such as the age, sex, marital status and the number of children living in the household, was also collected in the 1993, 1999, 2004 and 2009 surveys.

Because the GSS and the CUVS are carried out over the telephone, there is a finite amount of time that a respondent can be expected to be kept on the line speaking to an interviewer. As a result, these types of surveys are limited in terms of the number of questions respondents can reasonably be expected to answer. This is becoming increasingly problematic as most Canadian households are constantly being bombarded by irritating telephone calls from telemarketers and other telephone surveys; the Canadian public is becoming less tolerant of what are perceived to be invasions of time and privacy.

While large-scale national victimization surveys are useful for uncovering crimes that have not been reported to the police, they have been criticized because they are not able to focus specifically on those populations who may be the most vulnerable to crime. According to probability theory, every household in Canada with a landline telephone has an equal chance of being selected for participation in a victimization survey. The problem with this design is that these types of research instruments are unable to provide useful information about victimization in what are often described as "crime hot spots" where levels of victimization are well above the national average. Such hot spots often include communities where there is a high concentration of socially disadvantaged people. In fact, the 2004 GSS survey revealed that individuals who live in households with incomes of less than $15,000 per year are 1.5 times more likely to be a victim of a violent crime than individuals living in higher-income households (Gannon and Mihorean 2005). However, because national surveys like the GSS are based on random probability samples, only a relatively small number of individuals from crime-prone communities are included in these national surveys. This provides a barrier to those who wish to get a stronger sense of the dynamics within these higher-risk communities. In recognition of this problem, research by Jones et al. (1986) carried out a local victimization survey in a high-crime neighbourhood in Britain. This survey found levels of victimization for some offences were far greater than national data provided by the British Crime Survey. Not only are local surveys useful in gaining information about levels of criminal victimization in particular communities and how these levels may differ from provincial or national averages, but their results also have implications for service provision in these communities, including the police, assaulted women's help lines and shelters and other social service agencies.

A similar study has been carried out in Canada by DeKeseredy et al. (2003), who surveyed more than 325 people in a public housing community in eastern Ontario. The results of this local victimization survey showed that "public housing residents were much more likely to be victimized by most types of predatory crime than are members of the Canadian general population" (DeKeseredy et al. 2003: 44). For example, public housing residents were three times more likely than those surveyed in the GSS to report that someone broke in or attempted to break in to their residence. These results show that the more vulnerable people are socially and economically, the more likely they are to be harmed by predatory crime.

Another Canadian small-scale victimization survey carried out by Gaetz (2004) also focused on a marginalized population. In a study where 208 homeless youth (ages 15–24) were interviewed, Gaetz revealed findings similar to the study undertaken by DeKeseredy and colleagues. Examining six types of victimization, Gaetz found in almost every category that homeless youth reported more victimization than a sample of similarly aged youth who had been surveyed in the 1999 GSS. The GSS survey noted, for example, that 12 percent of youth (ages 15–24) had been the victim of an assault in the past year; the corresponding figure for the group of homeless youth was 62 percent. It should not come as a surprise that these two studies found that levels of criminal victimization are far greater among groups of people who face social and economic exclusion.

Both national and smaller-scale victimization surveys face certain problems that are difficult to rectify. First, surveys such as these are dependent on the ability of respondents to accurately place their experiences of crime in the proper time frame. This problem may occur both in terms of placing certain events further back in time than they actually took place, as well as situating other events further ahead in time than they actually took place. Criminologists refer to this problem as "telescoping," which refers to a respondent's mistaken specification of when an experience of victimization occurred relative to the reference period specified by a researcher. While there are no proven safeguards to prevent respondents from making these kinds of mistakes, the problem can be minimized through a technique called "bounding." Bounding is achieved by comparing incidents reported in an interview with incidents reported in a previous interview and deleting duplicate incidents. However, for this technique to be successful, it is necessary to interview each respondent twice over a given period of time. Since this practice is expensive, in Canada the gss interviews each respondent only once. In the United States, however, the National Crime Victimization Survey (NCVS) does practise this technique (NAJCD n.d.). In that survey, each visit to a household is used to bound the next one by comparing reports in the current interview with those given six months prior. When a report appears to be a duplicate, the respondent is reminded of the earlier report and asked if the new report represents the incident previously mentioned or if it is different. The first interview at a household entering the sample is unbounded, and data collected at these interviews are not included in NCS and NCVS estimates. However, if a household in sample moves and another [respondent] moves into that address, the first interview with the replacement household is unbounded but is included in NCS and NCVS estimates.

Victimization surveys face other limitations. For obvious reasons, these surveys exclude data such as homicide. They are also unable to collect information about crimes where there are arguably no clear-cut offenders. This would include circumstances related to prostitution, drug use and illegal gambling. Finally, for ethical reasons, victimization surveys normally stay clear of including those who are under the age of 15. For this reason, victimization surveys are unable to measure levels of crime that take place within many teenaged populations.

OBSERVATIONAL ACCOUNTS

The fourth method criminologists use to study and sometimes even to measure crime are observational accounts. Here, the researcher actually interacts with individuals on a face-to-face basis in a natural setting to gather information about crime within the context where crime or victimization occur. However, unlike UCR data, self-report and victimization techniques, observational accounts are not undertaken to gather information about crime so that estimates can be made about the volume or character of crime in the general population. These techniques are simply not applicable to the collection of this type of information. Observational research normally takes place on a relatively small scale so that a deeper understanding and appreciation of crime and victimization can be achieved. While there are some examples of research conducted from direct observation — where the activities of a group are observed but the presence of the researcher is unknown to the group (Humphries 1970) — most observational research in the field of criminology takes the form of what is called "participant observation." Participant observation generally involves a researcher interacting with a group while observing their behaviour. This method is a research practice that was first developed by anthropologists. However, criminological research early in the twentieth century also relied on the ethnographic approach to study crime. Research on gangs in Chicago in the 1920s conducted by Thrasher (1927), for example, used observational methods to understand how gangs were organized and the social function that gangs served. In fact, recent studies of gangs continue to favour this research method because of the difficulties inherent in gathering information about criminal subcultures using police statistics or surveys. Examples of this recent research include studies of male gangs by Huff (2002) and of female gangs by Campbell (1990) and by Chesney-Lind and Hagedorn (1999). Today, the ethnographic approach is used in many social science disciplines focusing on a wide range of research topics.

Quite a few criminological observational studies have taken place in Canada. A study by Wolf (1991), for example, examined an outlaw biker gang in western Canada. The technique has also been used to study punk rock subcultures in British Columbia (Baron 1989) and in Ontario (Dumas 2003) and "squeegee kids" in Toronto (O'Grady and Bright 2002). In addition, Visano (1987) studied male prostitutes in Toronto by interacting with them and observing the work of male street hustlers.

Participant observation also has been used to study the people who make and enforce our laws. While such a technique is less popular today, participant observers have examined policing practices by actually accompanying one or more police officers on patrol duty. One of the first studies of this kind carried out in the United States by Black and Reiss (1970) involved the policing of juveniles. Similar research has taken place in Canada by Ericson (1981, 1982) who observed detectives while they were on the job.

More recently, observation for research purposes of practitioners involved in other areas in the administration of justice in Canada has been undertaken using the ethnographic approach. One such study by Parnaby (2006) involves research on practitioners whose job is crime prevention through environmental design (CPTED). The basic premise behind CPTED is that proper design of the physical environment can be effective in preventing crime. Examples of CPTED practices would include the installation of lighting in outdoor areas that are frequented by women during hours of darkness. Not only did Parnaby observe the work of CPTED practitioners, but he fully immersed himself in that role by enrolling in and successfully completing the training required to become a certified CPTED practitioner. Other observational research in Canada by criminologists has studied the private security industry (Rigakos 1999) and bylaw informant officers responsible for enforcing Ontario's Tobacco Control Act (O'Grady et al. 2000). Work such as this does not only focus on lawbreakers; it carefully examines the processes and structures that are involved in the enforcement of criminal laws and other regulatory practices in society.

The strengths of the observational method clearly relates to the issue of validity. According to Neuman et al. (2004: 406), "Validity in field research is the confidence placed in a researcher's analysis and data as accurately representing the social world in the field." Thus, if the researcher's description of the social world that he or she is examining corresponds to the world of its members, then the work is valid. Given that the field researcher is observing first-hand the events that take place within the natural setting, observational techniques are more valid than UCR data, self-report or victimization surveys. Good ethnographic accounts produce information that is impossible to gather using the other techniques. For example, while a self-report survey may be a useful method for collecting information about how often a group of youth may have committed a set number of crimes over a specified period of time, surveys are not able to reveal very much about the details surrounding the contexts within which criminal activity takes place, or about the lifestyle of those who are involved in crime. Besides, ethnographic accounts are useful for collecting information from individuals in marginalized groups — like outlaw bikers — who would likely be suspicious of the motives of survey researchers. Gaining the acceptance from such a group can take time. And until a level of trust can be developed and nurtured between the researcher and participant(s), little useful information can be gleaned from the research experience.

As with the other methods criminologists use to study crime, observational research has some limitations. First, it is not a very useful technique if one wishes to make generalizations or inferences about the level and character of crime in a larger population. In other words, even data collected from a thorough and systematic investigation of the illegal activities of a motorcycle gang would be insufficient for making inferences about the activities of other biker gangs in Canada. To be sure, there would likely be a number of factors influencing the nature of gang activities of a biker gang in Quebec, for example, that may be different from biker gangs in western or Atlantic Canada. Another limitation with field research concerns the fact that the researcher may be putting him or herself in dangerous situations. Since criminological field researchers can find themselves interacting with groups and individuals who may engage in risky lifestyles, before researchers take to the field their projects must be granted ethical approval. Within the university environment, researchers must have work involving human subjects vetted by university research committees. Not only do ethical reviews demand that every possible step be taken

Table 1-3 Self-Reported Violent Victimization by Offence, 1999, 2004, 2009

Year	Sexual assault number (thousands)	rate[1]	Robbery number (thousands)	rate[1]	Physical assault number (thousands)	rate[1]
1999	502	21	228	9*	1,961	81
2004	546	21	274	11	1,931	75
2009†	677	24	368	13	2,222	80

† reference category
* significantly different from reference category (p < 0.05)
1. Rates are calculated per 1,000 population age 15 years and older.
Note: Excludes data from the Northwest Territories, Yukon, and Nunavut, which will be published at a later date.

Source: Statistics Canada, General Social Survey, 1999, 2004, and 2009

to ensure the safety of researchers, but researchers must ensure that those who are the subjects of their research will also be protected as much as possible from any deleterious physical or psychological events.

There is no getting around the fact that no ideal method exists to measure crime. Depending on the questions that are being asked, and the definition of crime being used, criminologists must decide to use one or more methods systematically and effectively to study the wide lexicon of crime and criminal justice.

IS CRIME IN CANADA ON THE RISE?

After reading the preceding discussion, we know it is not feasible to definitively answer whether crime in Canada is on the rise. This is especially the case if one is interested in tracking changes in all types of police-reported crime, or in types of crime collected by methods other than UCR statistics. This difficulty is due, of course, to the limitations associated with the four primary data sources that are used to measure crime in Canada that have just been reviewed. However, there are two ways in which changes over time in levels of certain types of crime in Canada can be systematically analyzed. The first is by using victimization data from GSS surveys. It is possible to determine whether or not there have been changes, over the short term, in certain types of crime, such as sexual assault, robbery and physical assault. The second method of analysis, which is appropriate for longer-term trends, is to rely on UCR data, specifically, the statistics that measure homicide. In fact, these are the only data regarded by the criminological community as providing a satisfactory (albeit imperfect) means of addressing the question of whether or not changes in levels of serious violent crime have occurred in Canada since 1962.

Beginning with GSS victimization data displayed in Table 1-3, rates per 1,000 of population for the years 1999, 2004 and 2009 indicate small increases in sexual assault and robbery, while levels of physical assault have fluctuated. In terms of property victimization, Table 1-4 shows that household victimization has also fluctuated, but theft of personal property has steadily risen from 1999 to 2009. Since victimization surveys have been carried out for only a relatively short period of time in Canada and because they are limited by measuring only a few types of crime, another information source must be found to learn the extent to which crime in Canada — in particular lethally violent crime — has been changing.

Not only have homicide statistics been systematically collected in Canada since 1962, these data also are regarded for a number of reasons to be reasonably valid and reliable measures of deadly interpersonal violence. First, homicide is one type of violent behaviour that is very likely to come to the attention of the police; virtually all homicides are reported to the police, partly because dead bodies are difficult to conceal. Second, unlike other police-reported crime, officials collect

Table 1-4 Self-Reported Victimization 1999, 2004, 2009

Year	Total violent victimization[1] number (thousands)	rate[3]	Total household victimization[2] number (thousands)	rate[4]	Theft of personal property number (thousands)	rate[3]
1999	2,691	111	2,656	218*	1,831	75*
2004	2,751	106	3,206	248	2,408	93*
2009†	3,267	118	3,184	237	2,981	108

† reference category
* significantly different from reference category (p < 0.05)
1. Total violent victimization includes: sexual assault, robbery, and physical assault.
2. Total household victimization includes: break and enter, motor vehicle theft/parts, theft of household property and vandalism.
3. Rates are calculated per 1,000 population age 15 years and older.
4. Rates are calculated per 1,000 households.

Note: Excludes data from the Northwest Territories, Yukon and Nunavut which will be published at a later date.

Source: Statistics Canada, General Social Survey, 1999, 2004, and 2009

considerably more information about homicide than about any other crime because homicide investigations are much more thorough and rigorous than most other criminal investigations.

As a result, more information is collected on homicide by the Canadian Centre for Justice Statistics than on any other crime in Canada. Finally, because homicide is similarly defined in most countries around the world, it is possible to compare levels of homicide in Canada with levels of homicide reported in other countries.

The Criminal Code of Canada classifies homicide as first-degree murder, second-degree murder, manslaughter or infanticide. In Canada, first-degree murder refers to homicide that is planned and deliberate. A person may also be convicted of first-degree murder if he or she is found guilty of killing an on-duty police officer or correctional officer. The final criterion for first-degree murder is a murder that is committed during the course of other criminal acts, such as hijacking, kidnapping, forcible confinement and sexual assault. The definition of second-degree murder is straightforward: It refers to all murder that is not first-degree murder. Most often the issue that would shift a first-degree murder charge to a second-degree murder charge or conviction would be the lower degree of intent legally attached to second-degree murder.

The punishment for both first-degree and second-degree murder is life imprisonment. There are important differences, however, between these two types of murder convictions in regard to the possibility of release on parole. For those convicted of second-degree murder, it is possible for the parole boards to grant early supervised release of the prisoner after he or she has served a designated period of time behind bars. Today, in Canada, parole boards are permitted to grant parole to second-degree murderers after their having served ten years of their sentence. However, for first-degree murder the convict must serve the full twenty-five years before being allowed the possibility of parole, but may apply for a judicial review after fifteen years

(Goff 2004). Although a rare occurrence, the court may designate certain inmates "violent offenders." Doing so would mean there is a strong possibility the offender would remain in jail until his or her natural death. The notorious Canadian serial rapist and murderer Paul Bernardo was designated a dangerous offender in 1995 and will likely never be released from prison. Interestingly, in 2010 when Russell Williams, the Canadian Armed Forces colonel who was the commanding officer at CFB Trenton, was convicted of dozens of crimes, including two for first-degree murder, the Crown attorney in that case did not seek a dangerous offender status for Williams because he felt that "it would be redundant" since the Crown's record against Williams was believed to be so strong that "the parole board will be satisfied that he will pose a danger for the rest of his life. A dangerous offender request is superfluous" according to Crown attorney Lee Burgess (CBC News Online 2010). Data from the Correctional Service of Canada indicated that there 486 inmates were designated as dangerous offenders as of April 2012.

A person guilty of manslaughter would have killed another human in the heat of passion or by sudden provocation. A person legally guilty of infanticide in Canada would be a female who by willful act or by omission causes the death of her newly born child. The child must be under the age of 12 months, and the mother must not have fully recovered from the effects of childbirth. Psychiatrists are usually given the responsibility of making this determination.

Punishments for convictions of manslaughter and infanticide normally involve shorter jail terms than convictions for murder. The maximum penalty for manslaughter is twenty-five years of imprisonment. However, those convicted by the courts of manslaughter are usually given sentences that are shorter than the maximum, and parole eligibility occurs after an offender serves one-third of his or her sentence. The median prison sentence/time served for men convicted of manslaughter in 1999–2000 was five years (Belanger 2001: 16). Mothers convicted of infanticide are liable to imprisonment for a maximum of five years.

Before turning to an analysis of the trends and correlates of Canadian homicide, it is important to place homicide within the broader context of how violent crime is defined in Canada. While homicide is conventionally taken to represent the most serious form of violent crime in Canada, and elicits the most attention in the mass media, according to Figure 1-1, homicides and attempted murders represented 0.4 percent of all violent crime in 2004. In fact, over 77 percent of all violent crime in Canada that comes to the attention of the police involves assault — the vast majority of which are "Assault level 1," or common assault. Thus, while homicide is certainly the most serious violent crime in Canada and receives the largest spotlight in the mass media, this offence represents a small fraction of all police-reported violence in the country (Gannon and Mihorean 2005).

Figure 1-1 Categories of Violent Crime, 2004

Category	% of Violent Crime
Abductions	0.2
Homicide/attempted murder	0.4
Other sexual offences	0.9
Other assaults	4.3
Sexual assault (levels 1, 2, 3)	7.8
Robbery	9.1
Assault (level 2 and 3)	16.3
Assault (level 1)	61.1

Source: Statistics Canada

TRENDS AND CORRELATES OF CANADIAN HOMICIDE

Homicide rates in Canada for the period 1981–2011 are presented in Figure 1-2. The overall trend in the Canadian homicide rate per 100,000 population has been one of slow but constant decline.

For the past several years the highest provincial homicide rates have been reported in Saskatchewan and Manitoba, followed by Alberta and British Columbia. Quebec's and Ontario's rates are below the national average, while the lowest rates are registered in Prince Edward Island and Newfoundland and Labrador. It is important not to overlook the fact that the homicide rates in Canada's three northern territories are higher than the rates in any province. The pattern whereby levels of homicide increase in Canada from east to west has been apparent for some time. Data showing these provincial differences in 2011 are displayed in Figure 1-3.

While several hypotheses have been generated by criminologists to explain this phenomenon, one reason that has been suggested for levels of homicide being higher in western Canada and in the North than is the case in other provinces (particularly in Manitoba and Saskatchewan) is the greater proportion of Aboriginal peoples who live in these areas of the country. Homicide is especially frequent on some First Nations reserves and communities that experience severe economic strain and cultural instability (LaPrairie 1987).

Not only is there provincial variation in levels of homicide across Canada, but as is evident in Table 1-5, homicide rates vary considerably in Canada's Census Metropolitan Areas (CMAs). Consistent with patterns of provincial homicide rates identified in earlier, CMAs with populations over 500,000 in western Canada (such as Regina, Winnipeg and Edmonton) have the greatest homicide rates in the

Figure 1-2 Attempted Murder and Homicide Rates Canada: 1981–2011, per 100,000 Population

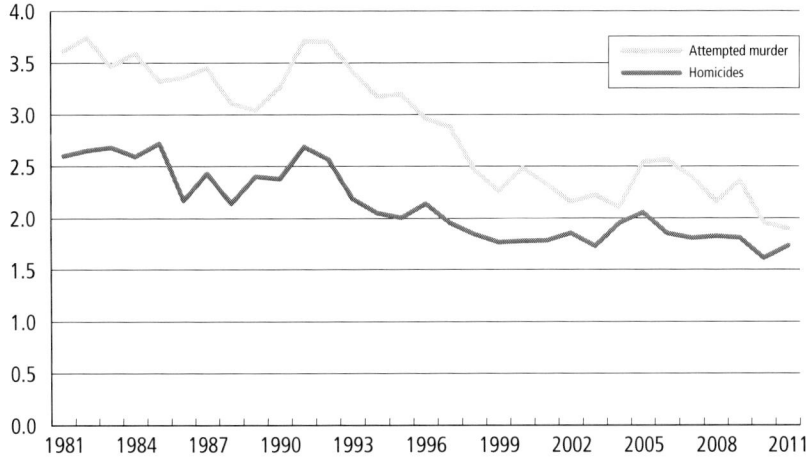

Source: Statistics Canada, Canadian Centre for Justice Statistics, Uniform Crimne Reporting Survey 2011

Figure 1-3 Homicides by Province/Territory, 2011

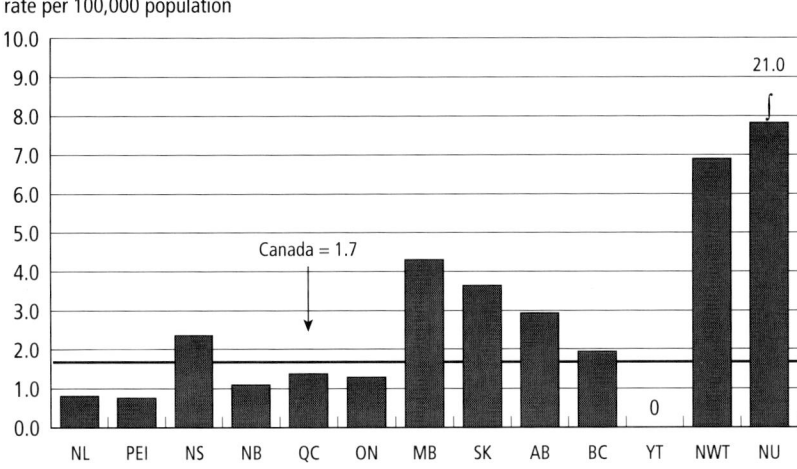

Source: Statistics Canada, Canadian Centre for Justice Statistics, Uniform Crimne Reporting Survey

country that were recorded between 2000 and 2009.

Table 1-6 presents homicide rates from 2006–10 on the basis of the age and sex of homicide victims. The most notable pattern displayed is that males are more likely to be victims of homicide in Canada than are females. In fact, males were, on average over this five-year period, victims of 73.6 percent of all homicides. Also evident in these figures is that there has been a rise in the total percentage of males

Table 1-5 Hmicides by Census Metropolitan Areas (CMAs), 2009–10

Census metropolitan area	2009 number	2009 rate[1]	2010 number	2010 rate[1]	2000 to 2009 average number	2000 to 2009 rate[1]
Thunder Bay	6	5.0	5	4.2	2	1.5
Saskatoon	6	2.3	10	3.7	7	2.8
Regina	4	1.9	8	3.7	7	3.7
Winnipeg	32	4.2	22	2.8	25	3.5
Halifax	12	3.0	11	2.7	7	1.9
Edmonton	30	2.6	32	2.7	32	3.0
Greater Sudbury	4	2.4	4	2.4	2	1.4
Abbotsford–Mission [2]	9	5.2	4	2.3	5	3.1
Moncton [3]	2	1.5	3	2.2	1	1.0
Saint John	0	0.0	2	1.9	1	0.8
Kingston [2]	4	2.5	3	1.9	3	1.7
London	3	0.6	9	1.8	6	1.2
Kelowna [3]	3	1.7	3	1.7	4	2.2
Hamilton	9	1.3	12	1.7	10	1.4
Peterborough [3]	1	0.8	2	1.6	1	0.6
Oshawa	3	0.8	6	1.5	3	0.8
Vancouver	61	2.6	36	1.5	54	2.5
Toronto	90	1.6	80	1.4	95	1.8
Victoria	3	0.9	5	1.4	4	1.3
Ottawa [4]	10	1.1	13	1.4	10	1.2
Montreal	44	1.2	49	1.3	59	1.6
Calgary	24	2.0	15	1.2	22	2.1
St John's	0	0.0	2	1.1	1	0.7
Barrie [3]	1	0.5	2	1.0	2	1.0
St Catharines–Niagara	5	1.1	4	0.9	6	1.4
Quebec	2	0.3	6	0.8	5	0.7
Kitchener–Cambridge–Waterloo	4	0.8	4	0.8	5	1.0
Brantford [3]	2	1.4	1	0.7	2	1.3
Sherbrooke	1	0.5	1	0.5	1	0.6
Gatineau [5]	2	0.7	1	0.3	3	1.2
Saguenay	5	3.5	0	0.0	2	1.0
Windsor	5	1.5	0	0.0	6	1.7
Trois-Rivières	3	2.0	0	0.0	2	1.1
Guelph [3]	1	0.8	0	0.0	1	0.8

1. Rates are calculated per 100,000 population.
2. Abbotsford–Mission and Kingston became census metropolitan areas (CMAs) in 2001. Average number and rate are calculated from 2001 to 2009.
3. Moncton, Kelowna, Peterborough, Barrie, Brantford, and Guelph became CMAs in 2006. Average number and rate are calculated from 2006 to 2009.
4. Ottawa refers to the Ontario part of the Ottawa–Gatineau CMA.
5. Gatineau refers to the Quebec part of the Ottawa–Gatineau CMA.

Source: Statistics Canada

who were victims of homicide: in 2006 males comprised 66 percent of all victims while in the following four years males averaged 73.6 percent of all victims. Table 1-6 also presents data for those who have been victims of homicide on the basis of age. For males, those aged 18–24 had the greatest number of homicide victims. For females, those in the 30–39 age groupings are where numbers are the highest.

The Canadian Centre for Justice Statistics also collects information on the numbers of homicides that involve firearms. While the overall rate of firearm homicides have fallen from 1979 to 2009, it is interesting to note that handgun homicides, as can be seen in Figure 1-4, have generally risen over this twenty-year period. Commencing in the early 1990s, handguns have consistently accounted for about two-thirds of all firearm-related homicides in Canada.

Compared to many other industrialized nations, levels of homicide in Canada are quite high. For instance, the Canadian homicide rate is about three times the rate recorded in Japan. This may come as a surprise if, as is often the case, homicide rates in Canada are compared only with homicide rates in the United States — which are just under three times as high as they are in Canada. But when a wide range of other industrialized countries are used for comparison, as is shown in Figure 1-5, homicide rates in Canada are by no means low. In fact, rates of homicide in

Table 1-6 Victims of Homicide, by Age and Sex, 2006–10

Victims	2006	2007	2008	2009	2010
Males	**444**	**431**	**465**	**450**	**400**
0 to 11 years	16	13	17	21	21
12 to 17 years	12	23	22	30	20
18 to 24 years	110	119	128	122	89
25 to 29 years	69	60	67	61	64
30 to 39 years	91	78	73	83	62
40 to 49 years	70	62	86	63	67
50 to 59 years	39	39	37	39	47
60 years and over	36	37	35	31	30
Age not known	1	0	0	0	0
Females	**162**	**163**	**146**	**160**	**152**
0 to 11 years	16	11	12	13	9
12 to 17 years	16	8	8	12	11
18 to 24 years	24	22	20	17	21
25 to 29 years	16	16	21	16	20
30 to 39 years	32	33	22	38	24
40 to 49 years	23	36	28	27	31
50 to 59 years	20	18	16	17	12
60 years and over	14	19	19	20	24
Age not known	1	0	0	0	0

Note: Homicide includes Criminal Code offences of murder, manslaughter and infanticide.

Source: Statistics Canada

Figure 1-4 Firearm Related Homicides, 1979–2009
rate per 100,000 population

[Line chart showing Total firearms, Rifles and shotguns[1], and Handguns rates from 1979 to 2009]

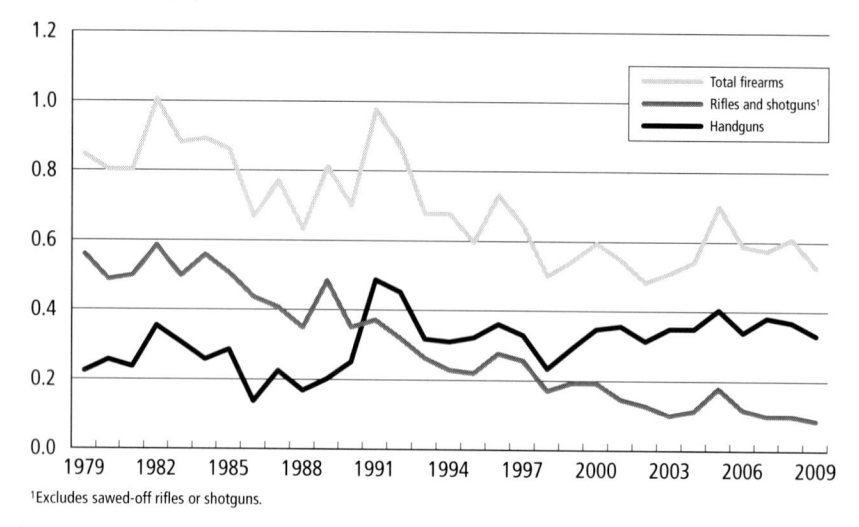

[1] Excludes sawed-off rifles or shotguns.

Source: Statistics Canada, Canadian Centre for Justice Statistics, Worldwide Survey

Figure 1-5 Homicide Rates for Selected Countries
Rate of homicides per 100,000 population

[Bar chart showing homicide rates for selected countries]

- United States[1]: ~5.2
- New Zealand[1]: ~3.0
- Turkey[1]: ~2.9
- Finland[1]: ~2.5
- Scotland[1]: ~2.2
- Canada[2]: ~1.8
- Hungary[1]: ~1.5
- Northern Ireland[1]: ~1.5
- France[1]: ~1.4
- Denmark[3]: ~1.4
- England and Wales[1]: ~1.2
- Australia[1]: ~1.2
- Sweden[1]: ~0.9
- Germany[1]: ~0.8
- Switzerland[1]: ~0.7
- Hong Kong[1]: ~0.5
- Japan[1]: ~0.5

rate per 100,000 population

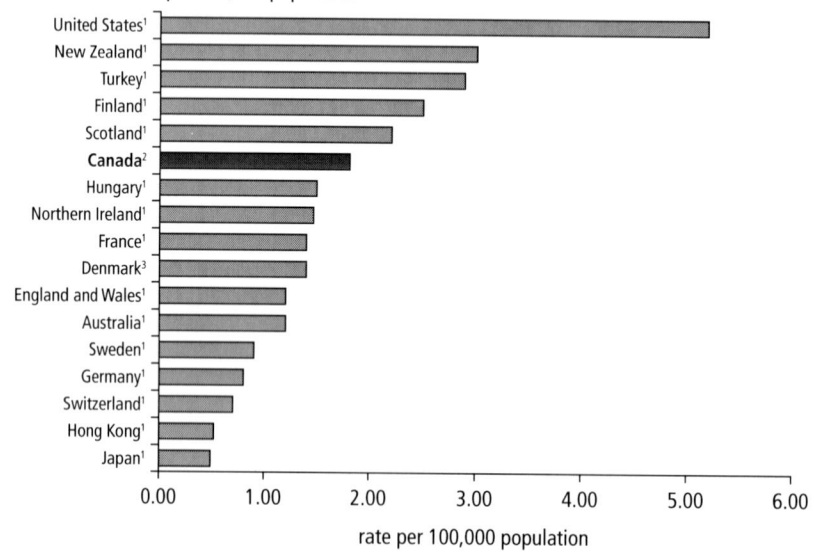

1. Figures reflect 2008 data.
2. Figures reflect 2009 data.
3. Figures reflect 2007 data.

Source: Statistics Canada, Interpol Ottawa and National Statistical Office website

economically developed countries such as Northern Ireland, France, Denmark, England and Wales, Australia, Sweden, Germany, Switzerland, Hong Kong and Japan are all lower than rates recorded in Canada.

CONCLUSION

Compared to the media messages about crime, the methods that criminologists rely on to study crime paint a different picture about the level and character of crime. Even though there are important limitations associated with UCR, self-report, victimization and observational accounts, there is no getting around the fact that any intelligent explanation or discussion about crime — its causes or how best to react to crime — cannot be arrived at unless crime is defined and measured in a systematic, yet critical, fashion. Even for those who take the position that scientific knowledge has no more claim to the "truth" than taken-for-granted or common-sense understandings, such a viewpoint demands an awareness of the strengths and weaknesses of all forms of information. Only a broad and open-minded approach to the study of crime can foster the sort of intellectual climate that will be effective in confronting crime.

References

Belanger, B. 2001. "Sentencing in Adult Criminal Courts, 1999/00." *Juristat,* 21, 10. Ottawa, ON: Statistics Canada.

Black, D., and A. Reiss. 1970. "Police Control of Juveniles." *American Sociological Review*, 35: 63–77.

Bowlby, J., and K. McMullen. 2002. *At a Crossroads: First Results for the 18–20-Year-Old Cohort of the Youth in Transition Survey*. Ottawa, ON: Human Resources Development Canada.

Byers, L., K. Menzies, and W. O'Grady. 2004. "The Impact of Computer Variables on the Viewing and Sending of Sexually Explicit Material on the Internet: Testing Cooper's Triple-A Engine." *Canadian Journal of Human Sexuality,* 13, 3/4: 157–169.

Campbell, A. 1990. *The Girls in the Gang, 2nd edition.* New York: Blackwell.

Carrington, P., and J. Schulenberg. 2005. *The Impact of the Youth Criminal Justice Act on Police Charging Practices with Young Persons: A Preliminary Statistical Assessment.* Ottawa, ON: Report to the Department of Justice.

CBC News Online. 2010. "Dangerous Offender: What the Label Means." <http://www.cbc.ca/news/canada/story/2010/ 10/21/f-dangerous-offender.html>.

Chesney-Lind, M., and J. Hagedorn (eds.). 1999. *Female Gangs in America: Essays on Girls, Gangs, and Gender.* Chicago, IL: Lakeview Press.

DeKeseredy, W., S. Alvi, M. Schwartz, and A. Tomaszewski. 2003. *Under Siege: Poverty and Crime in a Public Housing Community*. New York: Lexington.

Dobash, R., and R. Dobash. 2003. "Violence in Intimate Relationships." In W. Heitmeyer and J. Hagan (eds.), *International Handbook of Violence Research* (pp. 737–752). London, UK: Kluwer.

Dumas, M. 2003. "Punk in Drublic: Gender, Politics, Resistance and Producing Punk Rock in a Small Canadian Town." MA thesis, University of Guelph.
Elliott, D., and S.S. Ageton. 1980. "Reconciling Race and Class Differences in Self-Reported and Official Estimate of Delinquency." *American Sociological Review*, 4, 1: 95–110.
Ericson, R. 1981. *Making Crime: A Study of Detective Work*. Toronto, ON: Butterworths.
____. 1982. *Reproducing Order: A Study of Police Patrol Work*. Toronto, ON: University of Toronto Press.
FBI. n.d. "Uniform Crime Reports." <www.fbi.gov/ucr/ucr.htm>.
Gaetz, S. 2004. "Safe Streets for Whom? Homeless Youth, Social Exclusion, and Criminal Victimization." *Canadian Journal of Criminology and Criminal Justice* (July): 423–456.
Gaetz, S., and B. O'Grady. 2002. "Making Money: Exploring the Economy of Young Homeless Workers." *Work, Employment and Society*, 16, 3: 433–456.
Gannon, M., and K. Mihorean. 2005. "Criminal Victimization in Canada, 2004." *Juristat*, 25(7). Ottawa, ON: Statistics Canada Catalogue no. 85–002.
Goff, C. 2004. *Criminal jJustice in Canada*, 3rd edition. Toronto, ON: Thompson.
Hagan, J., and B. McCarthy. 1997. *Mean Streets: Youth Crime and Homelessness*. Cambridge, UK: Cambridge University Press.
Hagedorn, J.M. 1998. *People and Folks: Gangs, Crime, and the Underclass in a Rust-Belt City*, 2nd edition. Chicago, IL: Lakeview Press.
Hindelang, M., T. Hirschi, and J.G. Weiss. 1979. *Measuring Delinquency*. Beverly Hills, CA: Sage.
Huff, R. (ed.). 2002. *Gangs in America*, 3rd edition. Thousand Oaks, CA: Sage.
Humphries, L. 1970. *Tearoom Trade: Impersonal Sex in Public Places*. Chicago, IL: Aldine.
Jones, T., B. MacLean, and J. Young. 1986. *The Islington Crime Survey*. London, UK: Routledge.
LaPrairie, C. 1987. "Native Women and Crime in Canada: A Theoretical Model." In E. Adelbery and C. Currie (eds.), *Too Few to Count: Canadian Women in Conflict with the Law*. Vancouver: Press Gang.
Moyer, S. 2005. "A Comparison of Case Processing under the Young Offenders and the First Six Months of the Youth Criminal Justice Act: A Report to the Ministry of Justice." Ottawa, ON: Ministry of Justice.
NAJCD (National Archive of Criminal Justice Data). n.d. "National Crime Victimization Survey Resource Guide." <http://www.icpsr.umich.edu/NACJD/ NCVS/>.
Neuman, L., B. Wiegand, and J. Winterdyk. 2004. *Criminal Justice Research Methods: Qualitative and Quantitative Approaches, Canadian edition*. Toronto, ON: Pearson.
O'Grady, W., and R. Bright. 2002. "Squeezed to the Point of Exclusion: The Case of Toronto Squeegee Cleaners." In J. Hermer and J. Mosher (eds.), *Disorderly People: Law and the Politics of Exclusion in Ontario*. Halifax, NS: Fernwood Publishing.
O'Grady, W., M. Asbridge, and T. Abernathy. 2000. "Illegal Tobacco Sales to Youth: A View from Rational Choice Theory." *Canadian Journal of Criminology*, 42, 1: 1–20.
Parnaby, P. 2006. "Crime Prevention Through Environmental Design: Discourses of Risk, Social Control, and A Neo-Liberal Context." *Canadian Journal of Criminology and Criminal Justice*, 48, 1: 1–30.
Porterfield, A. 1943. "Delinquency and its Outcome in Court and College." *American Journal of Sociology*, 49: 199–208.

Rigakos, G. 1999. "Hyperpanoptics as Commodity: The Case of the Parapolice." *Canadian Journal of Sociology,* 24, 3: 381–409.

Sauvé, J. 2005. "Crime Statistics in Canada, 2004." *Juristat,* 25, 5. Ottawa, ON: Statistics Canada.

Short, J., and F.I. Nye. 1958. "Extent of Unrecorded Juvenile Delinquency: Tentative Conclusions." *Journal of Criminal Law and Criminology,* 49: 296–302.

Statistics Canada. 2009. *The Daily*. 21 July.

____. 2010. "General Social Survey: Victimization." *The Daily.* <http://www.statcan.gc.ca/dailyquotidien/100928/dq100928a-eng.htm>.

Tanner, J., and S. Wortley. 2002. *The Toronto Youth Crime and Victimization Survey: Overview Report*. Toronto, ON: Centre of Criminology.

Taylor-Butts, A. 2010. "When and Where Youth Commit Police-Reported Crimes, 2008." *Juristat,* 30, 2. Ottawa, ON: Statistics Canada. <http://www.statcan.gc.ca/pub/85-002-x/2010002/article/11241-eng.htm>.

Thornberry, T., and M. Krohn. 2000. "The Self-Report Method for Measuring Delinquency and Crime." *Criminal Justice,* 4. Washington, DC: US Department of Justice.

Thrasher, F. 1927. *The Gang*. Chicago, IL: University of Chicago Press.

Wolf, D. 1991. *The Rebels*. Toronto, ON: University of Toronto Press.

Chapter 2

MARGINALIZATION AND WRONGFUL CONVICTIONS

Dawn Anderson

From: *Manufacturing Guilt: Wrongful Convictions in Canada*, Chapter 1 (reprinted with permission of the author).

THE SOCIAL REALITY OF WRONGFUL CONVICTION

Looking at them, the casual observer would see nothing unusual about the men seated in front of an audience in the conference room of a downtown Toronto hotel in May 1995. They might have been business people, politicians, or academics. But David Milgaard, Donald Marshall and Guy Paul Morin were in fact men who had been wrongfully convicted of serious crimes. Milgaard served twenty-three years behind bars, Marshall served eleven years. Milgaard, Marshall and Morin have become public figures, symbols of a justice system gone wrong. We can now add more names to that list such as James Driskell and Bill Mullins-Johnson. After years of being ignored, their cases had been championed by the media. They had become household names. Many of them owed their freedom to the dedication of long-suffering family members who had pursued their cases for decades. Had they trusted in the justice system to identify and correct its own mistakes, they would still be in prison. Their presence at this national convention of the Association in Defence of the Wrongly Convicted, indeed the fact that such an organization is needed, raises troubling questions about the Canadian justice system. How many more innocent Canadians are locked behind prison bars? Can we blame their convictions on simple human error, or are there deeper problems in the Canadian justice system?

HOW MANY ARE WRONGFULLY CONVICTED?

There are many guilty people in prisons who insist they are innocent, hoping their claim will earn them their freedom. Unfortunately, there is no simple method for separating legitimate claims of innocence from those of the guilty or for determining the actual number of wrongfully convicted. In Canada very little research has been done in this area. The answer to the question of how many people are wrongfully convicted is therefore unknown and unknowable. We know only of cases that go to trial. As we will discuss later, there may be thousands of cases of wrongful conviction in Canada because, for a variety of reasons, innocent people may plead guilty during plea bargaining. Although justice officials stress that wrongful convictions are rare occurrences, the available evidence indicates that the cases that do come to our attention are only the tip of the proverbial iceberg. Those who have been wrongfully convicted may apply for a Ministerial Review of their case under 696.1 of the *Criminal Code*. These applications are received by the Criminal Conviction Review Group, a separate unit under the federal Department of Justice. In 2007 they received eighteen applications; in 2008 they received thirty-two applications for review (Department of Justice 2007; Department of Justice 2008).

A study conducted at Long Lartin maximum security prison for the National Association of Parole Officers in Britain revealed that as many as 6 percent of the inmates of that prison may be wrongfully convicted. The Association believed this figure was typical of British prisons (Carvel 1992). British inmates who proclaim their innocence all said they face enormous difficulties trying to get the judicial system to listen to their complaints. As in Canada, British prisoners who protest their innocence also find it much more difficult to gain parole. Harry Fletcher, who headed the study, noted:

> Many of the men have been trying to put together a case for up to ten years. All have experienced problems in getting adequate legal advice and some have been forced to draft their own appeal grounds, with no real hope of an adequate hearing. (Carvel 1992)

Only a few very committed lawyers were prepared to take on the tedious and time-consuming task of proving a miscarriage of justice with little prospect of any monetary reward.

A British Royal Commission report states that seven hundred to eight hundred cases of possible wrongful conviction are still waiting for review. The report also states that one-third of Britain's police departments are being investigated in connection with such cases. American criminologists Ronald Huff, Arye Rattner and Edward Sagarin (1986) reported that top justice officials in the United States believed that between 1 percent and 5 percent of all felony convictions were wrongful. In numerical terms, 1 percent translates into six thousand cases per year. Hugo Bedau and Michael Radelet (1987), in researching wrongful convictions, concluded that twenty-three innocent persons have been executed in the United States between 1905 and 1974. Edwin Borchard, in his classic 1932 book, *Convicting the Innocent*, discussed sixty known American cases of wrongful conviction. A Gannett News Service analysis found eighty-five instances over a twenty-year period in which American prosecutors used fabricated or questionable evidence to convict innocent people (*USA Today* 1994). Holmes (2001, cited in Denov and Campbell 2008) estimates that as many as 20 percent of all convictions in the United States may be wrongful.

Have Canadians bought the official message that there are too few wrongful convictions to be concerned about, that human error is bound to occur, and that in any event the justice system will self-correct? Do we naively assume that a democratic political system automatically guarantees us a fair and equitable system of justice, free of corruption and political intrigue? Has our search for truth and justice been allowed to regress into a vilification of the innocent? Have we let down our guard and permitted race and class distinctions, political corruption and professional self-interests to pervade our justice system? These are unpleasant questions for which there are no immediate answers. Yet, as we will see, questions like these must, in part, guide our investigation into the cause of wrongful convictions.

THE OFFICIAL EXPLANATION

When a wrongful conviction is exposed, police, judges, bureaucrats and politicians who bear responsibility for the design and maintenance of the system are quick to offer a ready explanation for why the system failed. This explanation is frequently echoed by academics in contemporary criminological literature. Miscarriages of justice are said to result primarily from poor witness reporting or from "unintended" errors committed by justice officials. Huff, Rattner and Sagarin (1996) note that most of the wrongful convictions they examined were the product of unintentional errors made by witnesses or by those who operate the American justice system. While Rattner (1983) indicates that many factors are involved in wrongful convictions, he notes that fully 52 percent of the cases he studied involved poor witness identification. Borchard (1932) emphasized the major role that witnesses can play in the wrongful conviction of the innocent. Jerome and Barbara Frank (1957) argue that a witness who gives false testimony frequently believes he or she is telling the truth. Philip Rosen (1992) noted the importance of bad eyewitness reporting as a causal factor in Canadian wrongful convictions. The true extent of the problems generated by eyewitness reporting can be seen in a *Globe and Mail* article, which reported that a review of one thousand American wrongful convictions found that half of these were due to eyewitness errors. The same report found that each year nearly eighty thousand trials in the United States rely on eyewitness testimony (*Globe and Mail* January 21, 1995).

Eyewitness reporting is crucial to any comprehension of wrongful conviction. A key witness to a crime is sometimes the only evidence the prosecution has to make its case. Without the testimony of a witness to the event, the prosecution may be forced to rely on circumstantial evidence, which most juries would find insufficient for a guilty verdict. An eyewitness to an event is a powerful weapon in the hands of the prosecution. History has shown that juries are inclined to accept the testimonies of witnesses as fact because they find it difficult to believe that people lie under oath. The end result is that tenuous eyewitness evidence becomes socially transformed into "fact."

Obviously, the official explanation that unavoidable human error is a prime cause of wrongful conviction cannot be discounted. Lawyers can be misinformed, witnesses may honestly believe they have seen something that they have not, judges may unconsciously give bad instructions to juries. People do make mistakes and that fact must be recognized. What we are suggesting here is that many of the official explanations for wrongful conviction miss the mark. The cases that we examine in this book demonstrate a consistent pattern of who becomes the victim and how they have been victimized. The official explanations ignore the fact that the underprivileged are most frequently the victims of this "human error."

At the most fundamental level, we must surely consider the possibility that those with wealth can retain the best of defence counsels who will ensure that such "human error" does not often happen to them. When David Milgaard, Thomas Sophonow and Guy Paul Morin were finally able to attract high-calibre lawyers to work on their cases, "human error" was "discovered" by the courts and their convictions were overturned. Furthermore, when a wrongful conviction is exposed and corrected, it is presented as evidence by the authorities that the system does work and is self-correcting. Ontario prosecutor Leo McGuigan put Guy Paul Morin behind bars for murder in 1993. When Morin was later proven innocent through DNA analysis, McGuigan told the press gathered outside the courthouse that "the justice system in this country is run by human beings. It does on occasion make mistakes. This was one of them" (Clayton 1995: 9). This audacious statement, from a man who only two years before had presented Morin to the jury as a sadistic mad killer, is typical of how those within the system rationalize wrongful convictions to the public. Overly-simplistic references to "unfortunate human error" do not capture the true nature of the unjust convictions studied in this book.

If we are to gain a comprehensive understanding of this phenomenon, we must subject our justice system to two levels of analysis. The first, "on-the-ground" level involves the "hands-on" work of the professionals and bureaucrats who run the legal and justice systems. Their actions are the immediate cause of all convictions, wrongful and otherwise. The second and higher level of analysis involves an understanding of how the systemic political, economic and social inequality endemic to Canadian society leads to the marginalization of large groups of Canadians, some of whom become wrongfully convicted. The two levels are interdependent, because bureaucratic and professional malfeasance generally occurs within the overarching context of social inequality and its commensurate marginalization of certain groups of peoples.

BUREAUCRATIC AND PROFESSIONAL WRONG-DOING

This on-the-ground level of analysis examines the targeting practices of the police, the suppression of evidence, police coercion and intimidation, falsified forensic evidence, judicial malpractice, jury tampering and prosecution and defence misconduct. Clayton (1995) contends that the most frequent causes of wrongful convictions in Britain include confessions obtained under pressure in the absence of a lawyer, fabrication of evidence, lack of forensic corroboration, untested alibis, unreliable prosecution witness, poor representation by defence lawyers and biased direction to the jury by judges.

Some American studies, while acknowledging the importance of Clayton's findings, emphasize the role of eyewitness identification as a factor in wrongful convictions. Rattner (1983, 1988) found that 52 percent of all wrongful convictions studied involved eyewitness misidentification; 11 percent, perjury by witnesses; 10 percent, the negligence of criminal justice officials; 8 percent, confessions coerced by the police; 4 percent, a "frame-up"; and 3 percent, perjury on the part of criminal justice officials. Other factors involved identification by police due to prior criminal record, forensic errors and "pure error" (Rattner 1983, 1988). Rattner (1983) also discovered that organizational and societal factors play a major role in wrongful conviction and that all levels of the criminal justice system tend to ratify earlier errors. Indeed, Rattner (1983) noted that the higher a case moved in the system, the less chance there was for an error to be recognized and corrected. This would seem to suggest that those at the highest level of judicial review close ranks and act as gatekeepers to sustain public perception of the system's integrity.

Because they are particularly sensitive to public pressure, it is in the police's interest to solve a case quickly. Under these circumstances the police may target for arrest the first individual who has even the remotest chance of being involved in the crime. Convinced of the suspect's guilt, they feel justified in using any legal as well as illegal means, such as threats, brutality, perjury and suppression of evidence, to build a case against this person (Huff et al. 1996). If this unfortunate individual has a previous criminal record, comes from a visible minority and is already living on the fringes of society, he or she will have few resources with which to defend him- or herself against police power and public indifference. Many of the wrongfully convicted have been the victims of "tunnel vision." Tunnel vision occurs when the police or prosecution's focus on one particular individual taints the interpretation and evaluation of any information received and results in the "unconscious filtering in of evidence that will 'build a case' against a particular suspect, while ignoring or suppressing evidence respecting the same suspect that tends to point away from guilt" (MacFarlane n.d.: 34).

Exacerbating the problem is the fact that the police feel that they do society's "dirty work" but receive no recognition for a job well done. This culminates in an "us against them" mentality and a tendency for the police to be secretive in their actions and suspicious of the public. Directed primarily against those of the lower class, this suspicion is one of the key factors leading to police coercion and brutality and the targeting of the poor that is endemic to wrongful convictions. Also, because promotion within police ranks is determined in part by an officer's clean record and the number of high profile arrests and cases completed, an officer may be tempted into wrongdoing in order to secure a conviction. In such an organizational culture and structure, winnable (and won) cases are a priority and become a self-maintaining process. We will see later how Donald Marshall Jr., a Nova Scotia Mi'kmaw, was quickly singled out by the Sydney police as a prime murder suspect. Guy Paul Morin was targeted as a prime murder suspect because he was considered "weird" by an Ontario regional police department. David Milgaard, a 16-year-old high school drop-out and self-professed hippie, became the prime suspect of a conservative Saskatoon police force headed by a chief who made it known that he had no use for hippies. All of these men, and others to be discussed in the case chapters, were marginalized in one way or another from mainstream middle-class society.

The police, in building their case against a prime suspect, may suppress, lose, misinterpret or overlook evidence that supports the defendant's claim of innocence. Once the police have convinced themselves that they have apprehended the guilty person, they proceed on the assumption that the accused and any witnesses whose evidence supports the accused's claims of innocence are lying. On the other hand, any evidence that appears to point to the defendant's guilt may be exaggerated out of all proportion. Furthermore, evidence or testimony that points to alternative suspects may be repressed or totally ignored. This form of police misconduct is much less likely to be detected or challenged if it is perpetrated against the powerless members of society rather than those in the middle and upper classes.

Another aspect of professional wrong-doing involves what is frequently referred to as "jailhouse testimony." Jailhouse confessions involve an alleged confession of guilt by an accused to a fellow inmate who has been planted in a cell by the prosecution or police. The "plant" later testifies in court that the accused confessed to the crime. In exchange for this testimony, the witness may be given special consideration by the police or the prosecution. The fact that the accused in this instance may have been "set up" and that a deal was made with the planted inmate may not be known by the judge, the jury, the accused's lawyer, or the public.

Coerced eyewitness testimony may also result from professional misconduct on the part of the judicial authorities. Testimony gained through coercion may be presented by a variety of people, including the friends and family of both the accused and the victim. These people will swear in court that they saw the accused at the scene of the crime or even committing the criminal act. Unfortunately, the process of coercion is made relatively simple if the witness already harbours racial or class-based attitudes concerning the accused that blur the distinction between truth and falsification. The police may also easily coerce a witness into giving false testimony against an accused if the witness expects to gain some favour by cooperating with the police. This is frequently the motivation of the typical "jailbird" confessor. Many witnesses to a violent crime may have gotten only a fleeting look at their attacker and be reluctant, initially, to identify a possible suspect from a police line-up or mug book. These witnesses may be encouraged or coached by the police to identify a person as the one they saw at the scene of the crime.

Expert witnesses for the prosecution, such as forensic scientists, may step over the boundary separating science from advocacy. Some forensic scientists see themselves as part of the prosecution team rather than as standing at arm's length from the state, in search of the truth. We will see later how forensic scientists have misrepresented the results of laboratory findings in a manner prejudicial to the accused but favourable to the prosecution's case. It is also possible for forensic scientists to repress forensic evidence that would be beneficial to the accused.

We must also consider the possibility of biased judges. These individuals are at the pinnacle of the judicial system and their job is to oversee the trial process and determine the sentence for those convicted of a crime. It is the responsibility of the judge to guarantee that all parties involved in a trial act according to the proscribed rules, ensuring a fair and impartial hearing for the accused. Judges therefore have a tremendous responsibility to maintain justice. However, they also have the very important task of maintaining public confidence in the judicial system. To this end, lawyer Alastair Logan (1995) asserts, the judiciary will act to preserve the reputations of police officers, prosecutors, expert witnesses, or others acting on behalf of the Crown when their reputation or the legitimacy of the system is called into question. The possibility therefore exists that a judge may unintentionally or maliciously conduct a trial or instruct the jury in a way that is prejudicial to the accused, if he or she perceives that to do otherwise would somehow jeopardize the integrity of the judicial system.

We must recognize that prosecution and defence misconduct may lead to a wrongful conviction. The Canadian system of justice is based on an adversarial process that pits the formidable forces of the state against a lone individual. In theory, the power of the state should be nullified by the skill of the defence lawyer as he or she does courtroom battle with the prosecutor. This adversarial system demands a winner and a loser but, unfortunately, the reasons for winning go beyond simply seeing justice done. For lawyers, winning becomes a means of building a reputation, of earning more money, of living a good life. Those lawyers who have mastered the techniques of examination, cross-examination and other courtroom mysteries will naturally be rewarded with a higher income and the respect of their peers. Unfortunately, the desire to win has caused many lawyers to engage in questionable, even unscrupulous, tactics, which are frequently condoned by the legal profession as a whole. Lawyers learn quickly what works well in the courtroom and what does not. What works are techniques that may distort the truth, confuse the jury and make apparent liars out of honest witnesses. Members of the highly structured legal system share a culture that emphasizes winning cases rather than doing justice. For too many lawyers, the courtroom has become a place for building reputations rather than a forum for discovering truth and serving justice. When the need to win takes precedence over truth, the seeds of wrongful conviction have been sown in the fertile soil of legal indifference, personal greed and public apathy.

The antithesis to the overly combative lawyers for whom winning is the ultimate goal is the defence counsel who does not defend. 40-four-year-old Wilbert Coffin was hanged in 1956 for the murder of three American bear hunters. Many people now believe he did not commit the crime. In a book on the case, the late Jacques Hebert argued that the incompetent performance of Coffin's lawyer contributed to Coffin's conviction and subsequent execution. Similarly, the legal counsel for Donald Marshall Jr. is regarded by many as having been ineffective. While most lawyers are skilled and responsible professionals dedicated to insuring the propriety of the legal system in all its ramifications, that even a few should deviate from this ideal and lead to convicting the innocent casts a dark shadow over the entire system. The causes of such problems may be more mundane than malevolent. The legal aid lawyer asked to defend a client who is not guilty may not have the financial and human resources needed to provide the appropriate defence for the accused against an aggressive and determined prosecutor with the resources of the state at hand.

The bureaucratic and professional wrong-doing described above does not happen in isolation from the mainstream of society. Such behaviour has its source in the systemic social inequality endemic in the Canadian social structure. The analysis of wrongful conviction must therefore focus on the social structure itself — on Canadian society — and it is here that we now turn our attention.

SOCIAL INEQUALITY, CRIME AND WRONGFUL CONVICTION

Canada, like other Western industrialized nations, is a country characterized by systematic social inequality. Vast differences in life chances between classes and racial groups are clearly evident. Most telling is the high level and persistence of poverty in Canada. From the 1970s to the 1990s, between 15 percent and 18 percent of Canadians were classified as poor by the federal government. In fact, by Statistics Canada's estimation, which many argue seriously understates the problem, over five million Canadians, 17.8 percent of our population, were poor in 1995 (Ross and Shillington 1989: 40; Battle 1998). In 2004, 3.5 million Canadians, representing more than 11 percent of the population, were still living in poverty (Canadian Council on Social Development n.d.). Moreover, it seems that the rich are getting richer. Between the 1970s and 1990s, the share of national income going to the bottom 50 percent of the population dropped from almost 28 percent to under 23 percent, while the top 10 percent saw their income increase by almost 14 percent (Yalnizyan 1994: 22). More recently, Yalnizyan (2007: 3) found that "In 2004, the average earnings of the richest 10 percent of Canadian families raising children was 82 times that earned by the poorest 10 percent. That is approaching triple the ratio of 1976, which was around 31 times." Aboriginal people in Canada are particularly likely to live in poverty: in 1991, for example, the average income for Aboriginal people was $14,561 compared to $24,001 for all Canadians. That gap continued in 2000, when the average income for the Aboriginal population was $22,332, compared to $38,011 for the non-Aboriginal population (Statistics Canada 2004). Similarly, in 1991, almost half of the Aboriginal population had incomes of under $10,000, more than twice that for all Canadians (Battle 1997). That gap remains: in 2000, over one-quarter of the Aboriginal population (26 percent) had incomes under $10,000 compared to 11 percent of the non-Aboriginal population (Statistics Canada 2004). It is in this context that we must view the operation of our criminal justice system.

Justice is essentially an abstract concept based on the rather vague ideas that people share about law and society, crime and punishment, good and bad. Justice will change as society itself changes. However, as our laws become institutionalized and regarded as natural truths — the very foundation of society itself — they become a powerful tool for maintaining the legitimacy of the social order by deflecting public attention away from state agencies and institutions and towards individual wrongdoers, emphasizing the fact that the activities of such people are detrimental to the stability of social order itself. Unfortunately, the majority of those singled out by the judicial system as being the most undesirable and dangerous wrong-doers are the poor, the unemployed and the visible minorities living on the fringes of society. These unfortunate people, frequently underprivileged since birth, thus become our criminals. Structured as it is, the judicial system permits select people with authority to pass judgment on others in a process that will officially certify them as criminal. In practice, the legal system becomes not only an extension of the social values and attitudes of a society at any particular point in time but also a powerful weapon used by the state to control the dispossessed groups, particularly during times of political and social upheaval (Bonger 1967; Scott and Skull 1978).

Scholars in both critical and mainstream criminology have extensively documented the fact that criminal law is not applied equally to all classes in society. This leads to the lower class being identified as the criminal class (Hogarth 1971; Mandel 1991; Myers 1991; MacLean 1986; Tepperman 1977; Bell-Rowbotham and Boydell 1972; Reiman 2004; Comack and Balfour 2004; Stern 2006; Brooks 2008). These researchers tell us that the lower class is convicted more frequently than the upper class because the ideology as well as the actions of the police and others in the justice system weeds out and protects higher status offenders from prosecution for the types of crimes that most frequently draw the attention of the police. It is the poor, the unemployed, the visible minorities, the powerless and those ostracized for their sexual orientation who are most frequently criminalized by the system. It is members of these groups we most often mean when we speak of marginalized peoples. However, under some circumstances, the category expands. Guy Paul Morin was middle class, but the police questioning him considered him "weird." He was also marginalized because his lifestyle was not acceptable to his community.

To complicate the problem, many marginalized people are sensitive to the fact that what does and does not become defined as "criminal" may work against them. Understanding that the law and its application are frequently biased, insulting and injurious towards them, the marginalized may behave in ways that bring them into direct conflict with the law. This is a classic example of the self-fulfilling prophecy.

In the United States, the corrections system handles about 1.3 million offenders per day. Eighty percent of the people in this group come from the lowest 15 percent income group. Looked at another way, of the approximately 1.2 million people in state prisons in 1998, 30 percent were not employed at all and nearly half were without full-time employment prior to their arrest (Myers 1991; Reiman 2004). Beverley Bell-Rowbotham and Craig Boydell (1972) found that the highest rates of conviction in Canada were for people with little or no schooling and low-status occupations, with labourers having the highest rate. Lorne Tepperman (1977) noted that the police, prosecutors, judges and probation officers working within the Canadian justice system have been given a great deal of discretion in carrying out their duties towards the accused. Whenever this discretion is available it will be used in ways detrimental to the poor. William Chambliss and Robert Siedman (1971) agree with Tepperman, arguing that this discretion will be utilized by the legal and judicial authorities to bring the poor and powerless into the purview of the law. As a result, the laws prohibiting certain types of behaviour popular among the lower class are the most likely to be enforced.

Lower-status offenders are also less likely to be granted bail or recommendations for leniency from probation officers and others within the system. Accused persons who are not granted bail face severe problems. First of all, they are kept in jail, as if they had already been convicted. While in jail an accused person cannot seek out witnesses and evidence that could help in their defence. Studies have shown that those released on bail while awaiting trial are more likely to be acquitted or receive lighter sentences than those who are incarcerated while awaiting trial (Ares et al. 1963; Friedland 1965).

Even where crimes are identical, the courts will frequently give a middle- or upper-class offender a lighter sentence than that given a lower-class offender. It is assumed and sometimes stated by the court that since the upper-class offender has already "suffered enough" through loss of status brought about by the arrest and trial, incarceration would be socially and psychologically destructive. There is no empirical evidence to support this prejudicial notion that the poor suffer less than the rich from the humiliation and degradation of prison. Michael Mandel (1991: 152) suggests, "the tender attitude displayed to high status offenders by sentencing judges merely betrays their sympathy for the problems associated with their own class and their insensitivity to those of the working and marginal classes."

Jeffrey Reiman (1990) notes that weeding out the wealthy from the criminal certification process starts with the police deciding who to investigate, arrest and charge. The decision is not made simply on the basis of the offense committed, but also through a systematic class bias that works against the poor. This weeding-out process on the part of the police, combined with the class sympathies of the judiciary, causes our jails and penitentiaries to be populated predominantly by those from the fringes of society.

Afro-Canadian and Aboriginal peoples in particular seem to be targeted by the system for arrest, conviction and punishment. When a member of a visible minority is murdered the criminal justice system does not give the case high priority, but the killing of a white person by a member of a visible minority will cause the justice system to act with the greatest urgency (Radelet et al. 1986). Although Canada's Aboriginal peoples represented only about 4 percent of the total population in 2006, they constituted 18 percent of the population admitted to Canada's federal prisons and 20 percent admitted to provincial/territorial institutions in 2006/07 (Babooram 2008). In the prairies, where the Aboriginal population is higher, the over-representation of Aboriginal peoples in prison is higher. Specifically, in Saskatchewan and Manitoba, Aboriginal peoples represent 15 percent and 16 percent of the total population but 79 percent and 71 percent of the admissions to provincial/territorial sentenced custody (Landry and Sinha 2008).

Crime is also an economic engine for society. It generates employment for the police, lawyers, judges, court officials, prison guards and all the ancillary agencies that work within and support the system. Even the state-funded legal defence systems, designed to close the obvious gap in the quality of justice between the classes, have met with only limited success. The poor still get young, overworked and inexperienced lawyers who have little time to prepare an adequate defence for their clients. These systems seem to benefit the legal profession by creating a new source of guaranteed income while legitimizing the state (Snider 1985). In the same vein, Friedenberg (1980: 283), commenting on the legal industry, notes:

> It all rests on the backs of about 25,000 poor — mostly very poor — souls in jail. Most of them are less than thirty years old and have never finished school; a disproportionate number of them are Native people. In what other way could these few — these gallant if not happy few — impoverished in body and mind and often in spirit, contribute so much to their country?

Justice is essentially a system of social control. Historically it has favoured the interests of the powerful who have determined the law's content and implementation. A state that acts on behalf of the ruling class determines the laws, who will be certified as criminal and what punishments will be levied (Panitch 1977). The majority of those caught and convicted for criminal activities have consistently been from the ranks of the disadvantaged. For any given crime, the poor are more likely to be arrested; if arrested, more likely to be charged; if charged, more likely to be convicted; if convicted, more likely to be sent to prison; and if sent to prison, more likely to receive a longer term than deviants from other classes (Reiman 1990). The explanation for these disproportionate conviction rates among Canada's marginalized population will not be found simply in the behaviour of the poor, but in the class and racial biases infesting our society. But what has this bias, which leads to the conviction and punishment of the poor, got to do with wrongful convictions?

If arrest, conviction and the type of sentence are biased against the poor and the minorities in our society, is it not logical to assume that wrongful conviction will be shaped by the same social forces? Our society is fraught with serious structural inequalities based on class and race, which frequently transform the Western ideal of justice into a utilitarian search for a conviction. As revealed in several studies carried out in Britain and the United States, this search for a conviction all too often ends with a marginalized individual becoming the victim of a miscarriage of justice (Carvel 1992; Huff et al. 1986; Bedau and Radelet 1987). Often poor, uneducated and powerless, these wrongly accused end up incarcerated or executed for a crime they did not commit.

Even factors as seemingly innocuous as eyewitnesses reporting of a crime may be jaundiced by social inequality. While this is a growing area of research, still more scientific information regarding the major causes of wrongful eyewitness reporting in criminal trials is needed. We should, however, be conscious of the fact that eyewitnesses themselves are frequently marginalized people who are easily coerced by the police and prosecution. Faulty eyewitness evidence led to the initial convictions of Donald Marshall Jr., David Milgaard and Thomas Sophonow. The faulty testimony was not the result simply of human error. The witnesses were pressured by police to the point where they abandoned their original testimony and presented false evidence. Witnesses are not immune to the socially structured prejudice that characterizes our society. The notion that because eyewitness give evidence under oath they are somehow free of prejudice and bigotry plays into the hands of the apologists who would have us believe that wrongful convictions are a product of chance error.

Eyewitnesses are influenced, consciously or unconsciously, by their personal notions of truth and reality. Thus, an eyewitness who harbours a fear or hatred of a particular minority or racial group may incorrectly think the suspect he or she saw at the scene of the crime was a member of that group when in reality the suspect was not. Ideological beliefs do influence our perceptions of reality, including what and who we may have seen at any given point in time. And as long as such ideologies and attitudes are sustained by the social structure, eyewitness reporting must be considered suspect. Similarly, the social inequality characteristic of Canadian society may be responsible for the fact that the police play such a dominant role in wrongful convictions. It was noted above that police activity concentrates on marginalized groups and has stereotyped them as criminal (Reiman 1990). This false stereotype discriminates against and ignores individual differences among marginalized peoples. Pre-judging by the police leads to increased surveillance, harassment, arrest and conviction of members of these groups, in turn almost guaranteeing that those who are wrongfully convicted will come predominantly from the marginalized sectors.

It is no longer acceptable to suggest that wrongful conviction resulting from police activities is simply the result of numerous bizarre elements coincidentally coming together. Wrongful convictions are frequently the result of the mundane and malevolent behaviour of various state agents, including the police, which is directed against minority groups and marginalized peoples. This is not to suggest that the police are ideologically unique in their attitudes towards marginalized groups. They simply reflect the values and culture of which they are part. Indeed, R.H.D. Head, then Assistant Commissioner of the Royal Canadian Mounted Police, has acknowledged that "We have a racial intolerance within the force because, as a product of a larger Canadian society we enter its ranks with all the usual bias, prejudice and racism baggage that this society generates" (quoted in Harding 1991: 363–383).

Regardless of this frank confession, police officers who have targeted the underprivileged will deny this activity to protect themselves from loss of promotion, loss of job and criminal charges. People who have been harassed or intimidated by the police must make their case against police officers who are generally regarded by the public and members of juries as stalwart, respectable defenders of the law. Marginalized individuals, on the other hand, are frequently regarded with suspicion or fear by a predominantly white, middle-class population. Their charges against the police are unlikely to be given serious consideration. Such public apathy plays a major role in the outcome of any investigation of police misconduct (Anderson and Winfree 1987).

Lawyers, judges and juries are also major players in the drama of wrongful convictions. Their actions are often rooted in an inequitable social structure. Marginalized peoples do not have the economic means to pay for top-level legal counsel. They must rely on young, inexperienced, underpaid and overworked legal aid lawyers to defend them. These people have neither the time nor the resources to mount a good defence for their client. As a result, the poor become the classic victims of plea-bargaining pressure. Reiman (1990) notes that the vast majority of criminal convictions in the United States are concluded through plea bargaining. In Canada, Ericson and Baranek (1982) found that over half the lawyers they interviewed admitted to plea bargaining. The police were frequently involved in these discussions. Many of those lawyers who plea bargained felt that the bargain they reached brought no real advantage for the accused since the police had overcharged their client in the first place. In the plea-bargaining process, people are often advised by their lawyers to plead guilty to crimes they did not commit in order to avoid going to trial for a greater charge.

Why do accused but innocent people agree to plea bargain their case? For one thing, these individuals may know that there is considerable circumstantial evidence against them, and that the probability of being found guilty and sentenced to a long prison term or death is high. They may feel, correctly or incorrectly, that they have little choice but to bargain with the prosecution for a lesser charge and sentence in exchange for their guilty plea. There is also the possibility of legal pressure being put on the accused to plea bargain. If, for example, the suspect is not a model citizen, has a criminal record, is of the lower class, or comes from a visible minority, there is a strong possibility he or she will be represented by an overworked and underpaid legal aid lawyer who will encourage them to make a deal with the prosecution so the lawyer can get on with the next case (Huff et al. 1996). Even if the defence lawyer is not from legal aid, a plea bargain may be encouraged because a lawyer will benefit financially by concluding as many cases as possible in the shortest period of time. Likewise, prosecutors and others in a cash-strapped justice system are anxious to move cases through the system as quickly as possible. An unspoken agreement exists among defence counsel, prosecutors, judges and others within the system to encourage the defendant to plead guilty (Hagan 1977). During pre-trial negotiations, which occur behind closed doors, judicial control and rules of evidence are not available to the accused (Tepperman 1977). The accused pleads guilty and does not protest his or her innocence. As a result, the miscarriage of justice goes undetected. Plea bargaining is a cheap and efficient method of dispensing justice, one which can lead to poor people being wrongfully convicted.

Prosecuting lawyers are vulnerable to charges of professional misconduct leading to wrongful conviction. A trial is an adversarial tournament between jousting lawyers played out before a judge and jury. Theoretically, the Crown prosecutor's paramount responsibility is to ensure that justice is done. If the prosecutor becomes aware of information that casts serious doubt on the guilt of the accused, the prosecutor is supposed to share such information with the court. If necessary, the Crown should drop all charges. Unfortunately, this does not always happen.

The Crown prosecutor has access to state funding, police services and forensic expertise. Counsel for the defence, by contrast, may be significantly hampered by the accused's inability to pay for services. The prosecution's discretionary privileges include the right to reduce a charge from the more serious to less serious, reduce the number of charges outstanding against the accused, order a stay of proceedings, or entirely withdraw the charges. Unfortunately, in many instances, the discretion exercised by the prosecution is not carried out in the interest of justice but may be influenced by the prosecutor's own attitude about the accused, the profile of the case and the political and personal implications of winning or losing (Tepperman 1977). While the majority of lawyers regard themselves as respectable middle-class professionals serving a necessary function in society, they are also individuals who have deeply ingrained middle-class views and values about crime and criminals. One may logically expect that prosecutors and defenders will be inclined to serve their own class-biased interests first, before dedicating their services to those on the fringes of society. Some lawyers have a profound understanding of the true nature of social injustice and dedicate their lives to serving the underprivileged, but they are a rare breed. Lacking the services of the most skilled of lawyers, those of the lower classes more quickly fall victim to the injustice of justice.

Judges as a group are near the top of the social structure, but this does not mean that they are isolated from the racism, classism, politics and other biasing realities of our society. Judges have a value system that shapes their worldview and the way in which they approach their work. John Hogarth (1971) notes that judges as a group have a perception of themselves as being in and of the Canadian elite. They are well-educated, prosperous, conservative and similar to the police in their intolerance for deviants and their belief in the efficacy of penal servitude. In 1974 the Law Reform Commission of Canada noted that the treatment of accused individuals by judges reflects the concern of any prosperous person for life and property when dealing with the poor. Aware of their privileged social position, judges are not about to advocate changes to the system that is the source of their power. As a general rule, however, the public, including those serving as jury members, are unaware of potential judicial bias. They regard judges as wise and impartial adjudicators concerned only with seeing justice served. This public attitude toward the judiciary gives judges the social and legal power to greatly influence any decision rendered by a jury.

The outcome of many trials is determined by evidence presented in court by forensic experts, who frequently work closely with the police, prosecutors and Crown lawyers. These specialists take pride in telling us that forensic evidence is not tainted by the subjectivity that can plague social science research and the law. It is true that the tremendous advances made in forensics in recent years have caused much of the scientific evidence presented in court to be accepted as virtual truth. Unfortunately, while the science itself may be highly objective, the same cannot be said for all the scientists who interpret the evidence and present their opinions on the findings. Forensic pathologist Dr. Smith's mistakes went unchallenged for a number of years, resulting in the conviction of innocent people. Barry Tarlow (1995) cites numerous cases of evidence tampering by forensic experts who were acting on behalf of the prosecution. For example, Fred Zain was Chief Physical Evidence Officer of Bexar County, Texas, from 1989 to 1993, during which time he "systematically falsified, misinterpreted and exaggerated forensic tests and results which may have led to the conviction of hundreds of individuals" (Tarlow 1995: 18). This is perhaps an example of how the personal beliefs and values of a forensic scientist may interfere with the supposed value neutrality of science. In San Francisco, as many as one thousand people may have been convicted of drug-related offenses over a five-year period because a police department chemist falsified drug tests and results (Tarlow 1995). Stephanie Nyznyk, a laboratory technician working out of the Centre for Forensic Sciences in Ontario, suppressed the fact that hair and fibre samples used by the prosecution to convict Guy Paul Morin of murder had been contaminated and should have been discarded as evidence. The cases of James Driskell and William Mullins-Johnson also demonstrate the role of forensic science in wrongful convictions; for example, in the case of Driskell, faulty hair analysis contributed to his wrongful conviction. Despite the belief that forensic science is infallible and always one hundred percent accurate, a belief popularized by the recent fascination with crime shows based on forensic science (such as CSI), we have to remember that sometimes the science can be wrong, and can lead to a miscarriage of justice.

The British and American research noted above proves beyond any reasonable doubt that serious miscarriages of justice resulting in wrongful convictions are not isolated events. The only evidence we have about how such convictions occur, however, emerges from the more sensational crimes that generate media attention, primarily murder. Unfortunately, the factors of powerlessness and inequality that are the root cause of wrongful convictions in the first place are also the factors preventing the wrongfully convicted from establishing their innocence. Proving one is wrongfully convicted requires money, but it also requires many middle-class social attributes and skills unfamiliar to marginalized people. Consequently, for most of the wrongfully convicted, it is a classic case of "out of sight, out of mind." Only the most fortunate among them will gain their freedom.

The Canadian justice system is class based. Laws are made by middle-class politicians for middle-class people, enforced by middle-class police, argued over by middle-class lawyers and arbitrated by middle-class judges who sentence mostly lower-class people to prisons run by middle-class administrators. At no point do marginalized peoples play a role in developing or administering the system. Excluded from the mainstream, they are frequently swept up in the net of social injustice by the very institution that should protect them. Systemic inequalities ensure that the marginalized will be the criminals and the wrongfully convicted.

The eight case reviews we examine in *Manufacturing Guilt* are only a sample of the many known instances of wrongful conviction in Canada. They should give the reader a deeper insight into the contributing factors leading to this unfortunate phenomenon. The cases presented were purposely selected for several reasons. Some have received extensive media exposure, but this exposure, while long on description and sensationalism, has been short on analysis regarding the social forces that led to the convictions. The less well-known cases were selected, not because they supported a particular theoretical point of view, but because they are truly representative of the vast majority of wrongful convictions. Had space permitted, other cases such as those of William Nepoose, Eric Biddle, Tommy Ross, Kyle Unger and Romeo Phillion, as well as countless documented British and American cases, would have been included. These, too, would confirm what the cases presented here clearly show: the root cause of wrongful convictions is to be found primarily in the social structure itself, not in individual failings.

It is consistently denied by judges, lawyers, prosecutors and the police that politics, racism, sexism and professional interests influence their respective actions within the justice system. As the cases of Donald Marshall, Guy Paul Morin and others attest, this is a myth perpetrated on an unsuspecting public. Regardless of what those who control the justice system tell us, it is a fundamentally flawed system infected with overt secrecy, corruption, brutality, racism and class prejudice on the part of some police, lawyers, judges and others who work within the system. It is not surprising, therefore, that those who are wrongfully convicted are the marginalized of society, the direct victims of the systemic biases inherent in our social structure. As Radelet et al. (1986) note, the ideal that all people are born with an equal chance of dying in the electric chair is a myth. Alastair Logan (1995: 7) says it best when he states that the racism that was so much a part of Donald Marshall's life "walked ahead of him into the police station, into his lawyer's office and into his court of trial. It directed the quality of justice he received."

References

Anderson, Patrick R.L., and Thomas Winfree Jr. 1987. "Criminal Justice Scholars as Expert Witnesses: A Descriptive Analysis." In Patrick R.L. Anderson and Thomas Winfree Jr. (eds.), *Expert Witness: Criminologists in the Courtroom*. Albany, NY: University of New York Press.

Ares, C.E., A.A. Rankin, and J.H. Sturtz. 1963. "The Manhattan Bail Project: An Interim Report on the Use of Pre-Trial Parole." *NYU Law Review*, 38.

Babooram, Avani. 2008. "The Changing Profile of Adults in Custody, 2006/07." *Statistics Canada Juristat*. <http://www.statcan.gc.ca/pub/85-002-x/2008010/article/10732-eng.pdf>

Battle, Ken. 1998. "Poverty and the Welfare State." In Les Samuelson (ed.), *Power and Resistance: Critical Thinking about Canadian Social Issues, 2nd edition*. Halifax: Fernwood Publishing.

Bedau, H.A., and M.L. Radelet. 1987. "Miscarriages of Justice in Potentially Capital Cases." *Stanford Law Review*, 40.

Bell-Rowbotham, Beverly, and Craig L. Boydell. 1972. "Crime in Canada: A Distributional Analysis." In Craig Boydell, Carl F. Grindstaff, and Paul C. Whitehead (eds.), *Deviant Behaviour and Societal Reaction*. Toronto: Holt.

Bonger, Willem. 1967. *Criminality and Economic Conditions*. Boston: Little.

Borchard, Edwin M. 1932. *Convicting the Innocent*. New Haven: Yale University Press.

Brooks, Carolyn. 2008. "The Politics of Imprisonment." In Carolyn Brooks and Bernard Schissel (eds.), *Marginality and Condemnation: An Introduction to Criminology, 2nd edition*. Halifax: Fernwood Publishing.

Canadian Council on Social Development. n.d. "Economic Security Fact Sheet #2: Poverty." A Profile of Economic Security in Canada. <http://www.ccsd.ca/factsheets/economic_security/poverty/index.htm>.

Carvel, John. 1992. "Many Prisoners Could Be Wrongly Jailed." *Guardian Weekly*, April 5.

Chambliss, William J., and Robert B. Siedman. 1971. *Law Order and Power*. Reading, MA: Wesley.

Clayton, Mark. 1995. "Captives of a Flawed Justice System." *Christian Science Monitor*,

March 27.
Comack, Elizabeth, and Gillian Balfour. 2004. *The Power to Criminalize: Violence, Inequality and the Law*. Halifax and Winnipeg: Fernwood Publishing.
Denov, Myriam, and Kathryn Campbell. 2008. "When Justice Fails: Understanding Miscarriages of Justice." In Julian Roberts and Michelle Grossman (eds.), *Criminal Justice in Canada: A Reader, 3rd edition*. Nashville, TN: Thomson Nelson.
Department of Justice. 2007. *Applications for Ministerial Review — Miscarriages of Justice: Annual Report 2007*.
____. 2008. *Applications for Ministerial Review — Miscarriages of Justice: Annual Report 2008*.
Ericson, R.V., and P.M. Baranek. 1982. *The Ordering of Justice: A Study of Accused Persons as Dependents in the Criminal Process*. Toronto: University of Toronto Press.
Frank, Jerome, and Barbara Frank. 1957. *Not Guilty*. Garden City, NY: Doubleday.
Friedenberg, E.Z. 1980. "The Punishment Industry in Canada." *Canadian Journal of Sociology*, 5, 3.
Friedland, Martin L. 1965. *Detention Before Trial: A Study of Criminal Cases Tried in the Toronto Magistrates' Courts*. Toronto: University of Toronto Press.
Globe and Mail. 1995. "Picture Imperfect." January 21: D8.
Hagan, John. 1977. *The Disreputable Pleasures*. Toronto: McGraw-Hill.
Harding, Jim. 1991. "Policing and Aboriginal Justice." *Canadian Journal of Criminology*, 33, 3–4.
Hogarth, John. 1971. *Sentencing as a Human Process*. Toronto: University of Toronto Press.
Huff, C. Ronald, Ayre Rattner, and Edward Sagarin. 1986. "Guilty Until Proven Innocent: Wrongful Convictions and Public Policy." *Crime and Delinquency*, 32, 4.
____. 1996. *Convicted but Innocent: Wrongful Conviction and Public Policy*. Thousand Oaks, CA: Sage.
Landry, Laura, and Maire Sinha. 2008. "Adult Correctional Services in Canada, 2005/2006." *Juristat*. <www.statcan.gc.ca/pub/85-002-x/85-002-x2008006-eng.pdf>.
Logan, Alastair. 1995. "What Causes a Miscarriage of Justice?" AIDWYC *Journal*, 1, 1.
MacFarlane, Bruce. n.d. "Wrongful Convictions: The Effect of Tunnel Vision and Predisposing Circumstances in the Criminal Justice System." <www.canadiancriminallaw.com/articles/articles%20pdf/Wrongful-Convictions.pdf>.
Maclean, Brian. 1986. *The Political Economy of Crime*. Scarborough, ON: Prentice.
Mandel, Michael. 1991. "Democracy, Class and Canadian Sentencing Law." In Elizabeth Comack and Stephen Brickley (eds.), *The Social Basis of Law: Critical Readings in the Sociology of Law*. Toronto: Garamond.
Myers, Martha. 1991. "A Structural and Judicial Discrimination in Sentencing." In Les Samuelson and Bernard Schissel (eds.), *Criminal Justice Sentencing Issues and Reform*. Toronto: Garamond.
Panitch, Leo. 1977. "The Role and Nature of the Canadian State." In Leo Panitch (ed.), *The Canadian State: Political Economy and Political Power*. Toronto: University of Toronto Press.
Radelet, Michael L., Hugo Adam Bedeau, Constance Putnam, and Margaret Vandiver. 1986. "Race and Capital Punishment: An Overview of Issues." *Crime and Social Justice*, 25.
Ratner, Robert, John L. McMullan, and Brian E. Burtch. 1987. "The Problem of Relative Autonomy and Criminal Justice in the Canadian State." In Robert Ratner and John L.

McMullan (eds.), *State Control: Criminal Justice Politics in Canada*. Vancouver: University of British Columbia Press.

Rattner, Ayre. 1983. "Convicting the Innocent: When Justice Goes Wrong." Unpublished PhD dissertation, Ohio State University.

____. 1988. "Convicted but Innocent: Wrongful Convictions and the Criminal Justice System." *Law And Human Behaviour*, 12, 3.

Reiman, J. 1990. *The Rich Get Richer and the Poor Get Prison*, 3rd edition. New York: Macmillan.

____. 2004. *The Rich Get Richer and the Poor Get Prison*, 7th edition. Boston, MA: Allyn and Bacon.

Rosen, Philip. 1992. *Wrongful Convictions in the Criminal Justice System*. Ottawa: Library of Parliament Research Branch. BP 285E, January.

Ross, David, and Richard Shillington. 1989. *The Canadian Fact Book on Poverty, 1989*. Toronto: Canadian Council on Social Development.

Scott, Robert, and Andrew Skull. 1978. "Penal Reform and the Surplus Army of Labour." In William K. Greenaway and Stephen L. Brickey (eds.), *Law and Social Control in Canada*. Scarborough, ON: Prentice.

Snider, Laureen. 1985. "Legal Aid, Reform, and the Welfare State." *Crime and Social Justice*, 24.

Statistics Canada. 2004. "Family Income Groups (21), Sex (3) and Aboriginal Group of Lone Parent (11) for Lone-Parent Census Families in Private Households, for Canada, Provinces and Territories, 2000 — 20% Sample Data." 97F0020XCB2001065. <www12.statcan.ca/english/census01/products/standard/themes/RetrieveProductTable.cfm?Temporal=2001&PID=60146&APATH=3&GID=355313&METH=1&PTYPE=55496&THEME=54&FOCUS=0&AID=0&PLACENAME=0&PROVINCE=0&SEARCH=0&GC=0&GK=0&VID=0&VNAMEE=&VNAMEF=&FL=0&RL=0&FREE=0>.

Stephens, Sam. 1991. "Aboriginal People and the Canadian Justice System." In Les Samuelson and Bernard Schissel (eds.), *Criminal Justice Sentencing Issues and Reform*. Toronto: Garamond.

Stern, Vivien. 2006. *Creating Criminals: Prisons and People in a Market Society*. Halifax: Fernwood Publishing.

Tarlow, Barry. 1995. "The Truth May Set You Free." AIDWYC *Journal*, 1, 1.

Tepperman, Lorne. 1977. *Crime Control*. Toronto, ON: McGraw.

USA Today. 1994. "Convicted on False Evidence?" July 19.

Yalnizyan, Armine. 1994. "Securing Society: Creating Canadian Social Policy." In Armine Yalnizyan, T. Ran Idle and Arthur Cordell (eds.), *Shifting Time: Social Policy and the Future of Work*. Toronto: Between the Lines.

____. 2007. "The Rich and the Rest of Us: The Changing Face of Canada's Growing Gap." Canadian Centre for Policy Alternatives. <www.policyalternatives.ca/documents/National_Office_Pubs /2007/The_Rich_and_the_Rest_of_Us.pdf>.

Chapter 3

CRIME, JUSTICE AND THE CONDEMNATION AND EXPLOITATION OF THE YOUNG

Bernard Schissel

From: *Still Blaming Children: Youth Conduct and the Politics of Child Hating*, 2nd edition, Chapter 1 (reprinted with permission of the author).

A crescendo of anxious voices lamented the proliferation of the poor and unproductive in the towns and villages of England. Moralists constantly complained about the swarms of idle and dissipated young people who were not being contained within the system of household discipline — the system on which, most people believed, social stability depended. Stability in the state, Tudor preachers never tired of reminding their congregations, rested on stability in the family. (Underdown 1992: 11–12)

THE DEVELOPMENT OF YOUTH JUSTICE AND THE EROSION OF CHILD PROTECTION

Whether Canadians like to admit it or not, Canada's war on crime, like the war on crime in many other countries, and in other eras (as described above), has, in an important sense, become a war against youth. With proposals to reintroduce the death penalty for young killers or implement mandatory boot camps for all young offenders, Canadian society is embarking on a crusade to increase punishment for children, ostensibly, in the hopes of curbing crime.

The focal point for this law-and-order campaign was the Young Offenders Act (1982), which was replaced by the Youth Criminal Justice Act (2003). The Young Offenders Act (YOA) was struck to give youth the same rights and freedoms as their adult counterparts. It replaced the Juvenile Delinquents Act (JDA) of 1908, which was based on the principle of *parens patriae*, that the state is the ultimate guardian of the child. The JDA gave the state the right to override the civil liberties of the child and the family and to intervene forcibly in family life. This welfare approach to childhood essentially gave juvenile authorities wide discretionary powers in the informal policing of juveniles.

In response, the Young Offenders Act was ordained to re-establish the legal rights of youth. The Act was intended to ensure several things: that accused youth would be adequately represented in court; that their parents or guardians would be informed of their arrest and would be directed to appear in court; that accused youth would be informed of their rights and every effort made to ensure that they are able to make informed decisions about their legal options; and that the names and other references of the accused would be kept in confidence, safe from public scrutiny. Most importantly, however, the YOA was supposed to ensure that young offenders, whenever possible, would be directed away from the formal legal process and toward alternative measures, including community-based programs of reparation and mediation. So, in the final analysis, the principles of the YOA were declared, in general, to protect the civil liberties of young people and specifically, to provide them with non-judicial options.

The 1984 implementation of the Young Offenders Act, however, did not ameliorate the concerns of critics, who argued that the youth justice system continued to avoid the issue of what they perceived to be an increase in crime rates for Canadian youth. They argued that it was too lenient, that youth were not deterred because of the soft punishments allotted under the Act and that it allowed for the release of dangerous adolescent offenders into society. The harshest critics, usually found within groups that followed a "law-and-order" ideology, such as police organizations and victim's rights groups, argued that the Act lacked punitive measures and placed undue emphasis on the rights of the offender while ignoring the rights of the victims of crime. Ex-police officer turned author Carsten Stroud (1993), in his book *Contempt of Court: The Betrayal of Justice in Canada,* underscores the position taken by these critics with his claim that police cynically refer to the Young Offenders Act as the Youth Protection Act. Less punitive-minded critics believed that the problems with the Act had roots, not so much in the legislation itself, but in its administration. They charged the provinces with failing to implement some of the Act's more treatment-oriented provisions. Provincial administrators countered by arguing that the yoa was a complicated piece of legislation and difficult to make work (Tanner 1996).

Numerous amendments were proposed to deal with the criticisms aimed at both administration and content of the yoa (Bell 2002). Bill C-106 was introduced in the House of Commons on April 30, 1986, and passed by the Senate on June 26, 1986. This first amendment to the Young Offenders Act focused mainly on technical and procedural aspects of the law (Winterdyk 2000). A further amendment, Bill C-12, which came into force in of 1992, increased maximum sentences for murder from three to five years, outlined continuation of custody provisions and clarified rules for transferring youth to adult court (Winterdyk 2000: 447).

Bill C-37, put forward in 1994 and declared in force on the first of December 1995, represented another attempt by the federal government to balance the demands of competing groups for changes to the Young Offenders Act. It increased the maximum sentences for murder to ten years, created a presumption of transfer to adult court for sixteen to seventeen year olds charged with serious offences and allowed written victim impact statements in youth court. In total, there were nine relatively punitive recommendations put forward by Bill C-37, which formed the basis for Bill C-68.

THE YOUTH CRIMINAL JUSTICE ACT

Bill C-68, introduced in the House of Commons on March 11, 1999, came into force as the Youth Criminal Justice Act (YCJA) in April 2003. The new Act attempts to address concerns put forward from both those who argue for more punitive actions and those who argue for the need for special considerations for youth who come into conflict with the law. Public safety and security are now at the core of youth justice. To ensure public safety, the new Act includes the possibility for strong punitive measures to be employed against youth who are considered dangerous, violent or habitual offenders. Ontario's Ministry of the Attorney General made over a hundred recommendations to the federal government on ways to make young offenders more accountable for violent acts, including to automatically try and sentence sixteen and seventeen year olds as adults when they are charged with a serious, presumptive offence such as murder, attempted murder or manslaughter (Ministry of the Attorney General 2000). According to Justice Canada the primary features of the new YCJA address the following issues: strong community sentencing measures for youth in conflict with the law; diversion by both police and prosecution; and new, intensive rehabilitation custody and supervision sentences, including custody in adult prisons, available for offenders convicted of presumptive offences. According to section 2 of the YCJA, presumptive offences are offences committed by a young offender over the age of fourteen and include first- and second-degree murder, manslaughter, aggravated sexual assault and violent offences equivalent to those for which an adult would be liable to imprisonment for more than two years. The new sentences also apply to youth with mental illnesses, psychological disorders and emotional disturbances, thus allowing youth justice court judges to direct treatment and programming but also to deal with offenders designated as dangers to public safety.

The new Act incorporates several other features: 1) the option for youth with patterns of repeat offending to receive adult sentences at the age of fourteen years and older; 2) the publication of names of youth convicted of a crime who receive adult sentences; 3) the provision for a sentence of up to two years in jail for a parent who willfully fails to supervise his or her children when the parent has an undertaking with the court (Department of Justice Canada 1999).

THE REPERCUSSIONS OF A MORE PUNITIVE FORM OF YOUTH JUSTICE

Youth justice reform in Canada, over several years culminating in the YCJA, has served to erode the protection/welfare philosophy towards children and youth and has replaced it with a societal safety, just-desserts agenda (Hogeveen and Smandych 2001). The historical development of a Canadian youth criminal justice system appears to represent a transfer from the notion that children were essentially "adults in training," to a belief that children were in need of protection and welfare, to an attempt to balance the needs of youth with the rights of society in regard to public safety. It is arguable that recent youth crime legislation reflects an increasingly tough attitude that youth should be held accountable for their deeds and that parents should be punished for the delinquent or criminal actions of their offspring. As a result, "the focus of policies to curb youth crime seems to be increasingly on families and individuals rather than society as a whole (Alvi 2000: 38). Further, Giroux (2003) has alerted us to the reality that the politics of individualization — the notion that crime lives within individuals — is accompanied by state policy that valorizes and privileges "privatization, deregulation, consumption, and safety" (xix). It is interesting in this context that increasingly punitive youth justice laws accompany increasing corporate sovereignty and increasing campaigns by corporations to target youth as the new super-consumers.

The generalized law-and-order mindset in Canada, and many other countries, that is typified by the YCJA, especially the provisions that are intended to protect the public, seems to stand in contradistinction to the overall principles of earlier incarnations of youth justice in Canada. Those early provisions held that prevention and rehabilitation were constructive, that young people needed their judicial rights protected and that punishment and public condemnation were ultimately destructive to the young offender and to society. Interestingly, the YOA and the YCJA, in their original conceptions, were both based on progressive, compassionate provisions that embodied like intentions: 1) to foster the use of community-based, non-carceral alternatives to formal punishment; 2) to provide short-term maximum sentences for even the most dangerous offenders; 3) to minimize labelling through the insurance of anonymity through publication bans; 4) to provide civil rights of the young offender through adequate legal and parental representation in court.

Fiscal and political realities have dictated that the progressive provisions of Canadian youth justice have become supplanted by orthodox law-and-order policies, which are driven by lack of funding and an obsession with public protection. The changes brought about by the new law insure that "soft," non-serious offenders are cut adrift because of lack of alternatives and more serious offenders are dealt with in a more draconian fashion than before, through longer sentences and transfers to adult facilities. Programs and organization systems that were supposed to replace the formal justice system under the YCJA have been poorly realized, and police and court officials have been left with little alternative but to use the formal legal code in ministering to young offenders, especially repeat and serious offenders. The state's inability to support the spirit and intent of the alternative measures provision of the YCJA has given right-wing political movements ample fodder for their "we told you so" agenda. With the rise in the number of "street kids" (which is certainly a social/political problem and not a criminological phenomenon) and with a profusion of highly publicized violent crimes committed by youth, the "war on young offenders" is a *cause celebre* that politicians seem unable to resist. And, as we will come to see, the discourse of "gangs" permeates the contemporary public consciousness.

STILL BLAMING CHILDREN

If we were in the beginning stages of a "moral panic" that indicted children and adolescents, especially the marginalized and disadvantaged, for their dangerousness and their growing disrespect of adults (as I argued in *Blaming Children*), I contend that the *fin de siecle* moral panic has grown into a much more subtle and powerful social movement against kids. The end result of the condemnation of young people is the continuing scapegoating of youth for political purposes, and, in keeping with the irony of punishment, the alienation of a more uncompromising, more disaffiliated youth population. Increasing punishment, while denying access to civic and political involvement, greatly increases the likelihood of alienation and ultimately of young people's antisocial behaviour. Despite the political rhetoric to the contrary, we do not collectively consider children our most valuable resource. In fact, we consider them one of our most dangerous threats.

Our collective disintegrating wish to protect children in our society is the focus of this book. I explain the nature and the extent of the moral panic about youth criminogenesis by discussing the role of the media and its affiliations with information/political systems, with its readers/viewers and with corporate Canada. The current political pastime of "blaming children" for all social evils is placed in the context of changing international, national and local agendas. I contend that public panics are predictable in that they have little to do with a criminogenic reality, but much to do with the economic and political context in which they arise. Furthermore, crime panics are targeted at vulnerable and marginal people. In fact, a critical analysis of media coverage brings us to a particular political moral position: the public perception of seriousness of crime is largely a matter of misjudgements and fear about race, geography and family constitution. I argue further that the panic that vilifies children is a coordinated, calculated attempt to nourish the ideology that supports a society stratified on the bases of race, class and gender and that the war on kids is part of the state-business mechanism that continually reproduces an oppressive social and economic order through both labour and consumer exploitation (Giroux 2003; Hall et al. 1978; Iyengar and Kinde 1987; Herman and Chomsky 1988).

Ironically, this country is prepared to ignore the reality that:

- there is little real increase in serious youth crime;
- that participation rates in criminal activities are relatively stable;
- that youth crime is comprised mostly of petty, unthinking acts;
- that the increase in official rates of youth criminal behaviour is largely the result of increased arrest rates;
- the courts have adopted a zero-tolerance mentality;
- that society is largely unable to provide effective alternatives to punishment; and
- that, most importantly, the things for which youth are arrested and incarcerated are matters of health much more than they are matters of criminality, drug abuse being the most obvious example.

I do not mean to imply that there are no habitual young offenders, some of whom are dangerous. However, not only does the general public perceive that youth crime is on the rise, but conventional analysts, including some progressive, critical ones defend the political move to a more punitive youth crime policy on the basis of a more dangerous, criminogenic youth population. Despite the analytical polemics, most Canadian cities are confronted by high-risk youth, many of whom are "on the street" and vulnerable to exploitation by adults. Such youth often retaliate aggressively. Habitual and potentially dangerous offenders are a small minority, but only their activities seem to inform the moral panic debates. And of course, their own victimization and disadvantage disappear in the accounts of their dangerousness.

As political movements come to terms with their "terror of adolescents," the debates seem to coalesce around the suffering of those who are victims of violent crime. The fear of crime, which seems to be forever increasing, is a powerfully personal and politically emotional tool. Ironically, the fear of kids in Canada has been fuelled by two phenomena that are largely the result of business as usual.

First, part of the problem has been the increased visibility of young people in public places. As industry "rationalizes" production by reducing employment costs, youth unemployment rises, to as high as 30 percent in some regions. Simply put, more youth have increasingly more idle time, and the work that is available is poorly paid, bereft of benefits and offers little in terms of meaningful apprenticeship. The typical employee at a fast food outlet is an adolescent, the typical wage is at or just above minimum wage, the work is typically hard and quite dangerous, and the typical benefits package is non-existent. Furthermore, centralized shopping centres built with profits rather than community solidarity in mind, have become gathering placed for unemployed adolescents. While their presence is not discouraged by private interests, large numbers of youth in places such as shopping malls fuel the panic that kids are loitering with intent. The reality for children and youth in a global world is labour exploitation and consumer "abuse." The irony is that youth are badly needed in bourgeoning capitalism, but they are condemned either through omission or by commission.

Second, most people gain their images and opinions about the nature and extent of crime through the media. In Canada, much of our vicarious experience with youth crime is filtered through Canadian and American television. American news, much of which teeters on the brink of fiction, is highly sensational, selective to time and place, and focuses primarily on dangerous individuals. I argue that such depictions are not based on reality but rather on the wants of a presumed audience. The news industry argues that their function is to present news accounts that are based on an objective reality. More likely, however, the industry constructs the news to appeal to the demands of a frightened audience and a political-economic system that casts blame. Especially in a post–9/11 era, news is more controlled than in the past and the freedom of speech that journalists traditionally depended upon to be good journalists is much more tenuous (Chomsky 2002).

What we are left with is a gulf between reality and perception. The reality is that youth are mostly disenfranchised from the democratic process at all levels of governance, they are disadvantaged in the labour market and they have few services available to them, unlike their adult counterparts. When they do break the law, they are most likely to victimize other disadvantaged youth. Although youth crime has not increased significantly in recent years, the prosecution of youth crime has.

That reality stands in stark contrast to the singular collective perception that kids are out of control, that they are more dangerous now than ever and that youth crime is expanding at an alarming rate. How do we explain the existence of a belief system that moralizes about and condemns children in the face of contradictory evidence? Are we, as a society, so uncertain about our ability to raise children that we constantly question the culture of youth? Are we, in an adult-created and based world, so unfamiliar with adolescent social conventions that we are frightened by the unfamiliar? Or, are there structural forces at work that construct, communicate and perpetuate a belief system that benefits those who have access to power and indicts those who live on the margins of society? Fear is a great motivator. Society's growing fear of kids, its moral panic about their criminogenesis, has significant power to marginalize and disenfranchise young people.

MORAL PANICS AND POWER

One of the important considerations in understanding moral panics as historical and socio-political phenomena is that they are not unique and evolutionary, but that they occur regularly and predictably throughout history. Much of the moral panic literature, common in critical criminological research of the late sixties and early seventies, used historical analyses to study the phenomenon of putative crime waves and the origins of public panics about crime (Hall et al. 1978; Cohen 1980). The research concentrated on how atypical or rare events at particular historical junctures came to raise the collective ire to the point where the public demanded law reform. In addition, the literature concentrated on how official and popular culture accounts of criminality were based on over-generalized, inaccurate and stereotypical descriptions of criminals and their associations, and how the public panics that resulted were mostly directed at working class or marginalized people. Much of the research, in addition, concentrated on moral panics over youth crime, especially in relation to alienated, organized, gang-based delinquents.

Stanley Cohen's (1980) influential work developed the concept of moral panic to study and make sense of British society's alarm and attack on youth in the 1960s and early 1970s. His analysis of the construction of the "Mods and Rockers" illustrated how this political/linguistic device, based on social stereotyping, came to circumscribe youth misconduct. He also illustrated how the media, through their abilities to use evocative language and imagery, alerted the public to a potentially criminogenic youth, coined by Cohen as "folk devils." Cohen discovered that once the folk devil was identified by the mainstream media, the context for understanding youth crime was established. For example, the judiciary and the police overreacted to those identified as gang members and came to view the Mods and Rockers as a conspiratorial, well-organized force. The media as well were inordinately preoccupied with understanding the youth malefactor as a gang member and dangerous youth as organized conspiracies of defiance.

Equally important as the critical analysis of the media and political motives, however, was Cohen's specification of the connection between the particular moral panic he described and the social, political and economic atmosphere of 1960s England:

> The sixties began the confirmation of a new era in adult-youth relations ... What everyone had grimly prophesied had come true: high wages, the emergence of a commercial youth culture 'pandering' to young people's needs ... the permissive society, the coddling by the Welfare State ... The Mods and Rockers symbolized something far more important than what they actually did. They touched the delicate and ambivalent nerves through which post-war social change in Britain was experienced. No one wanted depression or austerity ... Resentment and jealousy were easily directed at the young because of their increased spending power and sexual freedom. (1980: 192)

Hall et al. (1978) lent a more Marxist interpretation to the historical understanding of moral panics by suggesting that panics serve a decidedly elitist purpose. Their study of mugging in England in the 1970s suggested that the public and political alarm over street crime was created by the ruling elite to divert attention away from the crisis in British capitalism. As in other capitalist countries, increasing unemployment was being deliberately used by business and government to re-establish general profit levels and fight inflation. In essence, high profits and high employment are anathema and inflationary. The British industrial state was in fiscal and social distress. To deflect attention away from the real causes of the fiscal crisis, according to Hall et al. (1978), authorities exaggerated the threat posed by street crime.

The work of Hall and his co-authors is particularly instructive in that it studies the connections between ideological production, the mass media and those in positions of power. Without this type of critical perspective, we are left with the presumption that the media act alone, isolated from economy and politics, and that their mistaken mandate is the result of poor journalism and the requirement to compete in the supply and demand world of news. Just as I argue in this book, Hall et al. contend that one of the primary functions of the news is to give political significance to events. In fact, the media both draw on and re-create consensus. This contention becomes apparent when we realize that the "media represent the primary, and often the only source of information about many important events and topics" (1978: 56). Furthermore, "the media define for the majority of the population what significant events are taking place, but, also, they offer powerful interpretations of how to understand these events" (1978: 57). (For more current debates, see Roberts and Foehr 2004; Fleras and Kunz 2001.) One of the important ways in which the news media maintain their power is by claiming journalistic objectivity as *a priori*. The ostensible task of news media is to sift fact from fiction, and they do this by drawing on expert opinion. As we will come to see later in this book, expert opinion is an extremely common journalistic device and such opinion is generally as wide and varied as it is numerous.

The discourse of news media is, first and foremost, ideological, that is, the language is morality-laden and belongs to privileged, powerful people. There is a structured relationship between the media and the ideas of the powerful sectors of the society. The creation, control and proliferation of journalistic discourse is constrained by definitions of right and wrong that are governed by powerful people, even if such people do not hold with such definitions. Capitalist power is able reproduce a morality that implies that certain people are better and more valuable than others on the basis of their place in the economic system. Such discourse serves to reproduce the relations of production (the socio-economic system that allows some to live in mansions while requiring others to live on the streets) by organizing the way we think of crime and punishment in relation to poverty and wealth. Crime, as it is constructed and framed in public discourse, functions to legitimate and maintain class differences in all sectors of the society. Rarely do media accounts that equate crime with privation do so without discussing related issues of visible minority group membership (and immigration) along with the problems that single motherhood poses to traditional family values.

Many of the panics that typified the sixties and seventies appear today in similar form, if not content. In moral panics, public perceptions of the degree and form of violent crime are largely inaccurate and exaggerated (Kappeler, Blumberg and Potter 1993; Painter 1993; Jenkins 1992). While traditional research on moral panics dealt with "mainstream" deviances — drug use, witchcraft, for example — current research tends to concentrate on what might be labelled shocking or lurid deviances: ritual abuse, serial killers, pedophilia and child abuse. While not to diminish the seriousness of these crimes, it is important to note that, with the exception of child abuse, most of these phenomena are quite rare. And as typified by past moral panics, the rare occurrences nourish a general alarm over individual safety.

There is, on the other hand, a rapidly expanding body of literature that focuses on youth gangs, studying either the origins and activities of such gangs or the public reactions to them. This rather orthodox, narrow-focused literature tends to endorse public panic discourse and, distressingly, discourse about the racialized nature of crime. By ignoring the moral outrage that greets all youth, not just identifiable gang members, it uses race and gang membership to underscore the presumed violent and organized nature of youth crime. This is not to suggest that the moral panic surrounding youth crime is subtle or hidden. On the contrary, the attack on youth has been vocal, concerted and politicized, fostered by the portrayal of idiosyncratic examples of youth crime as typical. The existing public debates on youth crime, while largely uninformed, have the potency and the scientific legitimacy to direct public opinion and to effect social control policy that stigmatizes and controls those who are most disadvantaged and most victimized.

The primary effect of media and official accounts of youth crime is to decontextualize such acts for public consumption. Although the media may not directly control public opinion, they are certainly able to contain the nature of discourse by establishing parameters of discussion and by giving the appearance of consensus on public issues. The portraits of youth criminals that public crime accountants paint are largely of nihilistic, pathological criminals who act alone or as members of gangs, criminals who are devoid of a moral base. The decontextualization of youth crime, however, misses a fundamental consideration in understanding crime: most repeat young offenders and their families are victims of socio-economic conditions beyond their control, and they are more than likely to be repeatedly victimized as clients of the systems of law, social welfare and education.

The powerful benefit from a particular "truth" about young offenders. Media images push public discussions away from understandings of youth crime that include the effects of privation, disenfranchisement and marginalization, and toward misunderstanding youth crime as individual immorality and pathology. Those in power in a corporate or state context are largely responsible for creating conditions that are detrimental to those without power. The attack on government deficits and the unrelenting drive to cut taxes, which seem currently to drive considerable public policy initiatives, are detrimental to the least advantaged but advantageous to the already privileged. For example, state policy rarely attacks unfair or non-progressive taxation, ostensibly for fear of alienating business and driving it elsewhere, especially in the context of free trade zones, like NAFTA. The recourse then is to attack social support programs, employment initiatives and education. The system of profit is absolved from responsibility for making the lives of the disenfranchised poor more precarious, for destroying social support networks. The law, in its function as moral arbiter, has a significant input into the way that the public views connections between crime and economy. Accounts of youth crime and justice that are fostered in the media focus almost exclusively on individual conduct and rarely on the criminogenic effect of the partnership between corporate capitalism and the state. The following section illustrates how a moral panic about children and crime arises in a modern political-economic context and how and why the media fosters images of criminalized children.

THE MEDIA AND THE POLITICS OF MORALITY

Moral panics are characterized by their affiliations with politics, with systems of information and with institutions of social control, including the legal system. The operation of the moral panic is both symbolic and practical, and functions within the confines of an already existing orthodox state machinery that is closely tied to the mechanisms of production. And, most importantly for this chapter, moral panics are constituted within a discourse that has a profound effect on public opinion and on justifying punishment as a legitimate, moral form of social control. In the end, moral panics both drive public policy and are driven by policy decisions that, in part, respond to the "democratic will."

The Symbolic Crusade

Most youth-focused moral panics argue either to protect children or to condemn them. Constant warnings that children are in danger lead to lobbies against child abuse, child pornography, prostitution, paedophilia, serial killers, smoking and drunk driving. On the other hand, those who believe that all children are potentially dangerous have lobbied for the reform of the *Young Offenders Act*, implementation of dangerous offender legislation, the public security provisions of the *Youth Criminal Justice Act* and increased use of custodial dispositions for young offenders. Pessimism about and distrust of children are apparent in many news articles. Our ambivalence between protecting and condemning children is embodied in our cultural approach to child rearing, which advocates both affection/protection and physical punishment. Further, it is ironic that we tend to punish those who are both most dear to us, our children and those who are farthest removed from us, the hardened criminal — the former inside our homes, the latter by incarceration.

The growing focus on criminogenic children and delinquent youth tends to divert public debate away from the political actions of the powerful that create social stresses for the less powerful (for example, unemployment, welfare cuts, dangerous work environments, poorly paid and part-time labour). In addition, child-focused panics seem to set the limits of social tolerance and seek to change the moral and legal environment to reflect those limits. While harm to children is the threshold of tolerance, child-centred, symbolic lobbies reflect the belief that children are also unpredictable and volatile as a subculture. The attendant rhetoric invokes images of gangs and connections between nihilistic behaviour and music/dress (grunge as a typical example). The youth subculture is, in general, portrayed as aimless and calculating. The anti-youth lobby is a potent symbolic mechanism for framing youth crime — and ultimately all conduct — in ambivalent yet moralistic terms.

The Interdependence of Panics

Moral panics tend to emerge in groups and foster one another. The current movements in Canada directed against gun control, the drug trade, gang violence, car theft and dangerous offenders all make reference to youth involvement. Highly sensational incidents are interpreted as part of an overall social menace, and subsequent events are contextualized in this gestalt of fear and framed in fear-provoking language. The success of one panic lends credibility to another, and the result is a generalized lobby for increased social control at all levels. For example, when issues of youth crime and violence predominate on the airwaves, there are usually concurrent discussions of teen sexuality, youth prostitution and unwed motherhood. Issues of youth exploitation and disadvantage, then, become linked, by temporal association, to issues of youth menace and dangerousness, resulting in a generalized "problem of youth." The lumping together of adolescent issues transforms a problem that originates with the structure of society to one that appears to originate with youth themselves. The state and the adult world are absolved from responsibility for the exploitation of children and the social disadvantages that delinquent children represent.

The Role of the Mass Media

The North American newspaper and television industries seem to be continually moving toward monopolization by a few major media corporations. In effect, there is very little competition for the moral attention of Canadians and Americans. When I wrote the first edition of this book, Conrad Black, who at that time owned forty or more newspapers around the world, had purchased the four major daily newspapers in the province of Saskatchewan. And, in typical corporate rationalization, the company immediately laid off one quarter of the newspaper employees in the province. Since then, the Hollinger empire has sold its assets to another major Canadian newspaper conglomerate, CanWest Global, which owns 50 percent of the *National Post*, twenty-six other daily newspapers in Canada and television stations in the cities in which these newspaper are located. CanWest, along with other multi-national companies, including Rogers Media, Shaw Communications and Bell Canada, manage significant control of Canadian airwaves, and as dynamic and aggressive corporations, they have a tremendous influence on the editorial slant of major social phenomena. They do this, in part, as a result of horizontal convergence with other media forms. This "cross media ownership" entails the corporate integration of information, entertainment and retail companies. As Brownlee shows, from 1999 onward in Canada, "all but one of the major English-Canada newspapers was the property of a TV or communications giant," and the unimpeachable reality is that "Canada's largest media corporations are heavily interlocked with other dominant Canadian corporations" (Brownlee 2005: 44).

The fundamental problem in all this is that journalistic integrity and balanced public commentary suffer. As the Southern Ontario Newspaper Guild asked: "How can there be credible democratic discourse in Canada or any country when the major public information channels, television and newspapers are owned or controlled by a handful of individuals accountable only to themselves?" (Southern Ontario Newspaper Guild 2005)

The Communications, Energy and Paperworkers of Canada (CEP)[1] have recently launched an effort to return journalistic integrity to Canadian news media. Their policy package includes "public editor's contracts, media advisory councils, limits on ownership within each medium, and a ban on cross-ownership between legitimate private interests and the public interest" (Southern Ontario Newspaper Guild 2005: 1). The thrust of this lobby is to subject media owners, managers and journalists to formal public scrutiny and collective and personal accountability. This is an interesting and important grassroots movement that, unfortunately, may whither and die in a global context of neo-liberalism and unbridled free enterprise.

Herman and Chomsky (1988) argued several years ago that media of all kinds are becoming increasingly concentrated in the hands of fewer and fewer large corporations. As the media come to be more and more connected to the corporate world, the deregulated market provides opportunities for corporate takeovers of small companies. Further, the fundamental focus on profit — redefined as allegiance to stockholders — takes priority over objective, fair and factual journalism. Concurrent with the devastating effect on the newspaper labour market, as the analysis in this book illustrates, the newspaper industry's passion for profit results in the production of sensationalist, often uncontested, news accounts that appear fictitious and largely removed from the social and economic context in which they occur, but which are highly marketable. I discuss media presentations at length in a subsequent section, but I wish to iterate at this point that the primary functions of media portrayals of crime include: (a) the creation of a world of insiders and outsiders, acceptability and unacceptability in order to facilitate public demand and consumption; (b) the connecting of images of deviance and crime with social characteristics; and (c) the decontextualization of crime in anecdotal evidence, which is presented as omnipresent, non-complex truth.

The Interdependence of Institutions

Moral crusades are often typified by the collaboration of institutions of social control. On the issue of youth permissiveness, it is important to realize that institutions such as medicine, education, social welfare, religion and government are all involved in the work of understanding and controlling youth crime. It is not surprising, then, that public accounts of specific youth crimes, or of the youth crime epidemic generally, draw on experts from these institutions to lend credibility to their claims and to persuade audiences that the concern for growing youth crime is legitimate and widespread. And, politicians are quick to adopt a punitive stance toward youth, especially on behalf of conservative business and community leaders. As we will see, the interdependent and multi-institutional nature of moral panics is an important focus for the critical researcher in uncovering the claims to moral legitimacy that are made in public discourse and to revealing the actors who benefit from such claims.

CONCLUSION

The area of youth crime and justice has been inundated with a multitude of critical and consensus theories that have attempted to understand why youth choose to break the law or how a society is responsible for creating the conditions under which young people will end up at odds with that society. Conventional, consensus theories of youth crime especially predominate in the research and academic worlds. As they focus on the individual or cultural origins of crime and the ways to "correct" the offender, they support and foster the public's growing belief that youth are more disrespectful now than in the past, are more anti-social, especially towards adults, and ultimately are more dangerous. The policy implication of this "paradigm of panic" is to increase crime control and incarceration. And, this is no more evident than in the Canadian government's crime bill — one of the five platforms of Stephen Harper's Conservative government — which is based on increased reactive policing, standardized and harsh sentencing and increased use of incarceration for youth and adults. In contrast, and hopefully as an antidote to regressive and consequently oppressive, justice strategies, my orientation is both critical and social constructionist. The critical position draws on the debates surrounding the concept of the moral panic in the late sixties and early seventies. The corpus of that work attempted to unpack the hidden agenda behind the creation of a mythology of delinquency. I accept the challenge of that mythology, as well. I discuss the advantages that accrue to the influential players in this public debate, how they construct and produce images of deviance that absolve them from responsibility for social conditions and indict others who are less powerful, and how constructed images of good and evil infiltrate the public consciousness to the degree that young people are excluded from the common good. My work here is essentially a study of ideology, of a collective belief system that constricts the way we see the world, especially with respect to issues of good and evil. Ultimately, such a belief system ties the morality of good and evil to socio-economic characteristics.

The social constructionist approach presumes that knowledge (social or natural facts) is largely created, most often for a political purpose. Even the most objective-based knowledge is relative to time and place, and professionals/experts who are charged with understanding criminality are powerful constructors of portraits of crime. Discourse, knowledge and power are inextricably connected in a paradigm that awakens us to the need to deconstruct official and public opinions. Those who make claims to truth, and who often get their perceptions of reality translated into public opinion and public policy, are most often in positions of political and economic power. They have considerable ability to persuade the public that a condition exists and that it presents a threat to public security. I argue that the ongoing moral panic surrounding youth crime is a typical example of a constructed social problem: the objective threat is much less than the collective public sentiment would hold to be true. In addition, and most importantly, the powerful, economically advantaged members of our society gain considerable advantage by fostering a moral panic surrounding youth crime and dangerousness.

Overall, the sociological sensitivity to young offenders is important in unpacking the forces that would at once blame children for social ills and at the same time denounce anyone who would endanger children. I believe that this contradictory and unnerving posture towards Canada's youth can only be understood within a political-economic framework that poses the following question: If children are our most cherished resource, why then do we denounce and fear adolescence and ultimately discard children for political and moral ends?

Note
1. In 2013 CEP merged with the Canadian Auto Workers to form the union Unifor.

References
Alvi, Shahid. 2000. *Youth and the Canadian Criminal Justice System*. Cincinnati, OH: Anderson.
Bell, S.J. 2002. *Young Offenders and Juvenile Justice: A Century after the Fact, 2nd edition*. Toronto: Thompson Nelson.
Brownlee, Jamie. 2005. *Ruling Canada: Corporate Cohesion and Democracy*. Halifax, NS: Fernwood.
Chomsky, Noam. 2002. *Hegemony or Survival? America's Quest for Global Dominance*. New York: Metropolitan.
Cohen, Stanley. 1980 *Folk Devils and Moral Panics: The Creation of the Mods and Rockers*. New York: St. Martin's.
Department of Justice Canada. 1999. *Youth Criminal Justice Act: Backgrounder*. Ottawa: Government of Canada
Fleras, A., and J.L. Kunz. 2001. *Media and Minorities: Representing Diversity in a Multicultural Canada*. Toronto: Thompson Educational Publishing
Giroux, Henry. 2003. *The Abandoned Generation: Democracy Beyond the Culture of Fear*. New York: Palgrave MacMillan.
Hall, Stuart, Chas Critcher, Tony Jefferson, John Clarke and Brian Roberts. 1978. *Policing

the Crisis: Mugging, the State and Law and Order. London: Macmillan.
Herman, Edward S., and Noam Chomsky. 1994. *Manufacturing Consent: The Political Economy of the Mass Media.* New York: Pantheon.
Hogeveen, B., and R.C. Smandych. 2001. "Origins of the Newly Proposed Canadian Youth Criminal Justice Act: Political Discourse and the Perceived Crisis in Youth Crime in the 1990s." In R.C. Smandych (ed.), *Youth Justice: History, Legislation, and Reform.* Toronto: Harcourt Canada.
Iyengar, Shanto, and Donald R. Kinder. 1987. *News That Matters.* Chicago: University of Chicago Press
Jenkins, Philip. 1992. *Intimate Enemies: Moral Panics in Contemporary Britain.* New York: Aldine de Gruyter.
Kappeler, Victor E., Mark Blumberg, and Gary W. Potter. 1993. *The Mythology of Crime and Delinquency.* Prospect Heights, IL: Waveland Press.
Ministry of the Attorney General, Ontario. 2000. *2002–2003 Business Plan.* Toronto: Ministry of the Attorney General of Ontario.
Painter, Kate. 1993. "The Mythology of Delinquency: An Empirical Critique." Presented at the British Criminology Conference, Cardiff University.
Roberts, D., and U.G. Foehr. 2004. *Kids and the Media in America.* Cambridge, MA: Cambridge University Press.
Southern Ontario Newspaper Guild. 2005. *Journalistic Standards in Monopolized Media.* <www.song.on.ca/journalist_standards.html> (accessed October 5, 2005).
Stroud, Carsten. 1993. *Contempt of Court: the Betrayal of Justice in Canada?* Toronto: MacMillan.
Tanner, Julian. 1996. *Teenage Troubles: Youth and Deviance in Canada.* Toronto: Nelson Canada.
Underdown, David. 1992. *Fire From Heaven: Life in an English Town in the Seventeenth Century.* London: Harper Collins.
Winterdyk, John A. 2000. Issues and Perspectives on Young Offenders in Canada. Toronto: Thomson/Nelson.

Chapter 4

UNDERSTANDING CHILD-HATING

Bernard Schissel

> From: *Still Blaming Children: Youth Conduct and the Politics of Child Hating*, 2nd edition, Chapter 2 (reprinted with permission of the author).

There are two theoretical approaches that inform *Still Blaming Children*. The first falls under the broad rubric of social constructionism and assumes that public images of acceptable behaviour and the appropriate penalties for violations of social norms are highly variable, as is the definition of "normal" behaviour. As a result, what constitutes unacceptable behaviour changes over time and across social groups and societies. The social construction approach is informed largely by historical studies that track changing modes of social control. As we observe the public and political venom that is directed towards children and youth and as we think about youth misconduct in relation to the structure, culture and family of contemporary society, we are left with the gnawing question: "What is going on?" It is almost axiomatic that moral panics occur in troubled times. Our focus is on how power operates in defining and sanctioning virtuous and evil behaviour amongst youth.

The second theoretical concern attempts to understand the origins and intent of such power. The presumption is that fear, in its collective manifestation, becomes highly politicized as it is manipulated either inadvertently or deliberately for political and economic ends. This political economy/critical dimension of the theoretical framework, derived from Marxist philosophical principles, focuses on the structure of the society and, specifically, on the relationship between the media and the powerful sectors of the society. The presumption is that those in control of the economy manage to have their ideas transformed into general notions of morality and crime. They reproduce notions that become generalized belief systems, the bases of our ideology. The main presumption in this ideology is that some people are better than others by virtue of their place in the socio-economic structure of the society and that they have "merited" their advantage. The discourse of meritocracy and the attendant defamation of those who are dispossessed and marginalized are powerful mechanisms for legitimating a highly stratified society. Such an ideology serves to reproduce class relations by constraining the way that we think about issues of goodness and badness and their connection to poverty and wealth. The defamation of social groups through the discourse of crime and punishment is a powerful political mechanism.

In light of the two theoretical orientations above, I will focus on a social, legal and historical discussion for understanding Canada's current moral panic about youth to make sense of the paradoxical connection between child victimization and child blaming. I must also state that many youths who suffer economic, social and personal privation go on to become law-abiding and productive citizens. And, of course, much of the rhetoric of law and order is based on the presumption that everybody at one time or another has suffered victimization but only the truly bad engage in criminal behaviour. The theoretical sociological positions I address in this book ask how a stratified society not only creates criminal behaviour, but constructs certain types of behaviour and persons as unacceptable, not on the basis of an inherent morality, but rather on the basis of social signifiers.

THE SOCIOLOGY OF KNOWLEDGE AND THE DECONSTRUCTION OF CRIME MYTH

Fear and the knowledge that underpins that fear are important foci for this book. We are forced, as social analysts, to confront the task of deconstructing public opinion that we assume to be based on selected and biased knowledge. Further, we need to uncover the sources of information and assess the claims to legitimacy — or in journalistic parlance, the claims to objectivity — that inform and direct public opinion. Cohen (1980: 28) has made us aware that public opinion fluctuates and that it may cause social reform:

> Societies appear to be subject, every now and then, to periods of moral panic. A condition, episode, person or group of persons emerges to become defined as a threat to societal values and interests: its nature is presented in a stylized and stereo-typical fashion by the mass media: the moral barricades are manned by editors, bishops, politicians and other right-thinking people; socially accredited experts pronounce their

diagnoses and solutions ... Sometimes the panic is passed over and is forgotten, except in folklore and collective memory; at other times it has more serious and long lasting repercussions and might produce such changes as those in legal and social policy or even in the way society conceives itself.

The information contained in this book, gleaned from multiple media sources, identifies many of the characteristics of a typical moral panic. The massive and biased coverage of Canada's youth criminals and pre-criminals by the press and by politicians bears witness to the stability, persistence and power of a war against youth crime. Social constructionism, as part of the domain of post-modernism, is based on the methodological position that "deconstruction tears a text (all phenomena, all events, are texts) apart, reveals its contradictions and assumptions" (Rosenau 1992). We need to ask the following questions:

- What are the hidden messages that "objective journalism" conveys?
- Who are the originators of such ideological communiqués?
- How do these originators make claims to legitimacy?
- Who are the expressed and insinuated targets of the social/political attack?

The recurring focus in media and political accounts of youth crime are people who live on the margins. The manifest messages are that society is too lenient with children and that the only way to restore order and appropriate conduct is to become "tough" through law and order. The associated belief is that kids are inherently evil and that discipline and punishment are essential in the creation of normal, law-abiding children. The latent messages are much more damning. Youths who break laws belong to certain racial and ethnic categories, they are born and raised in the lower socio-economic strata of the society, their families are feminized and their lack of morality stems from their socio-economic positions in society. Simply put, the messages indict poverty and endorse wealth, blame the poor for being poor, condemn mothers almost exclusively for poor parenting and censure cultural difference as criminogenic.

The work of Michel Foucault is particularly instructive in understanding the nature of discourse surrounding young offenders. For Foucault, discourses are

> historically variable ways of specifying knowledge and truth — what it is possible to speak of at a given moment. They function (especially scientific discourses) as sets of rules, and the operation of these rules and concepts in programmes which specify what is or is not the case — what constitutes insanity, for example. Discourses are, therefore, powerful. Those who

are labelled insane, or hysterical women or frigid wives, are in the grip of power. This power may be exercised by officials through institutions, or through many other practices, but power is constituted in discourses and it is in discourses, such as those in clinical medicine, that power lies. Discourses produce truths and "we cannot exercise power except through the production of truth." (Foucault, in Ramazanoglu 1993: 10)

Foucault argues that historical periods are marked by particular discourses that constrain the types of knowledge that are produced. Knowledge is constructed and deployed on the basis of what types of people have access to the systems of knowledge, and it is this access to "legitimate knowledge" that gives people their power.

The basic tenets of a Foucauldian power/knowledge perspective are quite evident in the discourse of youth offenders. The ways of speaking about young offenders are restricted largely to individual or family-based accounts of the origins of crime. Rarely are the explanations based on structural inequalities or the injustice of people living on the margins of society. As Foucault has suggested, the discourses of historical periods are constrictive; they are rules under which "talk" can be carried out. The modern discourse of youth crime and punishment appear to be restricted to accounts based on individual blame. This contemporary medical/psychological discourse of goodness and badness sets youth crime in a context of orthodox criminology: individuals gone wrong, either inherently or culturally. The underlying ideological position is that society is structured correctly and that individuals who offend are individually or socially pathological and identifiable.

The discourse of individual or cultural blame receives its legitimacy primarily through the knowledge of experts. The language and accounts of youth criminality are often the products of testimonials by "scientists." Discourse operates as a powerful and oppressing mechanism, because it comes from the mouths of "legitimated speakers," who are almost without exception drawn from the privileged sectors of society. News articles are often infused with the voices of "professionals," who corroborate the claims made in the article. This strategy not only endorses the validity of the account, it also gives the media legitimacy by association. Furthermore, the "expert wisdom" of legitimated speakers is often accompanied by the folk wisdom of "ordinary people" and it is this technique of attaching common knowledge to expert knowledge that produces a generalized atmosphere of credibility.

In his treatises on power and knowledge, Foucault was generally unconcerned with the origins of discourses and what interests they served. Typical of postmodern orientations, his approach to the study of the social construction of truth focuses on how power and knowledge operate, not on what discourses mean, but rather on what makes them possible. This approach leaves us with the crucial questions of who controls the images of youth, who benefits from biased and incriminating portraits of offenders and why certain categories of people are the targets of journalistic and political abuse. To answer these questions we need to turn to the critical feminist and political economy-based theories of knowledge as it relates to criminality, and we need to harvest such theories for insights into and responses to the rhetoric of child-hating.

FEMINIST THEORY AND THE CONSTRUCTION OF GENDERED IMAGES

Law-and-order campaigns are also veiled attacks on women and feminism. Media presentations maintain that women are susceptible to victimization and poverty more so than men, but that they also, through their inadequate parenting, are the producers of criminality. In essence, women are the inadvertent victimizers of children. Such stereotypical and conventional explanations of criminality have focused on non-traditional families, non-traditional motherhood, single-parenthood and poverty as causal factors in youth criminality. Feminist responses to the conservative, traditional explanations of crime are that patriarchal ideologies frame the nature of women's crime and the imputed female role in criminogenesis. While feminism, as a generic theoretical position, is highly complex and multi-dimensional, feminist studies in general address the structure of society as disadvantageous to women: in hierarchical societies, men generally inhabit positions of privilege and domination over women. In such societies, women and men live in different experiential worlds, but the knowledge that underpins our understanding of gender issues is largely produced by men and is based on stereotypical and distorted ideas about women and men. And, importantly for this book, these stereotypical "sexist" images that connect maternity and motherhood to criminality are reproduced in the media. As Anderson (1988: 25) suggests,

> Although these institutions are not the exclusive sources of sexist ideas, they exert a powerful influence on the way we define reality and women's role within it ... In fact, it can be argued that in a highly complex technological-industrial society, these systems of communication and knowledge making play an increasingly important part in the generation and transmission of ideas ... Moreover, as the feminist movement has shown, images of women conveyed by the media and in educational materials have been based on distortions and stereotypes that legitimate the status quo at the same time that they falsely represent the actual experience of women in the society. Thus, the ideas we acquire regarding gender relations poorly prepare us for the realities we will face.

Public images of typical delinquents are primarily about males. When female youth are targeted, the depictions are couched in "paradox talk": it is so unusual for girls to act aggressively or anti-socially that bad genes must be at work. The "sugar and spice" understanding of femaleness is often the standard upon which young female offenders are judged, and the images of "bad girls" are presented as biological anomalies and/or the sinister products of the feminist movement. A general women-hatred appears to underlie the "sugar and spice" conception of femaleness in articles that discuss the wild, passionate, out-of-character woman who has to be constrained or held back always: a dual stereotype of women in western society — she is nice but emotional and unpredictable.

The second way that women are included and loathed in media accounts of youth crime is through speculations about the causal origins of delinquent behaviour. Specifically, the references are to "feminist women" trying to be more like men or to the inability of single mothers to raise "normal children" in the confines of the "abnormal family" living in conditions of privation. In the United States, much ink has been spent on fatherlessness, especially for black youth, who constitute the largest percentage of criminalized and incarcerated young people (Daniels 1998). The basic presumption in the collected works that comprise Cynthia Daniels' book is that conservative political and social pundits blame the criminogenesis of black youth on absentee fathers and by association, single mothers:

> The collapse of children's well-being in the United States has reached breathtaking proportions. Juvenile crime has increased six-fold ... One can think of many explanations for these unhappy developments ... But the evidence is now strong that the absence of fathers from the lives of children is one of the most important causes ... The proliferation of mother-headed families now constitutes something of a national economic emergency. (Popenoe 1998: 37)

The "family values" reference that has become so much a part of the conservative political creed is infused with references to the functional two-parent heterosexual family and the importance of male discipline and male role models. In contradistinction to public opinion and media hype, however, empirical evidence on street youth and youth who have been in contact with the courts indicates that single-parenthood shows little correlation with law-breaking behaviour. More to the point, living a life of poverty, which is often typical for single mothers, is a predisposing condition to contact with the law. Problems resulting from structural inequality and the unfairness of a market-based economy are transposed to problems of mothering and ultimately to problems created by feminism.

A feminist approach to studying the social construction of public knowledge is important for locating the sources of bias against women in the patriarchal structures that support media, politics, academia/education and the economy. As evidenced by the analysis in this book, condemnatory images of women are created and deployed in a rhetoric of fear, inherent criminality and unnatural predispositions. The constructed and gendered knowledge about youth crime originates in patriarchal political and economic systems. As the following section discusses, the fundamental issue in a critical analysis of social phenomena is that some people dominate others by virtue of their position of advantage in the political and economic structure, and that state policy is either directly or indirectly complicit in the system of domination and subordination.

IDEOLOGY, POWER AND THE IMAGES OF YOUTH

The theoretical orientation that directly addresses the issues of domination by powerful people over less powerful people as a primary focus can be subsumed under the broad category of Marxist (sometimes called, conflict) criminology. The primary assumption in Marxist-based theories is that certain groups of people gain advantage over others and dominate by virtue of their position of privilege and ownership in the system of production. In the context of this book we are concerned with understanding the creators of images of youth and those who are advantaged and disadvantaged by the social construction of knowledge. It is important to understand issues of power and economy in a contemporary context; the arguments I make in *Still Blaming Children* have to be placed in a context in which neo-liberal fiscal and social policies frame global politics.

As I have stated, global economics dictates constraints on government spending, which erodes the state's ability to provide for its citizens. The welfare and the civil liberties of the most vulnerable citizens become jeopardized. Canadian youth, as a formally disenfranchised group, are threatened most certainly by governmental policy, which promotes business group interests at the expense of social programs. In essence, business has the implicit right to set the social agenda (Bourdieu 1999; Giroux 2003). Males (2000) has argued that the baby boom generation, either through pension plans or through direct investments, has a profound interest in protecting its financial legacy and it does so by ensuring that social programs that support young people do not drain its collective resources. I argue, in addition, that young people bolster the economy to their own detriment as they provide cheap, unsecured labour and are targeted as vulnerable consumers. One of the basic arguments in this book is that the negative portraits of youth culture that occur in the news media serve an important function for business interests. If the general public views youth as dangerous and criminal they are less likely to be sympathetic to the increasingly dire economic situation that today's youth face and, are most likely to favour "law-and-order" approaches to youth misconduct rather than "social investment" approaches. The control of the media serves an extremely important legitimation function for business: through the media's sensationalist reporting, the general public comes to believe that the bad things that happen are the result of individual badness and not the result of social inequality and dispossession. The relationship between poverty levels and youth crime disappears from public discourse and is replaced with portraits of youth who are lazy, unwilling to work, immoral and criminally volatile.

The instrumental Marxist argument (Quinney 1974; Goff and Reasons 1978) has suggested that powerful people directly influence government policy and manipulate such policy to their advantage. Government is government for the wealthy and powerful. This understanding of power and corporate control of politics is somewhat difficult to envision in societies based on the democratic process. However, as nation states lose their autonomy to manage public spending through dictates from lending institutions like the World Bank and the International Monetary Fund and through trade agreements like the World Trade Organization, one could easily make the argument that powerful business interests do, in fact, dictate public policy. Nations that invest in public spending become "bad economic risks" (Bourdieu 1999; Carroll 2004; Robbins 2005).

The structural Marxist approach (Poulantzas 1972; Balbus 1973), on the other hand, allows for the reality that ordinary people, through the democratic process, can resist the neo-liberal world of global capital. The overall approach argues that the state is relatively autonomous from the power brokers, but that the role of the state is to create and maintain the conditions under which capital accumulation works most efficiently, for example, by putting a cap on spending on social programs. In so doing, the state must create the conditions under which the system of capital accumulation is held legitimate by the populace. Otherwise the democratic process would likely dictate the end of a system based on such domination and subordination. It is at this point where the question of the ideological role of the media needs to be raised:

> The media, then, do not simply "create" the news; nor do they simply transmit the ideology of the "ruling class" in a conspiratorial fashion. Indeed, we have suggested, in a critical sense, the media are frequently not the "primary definers" of news events at all; but their structured relationship to power has the effect of making them play a crucial but secondary role in reproducing the definitions of those who have privileged access, as of right, to the media as "accredited sources." (Hall et al. 1978: 59)

Hall and his colleagues took this structural Marxist position and applied it to the moral panics surrounding "mugging" in England in the 1960s and 1970s. They illustrated how the raw materials of crime facts get filtered to the media and are produced as "factual" stories, which ultimately serve to reproduce the ideologies of powerful people.

Stereotypical images of race, class and gender are created and employed to produce versions of goodness and badness attributable to class position. The obvious question is why news definers and makers conform to the dominant ideology of a modern day "ruling class," especially when the professed mandate of the media is objectivity and journalistic integrity.

Ownership
Observation of the ownership patterns of the Canadian news media reveals that newspapers and newsmagazines are monopolized by a few major corporate interests. As mentioned in Chapter 1, CanWest Global owns 50 percent of the *National Post*, twenty-six other daily newspapers in Canada and television stations in the cities in which these newspaper are located. CanWest, along with other large media corporations, including Rogers Media, Shaw Communications and Bell Canada, control a significant amount of Canada's airwaves (Brownlee 2005; Southern Ontario Newspaper Guild 2005). These aggressive and successful corporations have incredible influence on the editorial slant of Canadian social phenomena, with the result that journalistic freedom and balanced public commentary suffer. The arguments of Herman and Chomsky (1988) regarding media concentration and relatively simple regarding the loss of journalistic integrity. The fundamental focus on profit and the associated corporate agenda to control editorial policy dictate that journalistic accounts cannot be balanced. Corporate allegiance to stockholders takes priority over objective, fair and factual journalism. Through a variety of daily and mundane mechanisms (most of them indirect), a converging corporate domination and monopolization of the news creates narrowed comprehension and tolerance for issues that involve disaffiliated and marginalized peoples. John McMullen provides a poignant example of the corporate influence in the making of a news story. In *News, Truth and Crime* (2005), he describes the media focus on the human tragedy of the Westray mining disaster in Nova Scotia in 1992 and how the singular and unrelenting focus on the lives lost and the families disrupted diverted attention from the corporate lawlessness and state complicity in the explosion, the subsequent inaction and the cover up (McMullan 2005).

The influence that corporations have on the nature and content of journalism is enhanced by the tenuous nature of journalists' jobs. The threat of dismissal is a powerful compulsion for reporters to toe the corporate line, and this has certainly never been more true than after 9/11, when American reporters either lost or were threatened with losing their jobs for "non-party-line" reporting (Chomsky 2002). The controlled images are still produced in a framework of journalism and appear as objective, "factual" accounts of the social condition. The constructed images of goodness and badness that we see in media portraits of young offenders, for example, become the bases of the moral framework for the entire society.

Credibility

The legitimacy of the created moral framework is maintained not only by the ownership of the news but also by the credibility of the news. Only certain types of individuals are credited with the ability to comment on issues of badness and goodness. And, it is no coincidence that the primary commentators in news reports are generally professional, highly educated people who are obviously highly placed in the socio-economic system. Accounts that speculate on the causes of youth crime are created and endorsed by judges, lawyers, police officers, university professors, doctors and business owners. The credibility of these people results largely from their assumed superior knowledge and their links to science, in this case forensic and legal science. Part of their appeal is their unique access to the exclusive languages of law and science, which, to an uninitiated public, seems mystical, inaccessible and by definition, correct. It is no coincidence that the legitimate speakers are drawn from the higher echelons of society. Much of their understanding of crime and punishment, as a result, is based on the values and morals of privilege. Marx's aphorism that "the ruling ideas of any age are the ideas of its ruling class" is especially apt when we consider the socio-economic origins of "legitimate experts." Rarely are media accounts based on the insights and knowledge of marginalized or underclass people. Interestingly, the use of subverted knowledge is not an impossibility. In a rare instance in which a crime account was presented through the eyes of a young street person, the vision was especially poignant and as relevant as any so-called expert opinion that we have analyzed.

Process

The final method through which the ideas of dominant people get translated into dominating ideas is through selective media attention. Hall et al. (1978: 60) argue that

> not every statement by a relevant primary definer in respect of a particular topic is likely to be reproduced in the media; nor is every part of each statement. By exercising selectivity the media begin to impose their own criteria on the structured "raw materials" — and thus actively appropriate and transform them... the criteria of selection — a mixture of professional, technical and commercial constraints — serves to orientate the media in general to the "definitions of the powerful."

On this point, I agree with Hall et al. (1978: 60), and the work in this book lends support to their thesis. The authors, however, go on to state that

> each paper's professional sense of the newsworthy, its organization and technical framework (in terms of numbers of journalists working in particular new areas, amount of column space routinely given over to certain kinds of news items, and so on), and sense of audience or regular readers, is different. Such differences, taken together, are what produce the very different "social personalities of papers."

On this point, my analysis departs from the work of Hall and his associates. As I argue throughout *Still Blaming Children*, the stories, the visual and verbal images and the scientific accounts of youth crime are remarkably similar and constructed around a rigid set of journalistic/ideological rules. The newspapers and news-magazines, with some differences in the extent of inflammatory rhetoric, could be interchanged quite easily, with little change in content or intent. Hall et al. (1978) do concede that despite the different languages of newspapers, the accounts occur within certain ideological constraints. I would add that the constraints are so strong that the languages are one and the same.

Theoretical Synthesis
Overall, the Marxist and feminist perspectives allow us to understand the entire moral panic against youth in the context of power and social control. As Box (1983: 13) argues, crime and criminalization are social control strategies in that they:

> (i) render underprivileged and powerless people more likely to be arrested, convicted, and sentenced to prison, even though the amount of personal damage and injury they cause may be less than the more powerful and privileged cause; (ii) create the illusion that the "dangerous" class is primarily located at the bottom of various hierarchies by which we "measure" each other, such as occupational prestige, income level, housing market location, educational achievement, racial attributes — in this illusion it fuses relative poverty and criminal propensities and sees them both as effects of moral inferiority, thus rendering the "dangerous" class deserving of both poverty and punishment.

That images of poverty align with immorality and badness is manifest in media constructions, and the political economy-based moral panic literature is essential in understanding the origins of hate. What is less obvious, however, are the mechanisms through which racial minorities, women and poor people get reframed in the public's mind from people who lack privilege to people who are dangerous. Post-modern theoretical and methodological bases for unpacking commonsense language as the language of politics help us round out a theory of social constructionism of child-hating.

These theoretical positions help us understand a fundamental truth about crime, the news and the economy: when the general population is preoccupied with (and terrified of) street crime, the economic and social problems that disenfranchised people face virtually disappear from their consciousness. The construction and perpetuation of crime panics of any nature serve to pervade the consciousness of ordinary people, convincing them that street crime is the most imminent problem facing the society. The problems that our political economy has created — unemployment, the silencing of labour, record profits for major corporations at the expense of jobs (the Canadian banks exemplify this quite clearly), the continuing trend toward monopoly capitalism, decreased proportionate spending on health, education and welfare and a growing disenchantment with politics and politicians — become of marginal importance in the consciousness of the average Canadian when crime, criminals and lenient justice are the primary horror stories in the news. The effect of this "false consciousness" is that powerful people carry on with "business as usual," with little or no opposition from the general public. Many ordinary citizens, convinced that all social evils stem from bad economies, support conservative fiscal and social policies even during bad times. This study of the construction and management of a moral panic against youth helps us understand how institutions like the economy, law and politics maintain their legitimacy in light of clear evidence that they are largely responsible for a widening gap between the rich and the poor and for a growing underclass in North America. That ordinary people, including those of marginalized and oppressed classes, "buy into" arguments that we are at peril from street criminals and not the global economic activity of the privileged, suggests that hegemony works very effectively through the news media.

THE PLACE OF CHILDREN AND YOUTH IN THE GLOBAL ECONOMY

One of the difficulties in attempting to understand the exploitation of children and youth in the modern world is that we really do not have a sense of where young people fit in the continuum between work and play. Common sense and scientific evidence suggest that children and adolescents need to grow and develop in a protected world in which they can learn from their mistakes. Social convention suggests that young people are not to be exploited in any way, but that they should be involved in civic participation as a training ground for citizenship. Childhood and adolescence, then, are times for freedom from mental and physical trauma.

The reality, however, is very much dissonant with the perception. In many global contexts, children and youth have very little chance to develop without trauma. In the developing world, children and youth are exposed to war, sexual exploitation, disease and privation in unprecedented proportions (see, for example, Morris 1995; Newman 2000; O'Higgins 2001; International Labour Organization (ILO) 2002). In the developed world, children and youth are similarly exposed to trauma, albeit in a more subtle or concealed fashion. They are exploited in the labour market, with little access to the human rights that accrue to adults (see, for example, Reiter 1996; Glor 1989; ILO 2004; Basran, Gill and MacLean 1995; Human Rights Watch (HRW) 2000). They are exploited by merchandising industries that prey on the culture of youth (see, for example, Milner Jr. 2004; Sutherland and Thompson 2003). They are exploited in the sports arena, where fun is replaced by militaristic discipline in the guise of perfection and teamwork (see, for example, Robinson 1998; Miedzian 1998). They are exploited by the industry of medicine, in which "child" pathologies are a new breeding ground for medical research (see, for example, Green and Healy 2003; Diller 1998), and they are exploited in war, in which young people fight while older people sit in safety and watch (see, for example, Bourke 1999; Grossman 1995; Edelman 1985). And for children and youth in both developed and developing worlds, their exploitation occurs primarily in a political context in which they have virtually no input into what happens to them. If a portion of the population does not have the opportunity to engage in civic and political participation (at more than a superficial level) and if that population is exploited for their labour and for their consumption, what results is a modern form of slavery. Young people are indentured labourers, involuntary soldiers, guinea pigs for medical and pharmaceutical research, and victims of human trafficking for sexual and commercial exploitation. If this is true, how we have come to a point where we accept the deceit that children and youth are our most valuable asset.

The basic thesis of this chapter is that systems of public discourse, like news media, frame the way the general public thinks about social issues and that, with reference to children and youth, the framework is largely condemnatory. The basic question is why that should be. The answer lies with an understanding of the correlation between global corporatism and the condemnation of children and youth, accomplished in part through a punitive youth justice policy and a concomitant public discourse about dangerous young people. Essentially, the global context is one in which social policy and public discourse create the conditions under which children and youth lose their civil liberties to the vagaries and demands of global capital (Grossberg 2005). The global context in which public policy tends increasingly to condemn and marginalize youth is characterized by two aforementioned incontrovertible phenomena: the growing involvement of children and youth in a labour market — including the use of children and youth in the military — that provides low wage; poor working conditions and a denial of the rights and freedoms accorded to working adults; and the positioning of children and youth as super-consumers in both the developed and developing worlds.

To understand subjugation and exploitation of any kind, we need to understand how the discourse that legitimates exploitation evolves, becomes dispersed and takes on a peculiarly commonsense quality. To understand the "common sense" about children and youth, we need to look to institutions, particularly crime/justice and the media. Youth justice systems in Canada and the United States are particularly harsh. The public's perception of "criminal" youth and the magnitude of youth criminality come primarily through popular cultural depictions of youth crime, many of which are contained in so-called objective, journalistic contexts. As we will observe in the next four chapters, journalistic accounts have the potential to be extremely damaging to the image of youth. Common-sense perceptions about youth crime, however negative and unfounded, buttress a system of justice that is harsh, non-rehabilitative and ultimately supportive of the global exploitation of children and youth. In short, the ideological power of media (both fictional and non-fictional) fosters a context in which children are seen as incompletely developed non-citizens. Their exploitation, therefore, is implicitly justifiable. This is especially ironic in the developed world, in which human rights are ostensibly the most well-preserved.

References

Anderson, Margaret.1988. *Thinking about Women: Sociological Perspectives on Sex and Gender.* New York: MacMillan Publishing.

Balbus, Isaac.1973. *Dialectics of Repression.* New York: Russell Sage Foundations.

Basran, Gurcharn, Charan Gill and Brian MacLean. 1995. *Farmworkers and Their Children.* Vancouver: Collective Press.

Bourdieu, P. 1999. *The Weight of the World: Social Suffering in Contemporary Society.* Stanford: Stanford University Press.

Bourke, Joanna. 1999. *An Intimate History of Killing.* London. Granta.

Box, Steven. 1983. *Power, Crime, and Mystification.* New York: Tavistock.

Brownlee, Jamie. 2005. *Ruling Canada: Corporate Cohesion and Democracy.* Halifax, NS: Fernwood Publishing.

Carroll, William. 2004. *Corporate Power in a Globalizing World: A Study in Elite Social Organization.* Don Mills, ON: Oxford University Press.

Chomsky, Noam. 2002. *Hegemony or Survival? America's Quest for Global Dominance.* New York: Metropolitan.

Cohen, Stanley. 1980 *Folk Devils and Moral Panics: The Creation of the Mods and Rockers.* New York: St. Martin's.

Daniels, Cynthia. 1998. *Lost Fathers: The Politics of Fatherlessness in America.* New York: St. Martin's Griffin.

Diller, Lawrence H. 1998. *Running on Ritalin: A Physician Reflects on Children, Society, and Performance in a Pill.* New York: Bantam.

Edelman, Bernard. 1985. *Dear America: Letters Home from Viet Nam*. New York: W.W. Norton.
Giroux, Henry. 2003. "Public Time and Educated Hope: Educational Leadership and the War Against Youth." *The Initiative Anthology*. <www.muohio.edu/eduleadership/anthology/OA//OA03001.html> (accessed October 13, 2005).
Glor, Eleanor. 1989. "A Survey of Comprehensive Accident and Injury Experience of High School Students in Saskatchewan." *Canadian Journal of Public Health*, 80: 435–440.
Goff, Colin, and Charles Reasons. 1978. *Corporate Crime in Canada*. Toronto: Prentice-Hall.
Green, R.G., and K. Healy. 2003. *Tough on Kids: Rethinking Approaches to Youth Justice*. Saskatoon, SK: Purich Publishing.
Grossman, Dave. 1995. *On Killing: The Psychological Cost of Learning to Kill in War and Society*. Boston: Little Brown.
Hall, Stuart, Chas Critcher, Tony Jefferson, John Clarke and Brian Roberts. 1978. *Policing the Crisis: Mugging, the State and Law and Order*. London: Macmillan.
Herman, Edward S., and Noam Chomsky. 1994. *Manufacturing Consent: The Political Economy of the Mass Media*. New York: Pantheon.
HRW (Human Rights Watch). 2000. *Fingers to the Bone: United States Failure to Protect Child Farmworkers*. New York: Human Rights Watch.
ILO (International Labour Organization). 2002. *A Future Without Child Labour*. Geneva.
____. 2004. "Youth Employment at an All Time High." Press Release, August 11. Geneva.
Males, Mike. 2000. *Framing Youth: 10 Myths About the Next Generation*. Monroe, ME: Common Courage.
McMullan, John L. 2005. *News, Truth and Crime: The Westray Disaster and Its Aftermath*. Halifax, NS: Fernwood Publishing.
Miedzian, Miriam. 1998. *Boys will Be Boys: Breaking the Links Between Masculinity and Violence*. Toronto: Doubleday.
Milner Jr., M. 2004. *Freaks, Geeks, and Cool Kids: American Teenagers, Schools, and the Culture of Consumption*. New York: Routledge.
Morris, Nomi. 1995. "Kids at Work." *Macleans*, December 11: 28–29.
Newman, Tony. 2000. "Workers and Helpers: Perspectives on Children's Labour, 1899–1999. *British Journal of Social Work*, 30: 323–338.
O'Higgins, N. 2001. *Youth Unemployment and Employment Policy: A Global Perspective*. Geneva: International Labour Otganization.
Popenoe, David. 1998. "Life Without Father." In Cynthia Daniels. *Lost Fathers: The Politics of Fatherlessness in America*. New York: St. Martin's Griffin.
Poulantzas, Nicos. 1972. "The Problem of the Capitalist State." In Robin Blackburn (ed.), *Ideology in the Social Sciences*. New York: Pantheon Books.
Quinney, Richard. 1974. *Critique of Legal Order: Crime Control in Capitalist Society*. Boston: Little, Brown.
Ramazanoglu, Caroline. 1993. *Up Against Foucault: Explorations of Some Tensions Between Foucault and Feminism*. London: Routledge.
Reiter, Ester. 1996. *Making Fast Food: From the Frying Pan into the Fryer*. Montreal: McGill University Press.
Robbins, R.H. 2005. *Global Problems and the Culture of Capitalism, 3rd edition*. Boston: Allyn and Bacon

Robinson, Laura. 1998. *Crossing the Line: Violence and Sexual Assault in Canada's National Sport*. Toronto: McLelland and Stewart.

Rosenau, Pauline M. 1992. *Postmodernism and the Social Sciences: Insights, Inroads, and Intrusions*. Princeton, NJ: Princeton University Press.

Schissel, Bernard. 2006. *Still Blaming Children: Youth Conduct and the Politics of Child Hating, 2nd edition*. Halifax and Winnipeg: Fernwood Publishing.

Southern Ontario Newspaper Guild. 2005. "Journalistic Standards in Monopolized Media." Available at <www.song.on.ca/journalist_standards.html> (accessed October 5, 2005).

Sutherland, Anne, and Beth Thompson. 2003. Kidfluence: The Marketers Guide to Understanding and Reaching Generation Y: Kids, Tweens, and Teens. New York: McGraw-Hill.

Chapter 5

THE POWER TO CRIMINALIZE
An Introduction

Elizabeth Comack and Gillian Balfour

> From: *The Power to Criminalize: Violence, Inequality and the Law*, Chapter 1 (reprinted and slightly revised with permission of the authors).

To criminalize, according to the standard dictionary definition, means "to turn a person into a criminal." When you stop to think about it, of all the tasks assigned to law this one is perhaps the most formidable. It signals the power that law exercises in our society. This power to criminalize is something that law itself takes very seriously.

According to traditional legal doctrine, law's role in society is to dispense justice in an unbiased fashion, dispassionately and without favour or ill will. "Equality of all before the law" — regardless of class, race, sex or creed — is the hallmark of the rule of law. When criminal cases are brought before the court, law's task is to discern the "truth" of the matter by extracting the legally relevant facts of the case to determine the guilt or innocence of the accused. The Criminal Code contributes to the appearance of consistency, uniformity and precision in law. For instance, crimes against the person — such as assault, assault with a weapon or causing bodily harm and aggravated assault — are hierarchically ordered on the basis of their seriousness, with corresponding sanctions attached. When violence breaks out, the matter for law becomes one of imposing its definition on the event to render a judgment on who is to be criminalized. In the process, law imposes an order; it imputes reason and sensibility to the messiness of everyday life.

Critical legal theorists have argued that this business of criminalizing is much more complicated than it might first appear. Far from being an impartial and objective enterprise, law deals in ideology and discourse — through the meanings and assumptions embedded in the language that it uses, through its ways of making sense of the world and through its corresponding practices. While law's concern is ostensibly with making judgments on legal matters (such as culpability, admissibility or reasonableness), there is more at work. Extracting the legally relevant facts of a case from the messiness of people's lives involves a deciphering or translation. It also involves making judgments on the legal subjects themselves, in terms not only of what they have done, but also of who they are, and on the social settings or spaces in which they move. The net result is the reproduction of a very particular kind of order; and this order, as we will demonstrate, is one in which gender, race and class inequalities figure prominently.

In effect, two very different readings somehow need to be reconciled: law as a fair and impartial arbiter of social conflicts; and law as one of the sites in society that reproduces gender, race and class inequalities. As with most difficult issues, the reconciliation of these two readings is neither simple nor straightforward. Our purpose in this chapter is to offer an analysis that acknowledges the tensions between these two views of law.

The approach we take up here understands law as being premised on principles of fundamental justice (innocent until proven guilty, due process), principles that legal actors must strictly follow in the processing of criminal justice cases. Within this framework, the role of the Crown attorney is not to obtain a conviction, but rather to present credible evidence relevant to what is alleged to be a crime. The duty of the defence counsel is to ensure that the Crown proves every element of the alleged offence "beyond a reasonable doubt" and that the accused's rights are not violated during the investigation and prosecution of the offence. As officers of the court, lawyers are bound by professional codes of ethics and formal obligations that delimit their roles. Yet — and here is the crux — lawyers can exercise considerable agency in their work, not just in the interpretation and utilization of rules and procedures, but also in their case-building strategies.

The very nature of how legal actors choose to carry out their assigned tasks opens the way for particular constructions to enter the legal arena — constructions of the accused, complainant and witnesses in a criminal case, as well as of the event itself and the social space in which that event occurs. These constructions are built upon particular discourses (relating to masculinity, femininity, race, class and social space). But these discourses are not simply "invented" by law. Their salience draws, in large part, from the very strong resonance they have in the wider society. In these terms, the constructions on which lawyers frame their case-building strategies are conditioned by the particular socio-political context of the time: the assemblage of institutions, practices and discourses that legitimate the prevailing social order. One of our main premises, then, is that law is not just a set of rules and procedures, but a process that entails gendering, racializing and classing practices.

Law, then, is a complex and contradictory terrain, at once promoting an image of equality (and sometimes living up to that image) while also constituting those who stand before it in gendered, racialized and class-based terms (thereby reproducing social inequalities). This is our basic starting point for investigating law's power to criminalize. But there is more to be clarified before we proceed.

FOCUSING ON VIOLENT CRIME

While the power to criminalize extends to a variety of actions and behaviours, we choose here to concentrate on the criminalization of interpersonal violence.[1] Our choice is an obvious one for a number of reasons. Of all the offences that the criminal justice system is called on to adjudicate, it is crimes against the person — homicides, assaults and robberies, for instance — that are most likely to generate attention. Violent crimes feature regularly on the front pages of newspapers or as the lead item of evening TV news reports. Indeed, public concern over the issue of violent crime has heightened in recent years, even though crime rates have been on the decline (Statistics Canada 2003). The fear and anxiety invoked by violent crime — especially when it is featured so prominently in the media — lead to a scrutiny of law's ability to dispense justice in these cases. In this respect, violent crime is one area where the tension between the two readings of law is most acute.

Crimes involving interpersonal violence are presumably ones in which the seriousness of the charge is such an overriding consideration in the criminalization process that extra-legal factors (such as the gender, race or class of the accused) are not likely to invade the practice of law. In other words, given the nature of the offence, we would expect law's claims to impartiality, fairness and justice to be most in evidence in violent crime cases. At the same time, however, certain groups in our society are more likely than others to be criminalized for a violent offence. Aboriginal peoples, for instance, are overrepresented in the criminal justice system relative to their numbers in the general population:

- While Aboriginal peoples comprise 2 percent of the adult Canadian population, they make up 17 percent of the prison populations across the country (Statistics Canada 2000). In 1998–99, Aboriginal peoples represented 13 percent of admissions to probation and 11 percent of conditional sentence admissions (Statistics Canada 2001).

- The overrepresentation of Aboriginal persons is greatest in the Prairie provinces. In 1998–99 the proportion of Aboriginal persons admitted to adult provincial facilities in Saskatchewan (76 percent) was almost ten times higher than their proportion in the provincial adult population (8 percent). While Aboriginal peoples made up 9 percent of the adult population in Manitoba, they comprised 59 percent of admissions to provincial custody. In Alberta, where 4 percent of the adult population is Aboriginal, 38 percent of admissions to provincial facilities were Aboriginal persons (Statistics Canada 2001).
- While the majority of people incarcerated in Canada's jails are economically disadvantaged, this is especially the case for Aboriginal inmates; they have less education and are more likely to be unemployed than are non-Aboriginal inmates. Some 48 percent of Aboriginal inmates in provincial and territorial custody and 56 percent of those in federal custody have less than a Grade 10 education, compared with 31 percent of non-Aboriginal inmates in provincial and territorial custody and 43 percent of those in federal custody. Some 70 percent of Aboriginal inmates in provincial and territorial custody and 53 percent of those in federal custody were unemployed at the time of arrest, compared with 47 percent of non-Aboriginal inmates in provincial custody and 40 percent of those in federal custody (Statistics Canada 2001).
- Aboriginal women are even more overrepresented in Canada's jails than are their male counterparts. According to a one-day snapshot of prisoners conducted in October 1996, Aboriginal females accounted for almost one quarter (23 percent) of the adult female inmate population. Aboriginal males accounted for 18 percent of the adult male inmate population (Finn et al. 1999).
- The one-day snapshot also found that Aboriginal inmates were incarcerated more often for violent crimes than were non-Aboriginal inmates (42 percent compared with 31 percent in provincial and territorial facilities, and 79 percent versus 72 percent in federal facilities) (Finn et al. 1999).

Can these disproportionate incarceration rates of Aboriginal men and women be explained with reference to crime-producing conditions in their communities and families? Or do features of the criminalization process itself play a role?

Given that the Criminal Code, with its hierarchical ordering of crimes on the basis of seriousness, contributes to the appearance of consistency, precision and uniformity in law, the matter of what constitutes violent crime would appear to be relatively straightforward. Colin Sumner (1997: 1), however, makes the point that "even a serious matter like violence is not a simple fact which speaks loudly for itself." What counts as violence is culturally and historically variable. According to Sumner (1997: 3), violence is

> subject to the acculturated or political understandings and standpoints of the viewer. One man's "healthy aggression" is another woman's "mindless violence"; one society's blood feud is a system of social control, another's is dangerous vigilantism; one country's civilization is another's barbarism; one country's ethnic cleansing is another's war crime.

How law constructs violence in a particular case will be informed by culturally and historically specific understandings. The question is whether and in what ways these understandings of violence are gendered, racialized and class based.

Another way in which the issue of violent crime calls forth the tension between the two readings of law has to do with law's potential as a mechanism for realizing substantive change in society. Over the past three decades, feminists have been instrumental in bringing about legal reforms to redress women's inequality in society. Nowhere have these efforts been more pronounced than in the area of law's response to violence against women (especially in the form of rape and wife abuse). Concerted lobbying efforts by women's groups have led to changes to laws dealing with sexual violence and to the implementation of what Jane Ursel (2001) terms "a new paradigm of justice" for responding to cases of domestic violence. In effect the occurrence of violence against women has been transformed from a private trouble to a public issue worthy of law's attention, which reinforces Sumner's point — that what counts as "violence" is culturally and historically variable. At the same time, however, questions remain about whether the reforms have worked. Do recent reforms in the area of law's treatment of violence against women stand as a testament to law's claim to uphold principles of fundamental justice? Or do the case-building strategies of lawyers in these cases undermine efforts to bring about significant reforms?

STUDYING LEGAL PRACTICE

The role of gender, race and class in the processing of criminal justice cases has been a key area of concern within criminology. By far the most common approach used by criminologists to address this issue has been to focus on sentencing outcomes. Criminologists have employed quantitative methodologies to compare the severity of sentences accorded to men and women, whites and racial minorities and upper-class and economically marginalized groups (see, for example, Crow 1987; Daly 1987, 1983; Zatz 1984; Ericson and Baranek 1982). Yet such studies have produced inconclusive and inconsistent findings. Criminalization appears to be conditioned by case facts (the seriousness of the offence and prior record) and extra-legal factors (the age, race, ethnicity and sex of the accused), but not in a consistent fashion. Marjorie Zatz (1984: 147–148) captures the tentative nature of these findings: "The sum of our knowledge is that for some offences, in some jurisdictions, controlling for some legal and extra-legal factors, at some historical points and using some methodologies, some groups are differentially treated." Although sentencing studies may demonstrate disproportionate treatment of certain groups in society, the approach of focusing on outcomes misses much of what transpires in the criminalization process.

In a similar fashion, the study of widely publicized cases has provided insight into how gender, race and class play out in particular cases. For instance, the trial of former U.S. football star O.J. Simpson for the murder of his wife, Nicole Brown Simpson, and her friend, Ronald Goldman, raised issues around domestic violence, racial stereotypes and the extent to which money can be used to buy the best defence (Hutchinson 1996; Barak 1996). Similarly, the Canadian trials of Karla Homolka and Paul Bernardo for the sexual assaults and murders of two young women, Leslie Mahaffy and Kristen French, generated considerable commentary around gender and women's culpability (McGillivray 1998; Pearson 1997). Nevertheless, the more routine ways in which gender, race and class work in the criminal justice system have eluded criminologists.

Investigating the routine processing of criminal cases is no easy matter. As Sheilah Martin (1993: 32–33) notes:

> A major problem is getting access to the cases themselves. Relying on published cases means easier, less costly access but the available range of cases is limited and has passed through the filter of the publisher's assessment of relevance and their editing procedure ... Although reviewing every case on a selected subject matter is preferable, it is rarely feasible — even for defined geographical regions and within limited time spans. In many areas of concern ... there are no available written judgements. While transcripts of the proceedings can be created and ordered, they are exceptionally expensive.

Some researchers have relied on observation of court proceedings to examine the processing of criminal cases. Sue Lees (1994: 125) comments on the difficulties encountered with this methodology: "In the UK anyone can gain access to the public gallery. However, it is often difficult to hear, space is limited and access cannot be guaranteed, nor notes easily taken, so access to the press seats is essential, which can take a long time to negotiate." Lees (1994: 126) makes another important point: "The law often constitutes gender [and race and class] relations in its discretionary spaces rather than in its explicit rules." We need a methodology, therefore, that is capable of mining those spaces.

The two methodologies employed in this book attempt to do just that. The first involved gaining access to Crown attorney case files of men and women who had appeared before the Manitoba Court of Queen's Bench on violent crime charges (homicide, sexual and non-sexual assaults and robbery). A large percentage of criminal cases in Canada are disposed of without proceeding to the trial stage. As a superior court of criminal jurisdiction, however, the Court of Queen's Bench hears the most serious cases. For research purposes, this means that there is typically extensive documentation on each case.

We studied a total of ninety violent crime cases covering a four-year period (1996–99). We began by drawing an initial sample of forty-five cases involving women defendants, which represented 83 percent of the women who appeared before the Court of Queen's Bench on a violent crime charge during the four-year period. For comparative purposes, we also drew a random sample (stratified by offence type) of forty-five men.[2] The files on these cases included a number of documents: police incident reports, police notes, bail-hearing transcripts, transcripts of the preliminary hearing, notes written by the Crown, correspondence with the defence, pre-trial memos, pre-sentence reports, psychological assessments, medical reports, character letters, relevant case law and appeal court decisions. To gather as much information as possible, for several of the cases we ordered court transcripts of sentencing submissions and reasons for sentence. Because some of the cases were reported, we were also able to gain access to further information about them. In total, we produced over a thousand pages of detailed summaries and verbatim quotes on the ninety cases studied. Although it was a time-consuming process, our efforts in drawing together these legal documents afforded a unique opportunity to study how the justice system processes violent crimes.

Police incident reports, for example, show a distinct formulaic quality. Presiding officers are given the task of detailing a case's legally relevant facts, which together are meant to establish the basis for the criminal charge. Typically included are statements made by the accused, complainant and bystanders as well as comments by police on the demeanour of the accused. These reports form the starting point for the Crown attorney in building a case against the accused "beyond a reasonable doubt."

Most of the cases that reach the Court of Queen's Bench have a preliminary hearing, the purpose of which is for the judge to determine whether there is sufficient evidence to warrant committing an accused to trial. As André Marin (1995: 115) notes, the preliminary hearing is used by the defence "to test the strength and credibility of the evidence of the Crown witnesses and to take advantage of the hearing as a 'dry run' for the trial." In this respect, transcripts of the hearing offer a unique lens into the legal process. As a "dry run" for the trial, the preliminary hearing becomes a site in which the strategies used by defence lawyers to undermine the case against the accused are revealed. These strategies often involve the construction of alternative accounts or plausible scenarios. Given the standard of reasonable doubt, they also entail attacks on the credibility of the Crown's key witnesses in the case.

One document found in all of the Crown case files is a memo written by the Crown attorney in charge of the case to the Senior Crown attorney. The memo typically includes factual statements about the case, the defences that might be raised by the defence and descriptions of Crown witnesses (with special attention to their credibility). The Crown also often comments on what are perceived to be the strengths or weaknesses of the case against the accused.

Plea bargaining often occurs after the preliminary hearing, but if a case does go to trial, the files may also include court transcripts of sentencing submissions, judges' reasons for sentence, pre-sentence reports and the like. It is at the point of sentencing where competing accounts of the defendant are most likely to surface, as the Crown and defence put forward their justifications for a particular sentence and the judge makes a determination.

While each of these documents has been constructed with a particular purpose and a particular audience in mind, they can tell us a great deal about the process of criminalizing violence. We learn, for example, what is considered noteworthy about a particular case and, just as important, what is not. In the process, the gendered, racialized and class-based presuppositions that inform the law's construction of violent crime also come into view.

In addition to analyzing the Crown attorney case files, we interviewed twelve criminal defence lawyers. Our aim was to explore the case-building strategies they utilize in defending clients charged with violent offences. Because of solicitor-client privilege, lawyers cannot discuss details about specific cases they have taken on without violating professional codes of conduct and confidentiality. To circumvent this issue, we constructed a number of mock police reports that were designed to capture some of the typical situations and typical persons involved in violent crime events. We then used these mock reports as the basis for our discussions with the lawyers about the strategies they would employ to defend such cases.

In combination, the information obtained from a content analysis of Crown attorney case files and in-depth interviews with defence lawyers allows us to explore lawyers' strategies for translating the everyday experiences of defendants into legally recognized accounts. These data have the potential to reveal how lawyers negotiate their roles and strategies within the framework of procedural fairness, as well as the extent to which the prevailing socio-political context and discursive constructions based on gender, race and class inform their case-building work.

OUR ANALYSIS

In very general terms, there is a tension existing between law's claims to fairness and impartiality and law as a site for the reproduction of gender, race and class inequalities. Borrowing from radical, feminist, critical-race and post-structuralist theories, our approach situates lawyering as "structured action" and locates the agency of lawyers within three main dimensions: the Official Version of Law, the discursive nature of legal practice and the broader socio-political context in which law operates.

This tension and structured action is evident the gendering of violent crime. In legal practice, particular scripts of masculinity and femininity (albeit bounded by class and race factors) are played out in. Because the constructions of "normal crime" that Crown attorneys and defence lawyers use to inform their case-building strategies are premised on an equation of "aggression = male activity," men accused of violent crime do not necessarily betray their gender. Nevertheless, women defendants who appear before the court on violent crime charges are an anomaly; they breach not only the constructions of "normal crime," but also the feminine scripts typically held out to women.

Legal tension exists in the racialization of violent crime. Understanding how race (and class) work in law involves attending to complex and complicated processes that have to do with racist ideological representations and racialized spaces. Lawyers, for instance, rely on stereotypes of Aboriginal people as welfare recipients and "drunken Indians" and on assumptions of Aboriginal communities as places where violence, alcohol and drug abuse, welfare dependency and crime are commonplace. The language of space is used to signify the meaning of violence and the culpability of the accused, which can be seen in how lawyers and the law speak about violence that occurs in sexualized spaces of the inner city and in white, middle-class suburban spaces. Seeing through this lens raises questions of whether or not efforts to legislate equality — as in "special considerations" legislation designed to resolve the overincarceration of Aboriginal peoples — have the potential to realize significant change.

All of this leads to the issue of using law as a mechanism for realizing substantive change in society with respect to the feminist engagement with the law. We suggest that the agency of lawyers is a formidable element of the power of law that has been largely overlooked in debates about legal reform. Feminist-inspired legal reforms designed to protect women and children complainants through the criminalization of men charged with sexual assault and a "new paradigm of justice" promised by proponents of zero-tolerance policies in the criminalization of domestic violence have had mixed results. In the interest of defending their clients, lawyers can strategically subvert and sabotage the intention of law reforms that they believe are politically motivated. The irony is that while lawyers may resist efforts to use law to realize significant change in the area of women's inequality, lawyering strategies are themselves imbued with gendered, racialized and class-based stereotypes.

But, how do we work through the tensions in law? Traditional legal doctrine asserts that law's role in society is that of dispensing justice in a neutral, impartial and unbiased fashion. Yet law is a site in which gender, race and class inequalities are reproduced. What are the prospects, then, for challenging law to live up to its claims in order to realize a more just society?

Notes

1. We are mindful that concentrating on the processes involved in criminalizing interpersonal violence (as it is defined within legal practice) restricts our focus to only certain forms of violence in society. Corporate crime, environmental crime, workplace health and safety violations and the like cause untold damage to Canadians each year (see, for example, Snider 1999). In this respect, the issue of what is not criminalized is just as significant as what is.
2. The men's sample represented 6 percent of the cases involving male defendants who appeared before the court on violent crime charges.

References

Barak, Gregg (ed.). 1996. *Representing O.J.: Murder, Criminal Justice and Mass Culture*. New York: Harrow and Heston.

Crow, I. 1987. "Black People and Criminal Justice in the UK." *Howard Journal of Criminal Justice*, 26, 4: 303–314.

Daly, Kathleen. 1983. *Order in the Court: Gender and Justice*. Washington, DC: National Institute of Justice.

_____. 1987. "Discrimination in Criminal Courts: Family, Gender and the Problem of Equal Treatment." *Social Forces*, 66: 152–175.

Ericson, Richard, and Patricia Baranek. 1982. *The Ordering of Justice*. Toronto: University of Toronto Press.

Finn, Anne, Shelley Trevethan, Gisele Carriere and Melanie Kowalski. 1999. "Female Inmates, Aboriginal Inmates, and Inmates Serving Life Sentences: A One Day Snapshot." *Juristat*, 19, 5. Ottawa: Canadian Centre for Justice Statistics.

Hutchinson, Earl. 1996. *Beyond O.J.: Race, Sex, and Class Lessons for America*. Montreal: Black Rose Books.

Lees, Sue. 1994. "Lawyers' Work as Constitutive of Gender Relations." In M. Cain and C. Harrington (eds.), *Lawyers in a Postmodern World*. New York: New York University Press.

Marin, André. 1995. *The Guide to Investigations and Prosecutions*. Aurora, ON: Canada Law Book.

Martin, Sheilah L. 1993. "Proving Gender Bias in the Law and the Legal System." In J. Brockman and D. Chunn (eds.), *Investigating Gender Bias: Law, Courts and the Legal Profession*. Toronto: Thompson Educational Publishing.

McGillivray, Anne. 1998. "'A Moral Vacuity in Her Which Is Difficult if Not Impossible to

Explain': Law, Psychiatry and the Remaking of Karla Homolka." *International Journal of the Legal Profession,* 5, 2/3: 255–288.
Pearson, Patricia. 1997. *When She Was Bad: Violent Women and the Myth of Innocence.* Toronto: Random House.
Snider, Laureen. 1999. "Relocating Law: Making Corporate Crime Disappear." In E. Comack (ed.), *Locating Law: Race/Class/Gender Connections.* Halifax: Fernwood Publishing.
Statistics Canada. 2000. *Adult Correctional Services in Canada.* 21. 5. Ottawa: Canadian Centre for Justice Statistics.
___. 2001. *Aboriginal Peoples in Canada.* Ottawa: Canadian Centre for Justice Statistics Profile Series.
___. 2003. "Violent Crime. <http://142.206.72.67/04/04b/04b_002a_e.htm>.
Sumner, Colin. 1997. "Introduction: The Violence of Censure and the Censure of Violence." In C. Sumner (ed.), *Violence, Culture and Censure.* London: Taylor and Francis.
Ursel, Jane. 2001. "Report on Domestic Violence Policies and Their Impact on Aboriginal People." Submitted to the Aboriginal Justice Implementation Commission. February 21. Winnipeg: Aboriginal Justice Implementation Commission.
Zatz, Marjorie. 1984. "Race, Ethnicity and Determinate Sentencing: A New Dimension to an Old Controversy." *Criminology,* 22: 147–171.

Chapter 6

LAW AS A DISCURSIVE PRACTICE

Elizabeth Comack and Gillian Balfour

> From: *The Power to Criminalize: Violence, Inequality and the Law*, Chapter 2 (reprinted with permission of the authors).

Theorists who adhere to the reading of law as a discursive practice invariably express their indebtedness to the work of Michel Foucault (1977, 1979 and 1984), and especially his analysis of the relation between power and knowledge. Foucault rejected the notion of power as a "thing" or commodity that can be owned. Instead, he concentrated on the mechanisms of power that came with the development of what he called the "disciplinary society," characterized by the growth of new knowledges (such as medicine and criminology) that led to new modes of surveillance and regulation of the population. For Foucault, knowledge is not objective, but political; the production of knowledge has to do with power. A reciprocal relation exists between the two: power is productive of knowledge, and knowledge is productive of power. Furthermore, "It is in discourse that power and knowledge are joined together" (1979: 100).

Bodies of knowledge such as medicine, science, law, psychology and sociology are discourses, historically specific systems of meaning or ways of making sense of the world. These discourses are shaped by social practices and in turn shape social relationships and institutions. Because they join together power and knowledge, certain discourses — and their corresponding discursive practices or ways of acting — come to dominate society at particular points in history. Foucault was therefore interested in "discovering how certain discourses claim to speak the truth and thus can exercise power in a society that values this notion of truth" (Smart 1989: 9).

Socio-legal theorists have adopted Foucault's ideas as a means of understanding the power of law in society. Carol Smart (1989), for one, suggests that law is a form of knowledge, and therefore a form of power. That power derives, in part, from law's ability to impose its definition of events onto everyday life. It does this not simply through rendering judgments, but by disqualifying other accounts. For instance, within the courtroom, Smart (1989: 11) argues:

> Non-legal knowledge is … suspect and/or secondary. Everyday experiences are of little interest in terms of their meaning for individuals. Rather these experiences must be translated into another form in order to become "legal" issues and before they can be processed through the legal system … So the legal process translates everyday experience into legal relevances, it excludes a great deal that might be relevant to the parties, and it makes its judgement on the scripted or tailored account.

The process of the rape trial illustrates how legal practice translates people's experiences into "legal relevances." From a woman's standpoint, rape is, more often than not, an experience of humiliation, degradation and violation — a terrifying ordeal. The rape trial, however, involves sifting through that experience to extract those "facts" of the case that law views as being relevant to the determination of the guilt or innocence of the accused. For instance, did the woman complainant consent? As a key witness for the Crown, is her testimony credible? Is there physical evidence to support or corroborate her claim that it was rape? As one woman who experienced a rape trial notes, complainants are expected to speak in a legal language that is precise and exact, with times and dates attached:

> I was never allowed to describe the crime in my own words but was required to respond to a template designed to protect the rights of the rapist. I will never forget the final question put to me in defence of the man who had raped me. I was asked, as were the other four women [whom he had raped], whether my rape had been violent. Despite the knife, the threats against my life, the forced entry, the ghoul's mask and the binding of my eyes, he asked if my rape had been violent. Despite the police manhunt, the public outcry, the rapist's criminal history of violence, the packed courtroom, and the media scrutiny, the rapist's lawyer asked if my rape had been violent. Despite everything we know about the violent nature of rape, he asked if my rape had been violent. When I did not answer, could not answer, the judge instructed me that because I had

not been cut or stabbed with the rapist's knife, because he hadn't beaten or mutilated or (most decisive of all) killed me, I must answer that my rape had not been violent.

And my testimony was over. (Doe 2003: 72)

As a claim to power, law sets itself above other knowledges (such as psychology or common sense) and professes to have a method — the adversarial system — to establish the "truth" of events. In this sense, the practice of law is akin to a game constituted by certain rules (such as due process) and involving certain key players (lawyers, judges, complainants, the accused) (Chunn and Lacombe 2000: 15). Lawyers play the game using moves such as persuasion and negotiation, and they appeal to certain authoritative discourses to achieve their immediate aims. In these terms, the practice of law is more than just professional codes of conduct and prescribed roles of legal actors. Law is also a series of strategies that constitute both the identities of legal subjects and their social relations with each other.

In her later work, Smart (1992) turned her attention to the questions of how gender works in law and how law works to produce gender. She suggests that law is a "gendering strategy" — one of society's discourses that is "productive not only of gender difference, but quite specific forms of polarized difference." Law, she says, "brings into being not only gendered subject positions" but also "subjectivities or identities to which the individual becomes tied or associated" (34). These gendering strategies vary according to history and culture, and they can be strategies without authors "in as much as we should not imagine that strategy here implies a plan, masterminded in advance by extra-cultural (Cartesian) actors" (35).

For Smart (1995: 218), law is "a mechanism for fixing gender differences and constructing femininity and masculinity in oppositional modes." Her main interest is with the "Woman" of legal discourse. Law is a means by which "Woman" (in contradistinction to "Man") and "types of Woman" (the female criminal, the prostitute, the unmarried mother) are brought into being. These constructions work symbiotically, as a double strategy:

> Woman has always been both kind and killing, active and aggressive, virtuous and evil, cherishable and abominable, not either virtuous or evil. Woman therefore represents a dualism, as well as being one side of a prior binary distinction. Thus in legal discourse the prostitute is constructed as the bad woman, but at the same time she epitomizes Woman in contradistinction to Man because she is what any woman could be and because she represents a deviousness and a licentiousness arising from her (supposedly naturally given) bodily form, while man remains innocuous. (Smart 1992: 36)

While Smart elaborates on the significance of law as a gendering strategy for women, law also genders men's lives. The work of Robert Connell (1987, 1995 and 2000), for instance, has been instrumental in bringing the issue of masculinity to bear on criminological research and theorizing. Drawing from Gramsci's notion of hegemony — the "systems of domination which are formed through power struggles and become sedimented over time" (Howarth 2000: 84) — Connell theorizes that a certain culturally idealized form of masculinity becomes hegemonic in society. Emerging from socially organized power relations between men and women and among men, "hegemonic masculinity" is constructed in relation to women (what Connell calls "emphasized femininity") as well as various "subordinated" or "oppositional" masculinities (such as male homosexuality). In contemporary Western industrialized societies, hegemonic masculinity is characterized by "whiteness (race), work in the paid labor market (gender division of labor), the subordination of girls and women (gender relations of power), professional-managerial (class), and heterosexism (sexuality)" (Messerschmidt 1997: 10). As a culturally dominant discourse, hegemonic masculinity has a bearing on how men are constructed within law. As Smart (1992: 32–33) observes, "Law does not serve the interests of men as a homogeneous category any more than it serves the interests of women as a category." It follows, then, that law will make sense of men accused of criminal acts according to prevailing hegemonic scripts of masculinity. These scripts will also be informed by presuppositions of race, class and sexuality.

Working with Smart's typology of law as a gendering strategy, Kathleen Daly (1994: 460) suggests that we investigate law as a racializing strategy — that is, "how race and ethnicity are brought forth as racialized subject positions by criminal law and justice system practices." The term "racialization" is used to refer to the process by which discourses can become permeated with racial dimensions (Henry and Taylor 2002: 11). In adopting this view, we need not assume that justice system practices invariably exploit minority groups and serve the majority group. Rather, racializing discourses can be "everywhere apparent and move in cross-cutting ways" (Daly 1994: 460). For instance, because race is "not simply attached to people's bodies as a natural or stable characteristic" (Daly 1994: 461), racist imageries (relating to dangerousness, culpability and/or victimhood) can inform legal actors' constructions of crime.

The 1971 police investigation of the murder of Helen Betty Osborne reveals how racialization can profoundly influence the response of the criminal justice system to violent crime. Helen Betty Osborne, a young Aboriginal college student, lived in The Pas, a predominantly white town in Northern Manitoba. One night while walking home, she was forced into a car by four young white men who were "cruising" for an Indian girl. She was driven to an isolated spot outside of town, and there brutally beaten and stabbed to death with a screwdriver. The police investigation that followed the discovery of her body focused almost exclusively on Helen's Aboriginal friends. Police questioned Aboriginal youth in the community without the consent of parents, brought numerous people to the morgue to view Helen's battered body and widely distributed photos of her for the purposes of identification. Although the police were made aware of the suspicious activities of four white men following Helen's murder, the officers failed to follow up on that information. Instead they arrested, stripped-searched and detained two Aboriginal youth for questioning. In the words of the commissioners of the Aboriginal Justice Inquiry:

> It is clear that Helen Betty Osborne would not have been killed if she had not been Aboriginal. The four men who took her to her death from the streets of The Pas that night had gone looking for an Aboriginal girl with whom to "party." They found Betty Osborne. When she refused to party she was driven out of town and murdered. Those who abducted her showed a total lack of regard for her person or her rights as an individual. Those who stood by while the physical assault took place, while sexual advances were made and while she was being beaten to death showed their own racism, sexism and indifference. Those who knew the story and remained silent must share their guilt. (Hamilton and Sinclair 1991: 98)

Marlee Kline (1994) is another writer who locates law as one of the discourses in which racism is constructed, reproduced and reinforced in society. In her analysis of the "colour of law" with respect to First Nations people, Kline introduces us to an understanding of how judges and lawyers, as social actors, bring with them into the court racist ideologies that are rooted in the wider society. In these terms, racism flows from the ideological form of law rather than the isolated acts of individuals:

> Judges like other members of dominant society operate within discursive fields in which racist ideology helps constitute what is and is not to be taken for granted as "just the way things are." The appearance of racist ideological representations within judicial discourse may be more of a reflection of the power and pervasiveness of such dominant ideology in the wider society and the particular susceptibility of legal discourse to it, than individual racial prejudice on the part of judges. (Kline 1994: 452)

According to Kline, ideological representations of Aboriginal peoples developed out of the material relations of colonialism and continue to be constructed, reproduced and reinforced in a wide variety of discursive contexts, including what she refers to as the "abstracted and indeterminate form of law" (452). Inquiring as to how judges are allowed to import ideological frameworks into law, Kline suggests that it is the appearance of the neutrality of law (promoted by law's Official Version) that obscures law's power to naturalize and legitimize racist ideologies.

Sherene Razack (1998) further refines our discussion of law-as-racialized. She suggests that violence and drunkenness have come to be viewed as naturally occurring and inevitable features of places inhabited by Aboriginal peoples. According to Razack (2000: 117), violence is "an event that is routine when the bodies in question are Aboriginal." While violence has come to be associated with racialized spaces of the inner city — especially in the Prairie provinces, where inner-city neighbourhoods are heavily populated by Aboriginal peoples — violence in white, middle-class neighbourhoods is constituted as different from "other" (Indian) spaces (Razack 1998, 2000 and 2002).

Razack's analysis reveals how "legal and social constructs naturalize spatial relations of domination, highlighting in the process white respectability and Aboriginal criminality." Writing of the murder of Pamela George, a young Aboriginal woman who worked as a prostitute in Regina, Razack (2000: 6) argues that "because Pamela George was considered to belong to a space in which violence routinely occurs, and to have a body that is routinely violated, whereas her killers were presumed to be far removed from this zone, the enormity of what was done to her remained largely unacknowledged in the law." For instance, Razack (2000: 114) notes how lawyers described the site of the murder as "a romantic place where couples are often necking or petting in vehicles." She also acknowledges the historical and contemporary racial and spatial parallels between the murders of Helen Betty Osborne and Pamela George. In both the Osborne and George cases, "White men forcibly and fatally removed Aboriginal bodies from the city space, a literal cleansing of the white zone" (Razack 2000: 115). In the words of Justices A.C. Hamilton and C.M. Sinclair (1991: 96):

> To the people of The Pas, Osborne was not the girl next door; she was Aboriginal in a white town. Even though she had lived in The Pas for two years by the time she was murdered, she was a stranger to the community, a person almost without identity. She was unknown to those who heard the rumours. Because of the racial separation of The Pas, those who cared about Betty Osborne, her Aboriginal friends, were not privy to the rumours about those who took her life.

Throughout the trial, Pamela George was referred to as the "hooker" or the "Indian," whereas the accused men — two white, middle-class university students — were characterized by their lawyers as "boys who did pretty darn stupid things" (Razack 2000: 117). Razack maintains that these strategies constitute the identities of Pamela George and the men as well as the place where the death occurred in such a way that "no one could be really held accountable for her death, at least not to the extent that there would have been accountability had she been of [white] spaces within the domain of justice" (117).

The Pamela George case is significant because it highlights not only the role of race and gender in law, but also the role of class. The two male accused who were convicted of manslaughter in George's death were clearly privileged by their class position. They used their parents' credit cards to obtain cash to pay George for oral sex and later to purchase plane tickets to travel to Banff, where they hid from police.

Most writers who consider law as a discursive practice have not focused much attention on how law places value on a particular set of class relations. In large part, this is due to their adherence to a post-structuralist theoretical orientation. Post-structuralists — such as Foucault and Smart — are skeptical of theorizing premised on "totalizing structures" such as capitalism, imperialism or patriarchy. These vocabularies or concepts, they argue, are too cumbersome to capture the fragmented nature of social life; they also assume a reality that exists outside of or apart from individuals. Instead, post-structuralists place their emphasis on "agency and the habitat in which agency operates" (Smart 1995: 211). In response to this charge, we maintain that there are good reasons for retaining the notion that social structures exist, not the least of which is that systems like capitalism are "totalizing structures" (Fudge and Glasbeek 1992); they condition and contour the economic, social and political lives of the individuals who move within them (Comack 1999a: 66). In this regard, one of the advantages of adopting Messerschmidt's notion of "structured action" is that it acknowledges how social structures (like capitalism) are enacted in everyday interactions and in specific locations. And one of those locations is law.

Much goes missing, then, if gender and race are separated out from class. We need to be mindful of how class privilege and economic marginalization enter into legal practice. Nevertheless, given the ways in which gender, race and class so often intersect, clear lines of distinction are difficult to draw. Daly, for instance, notes how "whiteness" has both race and class dimensions:

> It includes notions of what constitutes appropriate dress, demeanor, ways of speaking, and child-rearing practices; it means believing that existing rules and authorities are legitimate and fair; and it implies trust that schooling is related to paid employment and that decisions in schools and work sites are based on meritocratic principles of ability and discipline. (Daly 1994: 451)

To the extent that the practices of criminal law and the justice system embrace such constructions, they will be "color-coded and class-compounded" (Daly 1994: 451).

By attending to the ways in which law operates as a discursive practice, we can begin to see how gender, race and class inequalities enter into the picture. While principles of fundamental justice and professional codes of conduct may constrain and enable the discretion of legal actors, lawyering also involves a series of strategies that constitute the identities of legal subjects, social relations and social spaces in gendered, racialized and class-based terms. Why is the rule of law susceptible to these strategies? How is it that certain truth claims come to have salience in the case-building strategies of lawyers? To address such questions we need to broaden our focus to include the wider socio-political context in which the criminalization process occurs.

THE SOCIO-POLITICAL CONTEXT: NEO-LIBERALISM AND NEO-CONSERVATISM

The socio-political context can be defined as the institutions, practices and discourses that legitimate modes of domination and control (Kellner 1989). In his own work, Messerschmidt (1997) explored slavery in the American South as a socio-political context that made the lynching of Black men possible by legitimating claims of white supremacy. In today's context we should assess how neo-liberalism and neo-conservatism can alter the practice of law.

Over the past three decades, the increasingly international or global nature of production and exchange has led to significant transformations within particular nation-states, including Canada. Corporate restructuring and downsizing — designed to keep up with these new forms of global production relations and financial systems — have led to heightened levels of inequality and immiseration. According to a United Nations report, "Worldwide, the top 20 percent of the world's population increased their share of total global wealth from 70 percent in 1960 to 85 percent in 1991, and the share 'enjoyed' by the poorest 20 percent actually declined from 1960 to 1991, falling from 2.3 percent to 1.4 percent" (quoted in Snider 1999: 184). Of the one hundred largest economies in the world, fifty-one are now corporations. Wal-Mart, the number twelve corporation, is bigger than 161 countries (Canadian Forum 1997: 48). Conditions in Canada are equally distorted. A Statistics Canada survey of assets, debts and wealth documented how millions of families and individuals were living on the brink of financial disaster at the same time as a small proportion of people were managing to accumulate huge slices of the wealth pie.

> All in all, Canadians had total personal wealth of more than $2.4 trillion in 1999, or an average of $199,664 for each family unit. The actual distribution of wealth, however, was anything but equitable. The wealthiest 10% of family units in Canada held 53% of the personal wealth, and the top 50% controlled an almost unbelievable 94.4% of the wealth. That left only 5.6% to be shared among the bottom 50%. (Kerstetter 2002: 1)

These economic transformations have occurred in tandem with a new political ethos: neo-liberalism. Premised on the values of individualism, freedom of choice, market security and minimal state involvement in the economy, neo-liberalism marks a dramatic shift in emphasis from collective or social values towards notions of family and individual responsibility. In their adherence to these neo-liberal ideals, governments have noticeably retreated from any professed commitment to social welfare. Instead of formulating policies and targeting spending on programs that would meet the social needs of the members of society (education, health care, pensions, social assistance), governments now focus on enhancing economic efficiency and international competitiveness. With the "privatization" of responsibility, individuals and families are left to look after themselves.

The impact of this shift is profound. As Janine Brodie notes, "This 'rebirth' of the individual marks the systematic erasure of structural factors in the formation of social policy. The poor become responsible for their own plight while the state becomes preoccupied with using its power to enforce the individualization of social costs." Joblessness becomes an individual rather than a social problem; the poor are stigmatized and made personally to blame for their own situation. According to Brodie (1999: 44), "Welfare dependency, similar to drug addiction, is a mark of individual weakness, irresponsibility and immaturity and, most of all, is avoidable." But it is not just the poor who feel the impact of these transformations. As Jock Young (1999: 8) notes, "The resulting effect of lean production and re-engineering is to remove a sizeable proportion of middle income jobs and to engender a feeling of precariousness in those previously secure." With the disappearance of secure, well-paying jobs and the stable communities that went with them comes increased anxiety and social unease.

While some writers have conceptualized neo-liberalism as a policy agenda adopted by nation-states that are ushering in new political regimes to match corporate globalization, others define neo-liberalism as "both a political discourse about the nature of rule and a set of practices that facilitate the governing of individuals from a distance" (Larner 2000: 6). Drawing on post-structuralist theories of "governmentality," these writers make a distinction between "government" and "governance." According to this view, while neo-liberalism may mean less government, it does not mean less governance. According to Wendy Larner (2000: 12), "It involves forms of governance that encourage both institutions and individuals to conform to the norms of the market." People are thereby encouraged to see themselves as "individualized and active subjects responsible for enhancing their own well being" (Larner 2000: 13).

How have these developments altered criminal justice policies and practices? Criminologists have noted the extraordinary expansion — especially since the early 1990s — in the scope and scale of penalization. One of the clearest indicators is the expansion of prison populations in most Western societies. In the United States, for example, the populations of state and federal prisons increased fivefold between 1970 and 1996, from less than 200,000 inmates to 1,182,000. In 1995 the United States spent some $55.1 billion on new prison construction (Taylor 1999: 186). In Canada the number of offenders in provincial institutions rose by 25 percent between 1986 and 1996, while federal inmates increased by an even more substantial 34 percent (Statistics Canada 1997). In 1999 more than twice as many offenders were admitted to prison than were placed under supervision in the community (Statistics Canada 2000). Accompanying this expansion in the use of prison has been a radical change in the discourses used to legitimate it.

Prior to the 1970s in North America and Western Europe, crime control strategies were rooted in the welfare state, or what David Garland (2001) calls the "penal welfare model": crime prevention through social engineering and rehabilitation. However, rising crime rates and a growing economic recession in the 1980s gave way to a crime control strategy that rejected liberal claims that poverty and racism caused crime. Rehabilitation, resocialization and "correction" were replaced with a concern for the policing and minimization of risk that offenders pose to the wider community.

"Risk management" is a neo-liberal strategy that relies on actuarial techniques of quantifying and assessing the risk that offenders pose; it is concerned not with changing offenders so much as with identifying and managing a person at risk of re-offending, while minimizing the potential risk to the community (Hannah-Moffat 2002). As such, offenders are depicted as "culpable, undeserving and somewhat dangerous individuals who must be carefully controlled for the protection of the public and the prevention of future offending. Rather than clients in need of support, they are seen as risks that must be managed" (Garland 2001: 175). Under this "responsibilization" model of crime control, then, criminals are made responsible for the choices they make. Those deemed to be unable or unwilling to manage their own risk or to exercise self-discipline are "the excluded." According to Nikolas Rose (2000: 331), the excluded are those individuals who inhabit "marginalized spaces," "savage spaces" and "anti-communities" because of an adjudged lack of competence or capacity for responsible, ethical self-discipline. Criminalization is intended to "transform and to reconstruct self-reliance in the excluded" (Rose 2000: 335).

Neo-liberalism is not the only ideology that informs criminal justice system policies and practices. As Kelly Hannah-Moffat (2000: 512) notes, neo-liberal strategies of government develop alongside and operate in conjunction with other forms of political rationalities. Indeed, as "vampire capitalism" replaces welfare capitalism (Chunn 1999: 256), increasing numbers of people are left to fend for themselves without the benefit of a social safety net. According to John Pratt (1999: 149), "The subjection of economies to market forces and the cutting back of welfare programmes of assistance has led to the re-creation of risk which welfarism had alleviated — poverty, unemployment and the formation of a new indigent class of vagrants, beggars, homeless, the mentally ill with criminal tendencies who now find themselves left to roam the streets." Added to this, the precariousness of middle-income families engenders a social anxiety that easily translates into fear of crime — and of "the excluded" — leading to calls for more law and order. Such calls for law and order solutions to crime are also aligned with demands by feminists and women's advocates, who see the criminalization of domestic violence as necessary for the safety of women and children (Schechter 1982; Martin 1993; Stanko 1985; MacLeod 1987; Walker 1990). Neo-conservative crime control policies — like zero-tolerance for domestic violence, "super max" prisons (complete with special handling units for dangerous offenders), parole-release restrictions, community notification laws and boot camps for young offenders — have become the order of the day.

Under the sway of neo-conservatism, police resources and practices have been strengthened and important aspects of the trial process have been altered to ensure the success of prosecutions. For example, since 1990 most provinces in Canada have implemented zero-tolerance policies on domestic violence. The programs include mandatory charging directives to police and vigorous prosecution policies. Laureen Snider (1998) points out that zero-tolerance has led to an overrepresentation of working-class men (and women) within the "net" of the criminal justice system, especially because these people often lack the resources necessary to acquire adequate legal counsel. Snider argues that these types of criminal justice policies are a form of "compulsory criminalization" in that they target groups — such as inner-city Aboriginal peoples — who are incapable of resisting the power of the state.

Neo-liberalism and neo-conservatism are not incompatible discourses. To the extent that neo-liberalism marks a retreat from social welfare and publicly funded commitments to equity and social justice, it advances in tandem with neo-conservatism's more hierarchical, patriarchal, authoritarian and inequitable vision of society (Knuttila and Kubik 2000: 151). What is more, the widening inequities of the neo-liberal market economy engender not only relative deprivation amongst the poor (which gives rise to crime), but also an anxiety amongst those better off — an anxiety that breeds intolerance and greater punitiveness towards the lawbreaker (Young 1999: 8). Given their concern for tradition, order, hierarchy and authority, conservatives place emphasis on family values and the need to restore individual responsibility. This focus on family and the individual meshes well with neo-liberalism's privatization of responsibility; it is not the state — but individuals and families — who are to be held accountable. While neo-liberals advocate deregulation and market freedom, conservatives call for a more orderly, disciplined and tightly controlled society. Nevertheless, the need for more social control is not a generalized one, but instead is a much more focused and specific demand, targeted on particular groups and behaviours. As Garland (2001: 99–100) notes, "The new conservatism proclaimed a moral message exhorting everyone to return to the values of family, work, abstinence, and self-control, but in practice its real moral disciplines fastened onto the behaviour of unemployed workers, welfare mothers, immigrants, offenders, and drug users."

The new global economy has thus given rise to a particular ideology — neo-liberalism — that appears to be anti-state in its rhetoric, yet relies on an expanding criminal justice system premised on risk management and "responsibilization." In harmony with neo-conservative calls to "get tough on crime," neo-liberalism rationalizes and legitimates the dismantling of the welfare state and the retrenchment of penalization. This socio-political context forms the backdrop in which lawyering takes place.

THE AGENCY OF LAWYERS

> Lawyers know they create law and are organized to police effectively the discursive mode of this creativity … the unanimity achieved by this policing enables them to see the law "itself" as unchanging, while in all its particulars it is infinitely malleable … Those wishing to understand lawyers should read what they say about themselves, no matter how pompous, tedious or self-adulatory the text may be. Lawyers are not wrong about themselves. The problem is rather that they do not understand the implications of their being so right. (Cain 1994: 20)

While Maureen Cain describes how instrumental lawyers are in the legal process, the role of lawyers in criminal litigation has actually received little attention in recent critical socio-legal theory.[1] Most of the focus has been on law as an "ideological terrain" or "discursive field," and within this context solicitor-client interactions are located as one of the more mundane aspects of law. But rather than being a merely mundane aspect of law, lawyers, we maintain, are powerful social actors in the administration of criminal justice. In his theory of crime as "structured action," Messerschmidt (1997: 5) notes that structures are enacted in everyday interactions by "people who know what they are doing and how to do it." In this respect, lawyering is one form of structured action in which lawyers exercise considerable agency.

Within their prescribed roles, Crown attorneys and defence counsel are empowered by the very form of law to legitimate normative definitions of gender, race and class. For instance, the form of law is premised upon the so-called "objective standard of reasonableness." This standard is used in criminal cases to judge whether a "reasonable" person would perceive an accused as intentionally committing a criminal act or failing to act, and the Crown is obliged to prove its case against an accused "beyond a reasonable doubt." Yet such criteria may not be as objective as they appear. As Sue Lees (1994: 125) notes, "An invitation to lawyers and judges to interpret what is reasonable is an invitation to them to fall back on their common sense, their culture, their class, race and gender-based stereotypes."

To suggest that lawyers exercise agency in their work also runs counter to professional codes of conduct that stipulate a lawyer's duty and obligation to his or her client. In theory, as Naffine (1990: 125) puts it, "The lawyer is the servant to the client, he is there to interpret the law and represent the client's interests, to act according to the client's view of the matter, not his own." But as Naffine goes on to note, this service model of the lawyer-client relationship does not accord with legal practice. Rather, the evidence suggests that in the criminal jurisdiction many lawyers regard their clients — "who are, in the main, socially disadvantaged" — as being "incapable of making decisions and so proceed to take control of the case." Naffine also finds evidence "that lawyers do not always present themselves in court in a neutral fashion, as the client's representative, but seek to establish a social distance between themselves and the individuals who hire their services" (126).

Indeed, in his classic study of the court process, Abraham Blumberg (1967) found that the practice of law was a "confidence game" in which defence attorneys acted as "double agents," pressuring their clients to reach a plea bargain in the interest of maintaining the efficiency of court procedures. According to Blumberg, defence lawyers identify not with their clients but with other members of the court. In particular, a working relationship emerges over time between Crown attorneys and defence counsel that "overshadows the relationship between clients and their lawyers." Blumberg argued that rather than participating in an adversarial system, the defence and prosecution become co-opted by the organizational goals of the criminal justice system; they come to rely upon one another's co-operation "for their continued professional existence and so the bargaining between them tends to be reasonable rather than fierce" (Blumberg 1967: 219).

A Canadian study by Richard Ericson and Patricia Baranek (1982) reinforced Blumberg's earlier findings. They found that court actors have a vested interest in maintaining mutually beneficial relationships amongst themselves, rather than in acquiring a satisfactory outcome for the accused. The common opinion of the lawyers they interviewed was that the lawyer should make the main decisions affecting the case, because the accused did not appreciate the processes of law.

Lawyering involves agency in an even larger sense as well. Crown attorneys and defence lawyers take turns presenting their competing accounts before the presiding judge, using techniques of persuasion and negotiation in the process of arriving at the "legal truth" of the matter. Cain (1994: 33) describes lawyers as "symbol traders"; they are imaginative traders in words. In a similar vein, Anita

Kalunta-Crumpton (1998: 568–569) describes lawyering as a "claims-making activity" whereby lawyers "negotiate knowledge through language in the bid to persuade." The legally relevant facts of a case form an important part of this claims-making process. Nevertheless, these are not facts that simply "speak for themselves." They require a translation or deciphering. In the process, judgments are made on the legal subjects, in terms not only of what they have done, but also of who they are and the social settings or spaces in which they move.

David Sudnow's (1968) work is instructive here (see also Worrall 1990). Sudnow uses the concept of "normal crime" to examine the criminalization process. He argues that over time prosecutors and defence lawyers develop proverbial characterizations of offences that encompass features beyond the statutory conception of an offence. These features include the typical manner in which offences are committed, the social characteristics of the persons who regularly commit them, the settings in which they occur and the type of victim often involved. In the course of their work, lawyers come to learn how to speak knowledgeably about different types of offenders and "to attribute to them personal biographies, modes of usual criminal activity, criminal histories, psychological characteristics, and social backgrounds" (Sudnow 1968: 162).

Sudnow's work carries a number of implications. The first is that — to the extent that Crown attorneys and defence lawyers come to agree on what is "normal" in their processing of criminal cases — they draw on similar stocks of knowledge for their case-building strategies. These shared understandings derive from their own specific visions or angles on the world, as well as from discourses that resonate within the wider society. Second, similar to Blumberg's (1967) analysis, the working relationship between the legal actors would appear to be not so much adversarial but more like a cartel. In this respect, Crown attorneys and defence lawyers will come to know and anticipate each other's moves as they go about the business of developing their case-building strategies. A third implication has to do with who lawyers are most likely to encounter in their routine work on cases. Rather than corporate embezzlers or environmental polluters, criminal lawyers are most likely to meet up with individuals whose lives are characterized by poverty, addiction and violence. The features and settings in which these individuals move will therefore come to form the conceptions of "normal crime" under which lawyers operate.

Finally, to the extent that criminal cases will be subject to a process of "normalization," when criminal cases reach the court both the illegal action and the person who commits that action are measured in relation to categories that are "already known and recognized" (Worrall 1990: 21). "Troubles are created," Sudnow (1968: 164) writes, "when offenses whose features are not readily known occur, and whose typicality is not easily constructed." Cases that do not conform to the constructions of "normal crime" will therefore require special explanation. If, for example, "normal violent crime" is premised on constructions of aggression as male activity, then what happens when the defendant is female? In these situations we might expect agency to be most evident as lawyers endeavour to constitute the identities of defendants who breach the known categories.

Sudnow's work centred on how guilty pleas are arrived at before cases go to trial. Lawyers, however, also have considerable agency during the course of a trial. Mike McConville and his colleagues explain the influence of lawyers at trial:

> It lies in their capacity to question witnesses, how hard they push certain points, their use of irony or ridicule and a whole range of rhetorical devices; the quality and thoroughness of their preparation; the astuteness of the way in which they use their knowledge not only of the law, but of jury reactions, those of a particular judge. In these ways, these agents materially affect the outcome of the cases in which they are involved and in ways which do not relate directly to substantive rules or principles of criminal law. (McConville et al. quoted in Lacey and Wells 1998: 76)

As McConville and his colleagues point out, the role expectations of lawyers enable them to choose or exploit particular strategies to influence the trial process. Yet, to be effective, the strategies of lawyers must also resonate with the wider socio-political context in which law rests — and today's socio-political conditions enable lawyers to normalize crime-producing conditions of inner-city communities and obscure the deepening of social inequality brought on by neo-liberal economic and social policies. Law is indeed a contested terrain on which various discourses operate to produce and reproduce certain claims to "truth." As Cain (1994: 20) points out, "In all its particulars [law] is infinitely malleable."

THEORIZING LAW

To unravel two apparently conflicting readings of law — as a fair and impartial arbiter versus a site for the reproduction of gender, race and class inequalities — we have laid out a theoretical synthesis that endeavours to capture the micro- and macro-processes that inform the practice of law. Messerschmidt's (1997) theory of structured action provides us with an analytical framework for situating gender, race and class within the nexus of individual agency and social structure. Specifically, we theorize criminalization as one site of structured action in which lawyers participate in the "making" of gender, race and class inequalities. Still, to locate lawyering as structured action requires going beyond Messerschmidt's work to identify how principles of fundamental justice sit uneasily with the gendering, racializing and class-based practices in which lawyers engage, and to consider how these practices are altered by the wider socio-political context in which they unfold.

Our main interest is to understand how law works to reproduce gender, race and class inequalities in the criminalization of interpersonal violence. To guide this analysis, we need to ask:

- How do gendered, racialized and class-based presuppositions influence the strategies that lawyers use in violent crime cases?
- How is violence normalized? How and where is it made atypical?
- Is the practice of law in violent crime cases structured by neo-liberal and neo-conservative values? What influence do socio-political conditions have on efforts to address violence in society?
- How do lawyers assert their agency under the procedural constraints of due process?

Note

1. Not everyone would agree with this statement. Robert Granfield (1996), for instance, begins his review essay on three books concerning the legal profession (none of which deal with criminal litigation) with the comment that "empirical investigation of lawyers has occupied a prominent site of inquiry within socio-legal studies." Nevertheless, the themes that Granfield indicates to be salient are "the relationship between the legal profession, capitalism and the state; the embeddedness of hierarchy across the distinct hemispheres of the legal profession; and the dark history of inequality within the legal profession that excluded the working class, ethnic minorities, and women from the practice of law." As we noted in Chapter 5 (this volume), the methodological difficulties encountered in researching the practice of law in criminal cases might account for some of this inattention.

References

Abell, Jennie, and E. Sheehy. 1998. *Criminal Law & Procedure: Cases, Context, Critique, 2nd edition*. Toronto: Captus Press.

Ashworth, Andrew. 1995. *Principles of Criminal Law, 2nd edition*. New York: Oxford University Press.

Blumberg, Abraham S. 1967. "The Practice of Law as a Confidence Game." *Law and Society Review*, 1 (June).

Boyd, Neil. 1998. *Canadian Law: An Introduction, 2nd edition*. Toronto: Harcourt Brace.

Brodie, Janine. 1999. "The Politics of Social Policy in the 21st Century." In D. Broad and W. Antony (eds.), *Citizens or Consumers?* Halifax: Fernwood Publishing.

Cain, Maureen. 1994. "Symbol Traders." In M. Cain and C. Harrington (eds.), *Lawyers in a Postmodern World*. New York: New York University Press.

Canadian Forum. 1997. "Index on Global Corporate Power." January/February: 48.

Chunn, Dorothy. 1999. "Feminism, Law and 'the Family': Assessing the Reform Legacy." In E. Comack (ed.), *Locating Law: Race/Class/Gender Connections*. Halifax: Fernwood Publishing.

Chunn, Dorothy, and Dany Lacombe (eds.). 2000. *Law as a Gendering Practice*. Don Mills,

ON: Oxford University Press.
Comack, Elizabeth. 1999a. "Theoretical Excursions." In E. Comack (ed.), *Locating Law: Race/Class/Gender Connections*. Halifax: Fernwood Publishing.
Connell, R.W. 1987. *Gender and Power: Society, the Person, and Sexual Politics*. Stanford, CA: Stanford University Press.
___. 1995. *Maculinities*. Cambridge: Polity.
___. 2000. *The Men and the Boys*. Berkeley: University of California Press.
Cunningham, Alison Hatch, and Curt T. Griffiths. 1997. *Canadian Criminal Justice: A Primer*. Toronto: Harcourt Brace.
Daly, Kathleen. 1994. "Criminal Law and Justice System Practices as Racist, White and Racialized." *Washington and Lee Law Review*, 51, 2: 431–464.
Doe, Jane. 2003. *The Story of Jane Doe: A Book about Rape*. Toronto: Random House.
Foucault, Michel. 1977. *Discipline and Punish*. New York: Vintage Books.
___. 1979. *History of Sexuality: An Introduction*. Vol. 1. London: Penguin.
___. 1984. *The Foucault Reader*, edited by Paul Rabinow. New York: Pantheon Books.
Fudge, Judy, and Harry Glasbeek. 1992. "The Politics of Rights: A Politics with Little Class." *Socio-Legal Studies*, 1, 1: 45–70.
Garland, David. 2001. *Culture of Control*. New York: Oxford University Press.
Granfield, Robert. 1996. "Lawyers and Power: Reproduction and Resistance in the Legal Profession." *Law and Society Review*, 30, 1.
Hamilton, A.C., and C.M. Sinclair. 1991. *Report of the Aboriginal Justice Inquiry of Manitoba*. 2 vols. Winnipeg: Queen's Printer.
Hannah-Moffat, Kelly. 2000. "Prisons That Empower: Neo-Liberal Governance in Canadian Women's Prisons." *British Journal of Criminology*, 40: 510–551.
___. 2002. "Governing through Need: The Hybridization of Risk and Need in Penality." Paper presented to the annual meetings of the British Society of Criminology, Keele University, England.
Henry, Frances, and Carol Taylor. 2002. *Discourses of Domination: Racial Bias in the Canadian English-Language Press*. Toronto: University of Toronto Press.
Howarth, David. 2000. *Discourse*. Buckingham: Open University Press.
Kalunta-Crumpton, Anita. 1998. "The Prosecution and Defence of Black Defendants in Drug Trials." *British Journal of Criminology*, 38, 4: 561–590.
Kellner, Douglas. 1989. *Critical Theory, Marxism and Modernity*. Baltimore: Johns Hopkins University Press.
Kerstetter, Steve. 2002. "Top 50% of Canadians Hold 94.4% of Wealth, Bottom Half 5.6%." *The CCPA Monitor*, 9, 6: 1 and 7.
Kline, Marlee. 1994. "The Colour of Law: Ideological Representations of First Nations in Legal Discourse." *Social and Legal Studies*, 3: 451–476.
Knuttila, Murray, and Wendy Kubik. 2000. *State Theories: Classical, Global and Feminist Perspectives*, 3rd edition. Halifax: Fernwood Publishing.
Lacey, Nicola, and Celia Wells. 1998. *Reconstructing Criminal Law: Critical Perspectives on Crime and the Criminal Process*, 2nd edition. London: Butterworths.
Larner, Wendy. 2000. "Neo-Liberalism: Policy, Ideology, Governmentality." *Studies in Political Economy*, 63 (Autumn): 5–25.
MacLeod, Linda. 1987. *Battered But Not Beaten: Preventing Wife Battering in Canada*. Ottawa:

Canadian Advisory Council on the Status of Women.

Martin, Sheilah L. 1993. "Proving Gender Bias in the Law and the Legal System." In J. Brockman and D. Chunn (eds.), *Investigating Gender Bias: Law, Courts and the Legal Profession*. Toronto: Thompson Educational Publishing.

Messerschmidt, James. 1997. *Crime as Structured Action: Gender, Race, Class, and Crime in the Making*. Thousand Oaks, CA: Sage.

Naffine, Ngaire. 1990. *The Law and the Sexes: Explorations in Feminist Jurisprudence*. Sydney: Allen and Unwin.

Pratt, John. 1999. "Governmentality, Neo-Liberalism and Dangerousness." In R. Smandych (ed.), *Governable Places: Readings on Governmentality and Crime Control*. Brookfield, VT: Aldershot.

Razack, Sherene. 1998. *Looking White People in the Eye: Gender, Race, and Culture in Courtrooms and Classrooms*. Toronto: Oxford University Press.

____. 2000. "Gendered Racial Violence and Spatialized Justice: The Murder of Pamela George." *Canadian Journal of Law and Society*, 15, 2: 91–130.

____. 2002. *Race, Space and the Law: Unmapping a White Settler Society*. Toronto: Between the Lines.

Rose, Nikolas. 2000. "Government and Control." *British Journal of Criminology*, 40: 321–339.

Schechter, Susan. 1982. *Women and Male Violence: The Visions and Struggles of the Battered Woman's Movement*. Boston: South End Press.

Smart, Carol. 1989. *Feminism and the Power of Law*. London: Routledge.

____. 1992. "The Woman of Legal Discourse." *Social and Legal Studies*, 1: 29–44

____. 1995. *Law, Crime and Sexuality*. New York: Routledge.

Snider, Laureen. 1998. "Towards Safer Societies." *British Journal of Criminology*, 38, 1 (Winter): 1–38.

Stanko, E. 1985. *Intimate Intrusions: Women's Experience of Male Violence*. London: Routledge and Keagan Paul.

Statistics Canada. 1997. *Juristat*, 17, 9. Ottawa: Canadian Centre for Justice Statistics.

____. 1999. *Crime Statistics in Canada*, 19. 9. Ottawa: Canadian Centre for Justice Statistics.

____. 2000. *Adult Correctional Services in Canada*, 21. 5. Ottawa: Canadian Centre for Justice Statistics.

Sudnow, David. 1968. "Normal Crimes: Sociological Aspects of the Penal Code." In E. Rubington and M. Weinberg (eds.), *Deviance: The Interactionist Perspective*. London: Macmillan.

Taylor, Ian. 1999. *Crime in Context: A Critical Criminology of Market Societies*. Cambridge: Polity Press.

Verdun-Jones, Simon. 2002. *Criminal Law in Canada: Cases, Questions and the Code, 3rd edition*. Toronto: Harcourt Brace.

Walker, Gillian A. 1990. *Family Violence and the Women's Movement: The Conceptual Politics of Struggle*. Toronto: University of Toronto Press.

Worrall, Anne. 1990. *Offending Women: Female Lawbreakers and the Criminal Justice System*. New York: Routledge and Kegan Paul.

Young, Jock. 1999. *The Exclusive Society*. London: Sage Publications.

Chapter 7

THE FEMINIST ENGAGEMENT WITH CRIMINOLOGY

Elizabeth Comack

> From: *Criminalizing Women: Gender and (In)Justice in Neo-liberal Times*, 2nd edition, Chapter 1 (reprinted with permission of the author).

The feminist engagement with criminology began almost fifty years ago, when pioneers in the discipline such as Marie-Andrée Bertrand (1967) and Frances Heidensohn (1968) first called attention to criminology's amnesia when it came to women. Heidensohn (1968: 171), for instance, described the analysis of women and crime as "lonely uncharted seas" and suggested that what was needed was a "crash programme of research which telescopes decades of comparable studies of males." Since that time, feminist work in this area has developed at a fast pace, to the point where it has become increasingly difficult to keep abreast of the research and publications on women and crime.

There is little doubt about the validity of Heidensohn's claim that women traditionally have been neglected in criminology. Like other academic disciplines, criminology has been a decidedly male-centred enterprise. Despite the use of generic terms — such as "criminals," "defendants" or "delinquents" — criminology has historically been about what men do, so much so that women have been invisible in mainstream criminological theory and research. This is not to say, however, that women have been completely ignored. From criminology's inception, there have been some (rather dubious) efforts to make sense of women and girls who come under the purview of the criminal justice system. Variously referred to as monsters, misfits and manipulators, women — and especially women who engaged in criminal activity — were relegated by early criminologists to the status of "other."

Historically, feminist engagement with criminology emerged out of the various ways in which women as an object of knowledge production were understood (or ignored) by the criminological discipline over time. Feminists have not only challenged these understandings but also promoted alternative claims about women and their involvement in crime. This kind of intellectual history is wide-ranging. Much has happened over the past five decades — both within academia and the wider society — that has played a role in instigating and contouring the kinds of work that feminists have undertaken in this area. Like all knowledge production, therefore, the rendering of an intellectual history in this chapter will at best be partial.

THE INVISIBLE WOMEN OF MAINSTREAM CRIMINOLOGY

To a certain extent, the male-centredness of criminology makes sense when you examine the official statistics on crime. In 2011 women comprised only 21 percent of adults charged with Criminal Code offences in Canada, while men made up the lion's share — 79 percent — of those charged (Brennan 2012: 20). In Australia, females made up 25 percent of individuals charged in three states (Victoria, Queensland and South Australia) in 2009–10 (Australian Institute of Criminology 2011: 69). A similar percentage exists for the United States, where females made up 25 percent of those arrested in 2010 (Snyder 2012: 2). Yet, even though this sex/crime ratio has long been recognized in the discipline, most mainstream criminologists have never really stopped to question it. Instead, they proceeded to develop theories of crime causation that took men — or, more accurately, poor inner-city Black men — as their subject, even when the theorist was intent on framing a general theory of crime ostensibly applicable to the whole population.

This invisibility of women can be easily demonstrated by examining some of the mainstream theories that make up the criminological canon. Robert Merton's (1938) anomie theory, for example, was offered as a general theory explaining crime in relation to the strain that results from the disjunction between culture goals (like monetary success) and institutionalized means (education, jobs). While Merton's theory reflected sensitivity to class inequalities, the same could not be said with regard to an awareness of gender inequalities. If lower-class individuals were more likely to engage in crime because of a lack of access to the institutionalized means for achieving monetary success, it follows, then, that women — who as a group experience a similar lack of access — should also be found to commit their share of crime as a consequence of this strain. But the statistics tell us that this is not the case.

Like anomie theory, Edwin Sutherland's (1949) differential association theory was presented as a general theory of crime. Sutherland focused on the processes by which individuals learn definitions of the legal code as either favourable or unfavourable, and posited the existence of a "cultural heterogeneity" in society with regard to social assessments that were pro- and anti- criminal. Yet, this "general" theory only applied to half the population. Sutherland suggested that while men were individualistic and competitive, women were more altruistic and compliant. So, while cultural heterogeneity could account for men's involvement in crime, it did not seem to apply to women, leading Sutherland to surmise that women were an exception or anomaly in his theory because they displayed a "cultural homogeneity."

Travis Hirschi's (1969) control theory was also characterized by a neglect of the female. While other criminologists focused their attention on explaining deviance, Hirschi turned the tables and set out to explain conformity. Since women appear to be more conformist than men (given, for example, their underrepresentation in crime statistics), it would have made sense for Hirschi to treat women as central to his analysis. Nevertheless, despite having collected data on females, he simply set these data aside and — like his colleagues — concentrated on males.

With the advent of labelling and conflict theories in the 1960s and 1970s, the potential for a more gender-inclusive approach to crime increased. Nonetheless, while Howard Becker's (1963) labelling theory raised the question of "Whose side are we on?" and advocated an approach to deviance that gave voice to those who were subjected to the labelling process, it was never fully realized in the case of women. Similarly, Ian Taylor, Paul Walton, and Jock Young's *The New Criminology* (1973), which offered up a devastating critique of traditional criminological theories, failed to give even a mention to women.

WOMEN AS "OTHER": MONSTERS, MISFITS AND MANIPULATORS

Women were not completely ignored in criminological thought. A small body of work, dating back to the nineteenth century, attempted to account for women's involvement in crime. What could be classified as the early approaches to explaining women's crime began in 1895 with Cesare Lombroso and William Ferrero's *The Female Offender*, followed by W.I. Thomas's *The Unadjusted Girl* in 1923, Sheldon Glueck and Eleanor Glueck's *Five Hundred Delinquent Women* in 1934, and Otto Pollak's *The Criminality of Women* in 1950. While differences exist between these approaches, they all share in common the view of women as "other" than men, and women who engage in criminal activity as even more so. For these theorists, it is women's "inherent nature" that accounts for both the nature and extent of their criminality. In particular, women are cast as sexual beings, and women's sexuality is at the root of their involvement in crime.

Lombroso and Ferrero based their theorizing on an examination of the physical characteristics of a group of 119 "criminal" women, which they compared with a control group of fourteen "non-criminal" women. In applying the concepts of atavism (the idea that some individuals were born criminals) and social Darwinism (the idea that those who get ahead in society are the most fit to survive), they suggested that women as a group possessed limited intelligence. Women were also less sensitive to pain than men, full of revenge and jealousy and naturally passive and conservative. These traits had a physiological basis. For instance, Lombroso and Ferrero (1985 [1895]: 109) assert that women's passivity was demonstrated by the "immobility of the ovule compared to the zoosperm." Atavistically, women offenders were considered to display fewer signs of degeneration than men. The reason, according to Lombroso and Ferrero, was that women (and non-white males) had not advanced as far along the evolutionary continuum as (white) males, and so could not degenerate as far. Given that women were relatively "primitive," the criminals among them would not be highly visible. However, those women who were criminal were cast as excessively vile and cruel in their crimes. They ostensibly combined the qualities of the criminal male with the worst characteristics of the female: cunning, spite and deceitfulness. Lacking "maternal instinct" and "ladylike qualities," criminal women were deemed to be "monsters":

> The born female criminal is, so to speak, doubly exceptional as a woman and as a criminal. For criminals are an exception among civilized people, and women are an exception among criminals … As a double exception, the criminal woman is consequently a *monster*. Her normal sister is kept in the paths of virtue by many causes, such as maternity, piety, weakness, and when these counter influences fail, and a woman commits a crime, we may conclude that her wickedness must have been so enormous before it could triumph over so many obstacles. (Lombroso and Ferrero 1985 [1895]: 151–152; emphasis added)

Like Lombroso and Ferrero, W.I. Thomas (1967 [1923]) framed his theorizing about women on presumed "natural" or biological differences between men and women. Thomas suggested that human behaviour is based on four wishes: desires for adventure, security, response and recognition. These wishes corresponded to features in the nervous system that were expressed as biological instincts of anger, fear, love and the will to gain status and power. However, Thomas asserted that men's and women's instincts differed both in quantity and quality. Since women had more varieties of love in their nervous systems, their desire for response was greater than men's. According to Thomas, it was the need to feel loved that accounted for women's criminality, and especially for their involvement in prostitution.

Sheldon Glueck and Eleanor Glueck (1934) continued in this same tradition with their book *Five Hundred Delinquent Women*. The Gluecks described the women in their study as a "sorry lot. Burdened with feeblemindedness, psychopathic personality and marked emotional instability, a large proportion of them found it difficult to survive by legitimate means." The view of criminal women as "other" is clearly evident: "This swarm of defective, diseased, antisocial misfits … comprises the human material which a reformatory and a parole system are required by society to transform into wholesome, decent, law-abiding citizens! Is it not a miracle that a proportion of them were actually rehabilitated?" (Glueck and Glueck 1934: 299, 303).

Two decades later, Otto Pollak attempted to account for what he described as the masked nature of women's crime. Skeptical of the official data on sex differences in crime, Pollak (1950) suggested that women's crime was vastly undercounted. He put forward the view that female criminality was more likely to be hidden and undetected. According to Pollak, women were more often the instigators than the perpetrators of crime. Like Eve in the Garden of Eden, they manipulated men into committing offences. Women, he claimed, were also inherently deceptive and vengeful. They engaged in prostitution and blackmailed their lovers. As domestics they stole from their employers, and as homemakers they carried out horrendous acts on their families (like poisoning the sick and abusing children). According to Pollak, woman's devious nature was rooted in her physiology. While a man must achieve erection in order to perform the sex act (and hence will not be able to conceal orgasm), a woman can fake orgasm (Pollak 1950: 10). This ability to conceal orgasm supposedly gave women practice at deception.

Pollak also argued that the vengefulness, irritability and depression that women encountered as a result of their generative phases caused female crime. For example, menstruation drove women to acts of revenge by reminding them of their inferior status (and their ultimate failure to become men). The concealed nature of their crimes, the vulnerability of their victims and their chivalrous treatment by men who cannot bear to prosecute or punish them combined to mask women's offences. When these factors are taken into account, according to Pollak, women's crimes are equal in severity and number to those of men.

For these early criminologists, then, the women involved in crime were monsters, misfits, or manipulators. While we can look back on these constructions of women with some amusement, it bears noting that these kinds of knowledge claims about women and the reasons for their involvement in crime have not disappeared. Throughout the 1960s, researchers continued to rely on the assumptions and premises of the earlier approaches. John Cowie, Valerie Cowie and Eliot Slater (1968), for example, in the tradition of Lombroso and Ferrero, looked for "constitutional predisposing factors" to explain female delinquency. In a similarly disparaging manner the same authors (1968: 167) characterized delinquent girls as "oversized, lumpish, uncouth and graceless." Gisella Konopka (1966), in extending Thomas's analysis, equated sexual delinquency in girls with a desperate need for love. Following on the footsteps of Otto Pollak, a more contemporary version of these theories links hormonal changes associated with women's menstrual cycles to their involvement in crime.

Premenstrual syndrome (PMS) has been described as a condition of "irritability, indescribable tension" and a "desire to find relief by foolish and ill-considered actions," something that is thought to occur during the week or two prior to the onset of menstruation (Frank, cited in Osborne 1989: 168). With no biomedical tests for determining its existence, PMS is the only "disease" not dependent on a specific type of symptom for its diagnosis. Nevertheless, PMS has been argued to be a cause of violent behaviour in women who suffer from it. Premenstrual syndrome gained popularity as an explanation for women's criminality in the 1980s, when it was introduced in two British court cases as a mitigating factor in homicide (Luckhaus 1985). Research linking PMS to women's criminality has been criticized for its methodological deficiencies (Morris 1987; Kendall 1991, 1992). As an explanation for women's involvement in crime, however, PMS clearly locates the source of the problem in women's "unruly" bodies. Because of their "nature," women are supposedly prone to madness once a month.

ENTER FEMINISM...

In its initial stages, feminist criminology took the form of a critique of the existing approaches to explaining crime. Writers such as Dorie Klein (1973), Carol Smart (1976, 1977), Eileen Leonard (1982), Allison Morris (1987) and Ngaire Naffine (1987) took issue with the sexism of criminological theories — socially undesirable characteristics were attributed to women and assumed to be intrinsic characteristics of their sex.

With regard to the early approaches to explaining crime (offered by Lombroso and Ferrero, Thomas, the Gluecks and Pollak), Heidensohn (1985: 122) noted how they lent an aura of intellectual respectability to many old folk tales about women and their behaviours. Their constructions of the "female offender" reflected the widely held assumptions about "women's nature," including the good girl/bad girl duality and a double standard that viewed sexual promiscuity as a sign of amorality in women but normality in men. Relying on common-sense, anecdotal evidence and circular reasoning — that is, "things are as they are because they are natural, and they are natural because that is the way things are" (Smart 1976: 36) — the early theorists failed to call into question the structural features of their society and the gendered roles of men and women. For these early criminologists, sex (a biological difference) and gender (a cultural prescription) were equated as one and the same, with the "ladylike" qualities of the middle-class and upper-class white woman used as the measuring rod for what is inherently female. Feminist criminologists castigated these early theories for being not only sexist, but also racist and classist.

Mainstream theories of crime (such an anomie, differential association, social control, labelling and conflict theories) came under a similar scrutiny. The invisibility of women and the failure to adequately explain or account for women's involvement in crime led feminist criminologists to label such theories as not just mainstream but "malestream." As Lorraine Gelsthorpe and Allison Morris asserted:

> Theories are weak if they do not apply to half of the potential criminal population; women, after all, experience the same deprivations, family structures and so on that men do. Theories of crime should be able to take account of *both* men's and women's behaviour and to highlight those factors which operate differently on men and women. Whether or not a particular theory helps us to understand women's crime is of *fundamental*, not marginal importance for criminology. (Gelsthorpe and Morris 1988: 103; emphasis added)

Kathleen Daly and Meda Chesney-Lind (1988) refer to one issue raised by the feminist critique of the mainstream theories as the "generalizability problem": can theories generated to explain males' involvement in crime be modified to apply to women? Several feminist criminologists responded to this problem by attempting to make the mainstream theories of crime "fit" women.

Eileen Leonard (1982), for example, in a reformulation of Merton's strain theory, suggested that females are socialized to aspire to different culture goals than are males, in particular relational goals concerning marriage and having children. Following this line of reasoning, women's low rate of criminal involvement compared to men could be explained by the relatively easy manner in which females can realize their goals. Nevertheless, as Allison Morris (1987) notes, such a formulation relies on an idealized and romanticized version of women's lives. Not only does it display an insensitivity to the strains and frustrations associated with women's familial role (raising children and maintaining a household), it fails to acknowledge the very real and pressing economic concerns that women confront in the process (making ends meet and paying the bills).

Such efforts to revise mainstream theories of crime to include women have been referred to as the "add women and stir" approach (Chesney-Lind 1988). Part of the difficulty with this project is that women are presented merely as afterthoughts, not as integral to the arguments being developed (Gelsthorpe and Morris 1988). Naffine (1997: 32) captures a more significant problem with this effort: "The point of these exercises has been to adapt to the female case, theories of crime which purported to be gender-neutral but were in fact always highly gender specific. Not surprisingly, the results have been varied and generally inconclusive."

A second issue raised by the feminist critique of mainstream criminology is one that Daly and Chesney-Lind (1988: 119) refer to as the "gender-ratio problem." Why are women less likely than men to be involved in crime? What explains the sex difference in rates of arrest and in the variable types of criminal activity between men and women? Attention to the gender-ratio problem sparked a multitude of studies in the 1970s and 1980s on the criminal justice system's processing of men and women (see, for example, Scutt 1979; Kruttschnitt 1980–81, 1982; Steffensmeier and Kramer 1982; Zingraff and Thomson 1984; Daly 1987, 1989). Much of this research was guided by Pollak's assertion of chivalry on the part of criminal justice officials. Are women treated more leniently than men? As in the generalizability problem, the results were mixed. For instance, research that supported this chivalry hypothesis indicated that when it does exist, chivalry benefits some women more than others — in particular, the few white, middle-class or upper-class women who come into conflict with the law. It also appears to apply only to those female suspects who behave according to a stereotypical female script, that is, "crying, pleading for release for the sake of their children, claiming men have led them astray" (Rafter and Natalizia 1981: 92). In this regard, Nicole Rafter and Elena Natalizia argue that chivalrous behaviour should be seen as a means of preserving women's subordinate position in society, not as a benign effort to treat women with some special kindness. Naffine (1997: 36), however, points to a larger problem with this research. By turning on the question of whether women were treated in the same way as men, or differently, the chivalry thesis (and its rebuttal) took men to be the norm: "Men were thus granted the status of universal subjects, the population of people with whom the rest of the world (women) were compared."

At the same time, in the 1970s and 1980s, another thesis was attracting considerable criminological attention. The "women's liberation thesis" posited that women's involvement in crime would come to resemble men's more closely as differences between men and women were diminished by women's greater participation and equality in society. As reflected in the work of Rita Simon (1975) and Freda Adler (1975), the thesis suggested that changes in women's gender roles would be reflected in their rates of criminal involvement. Simon argued that the increased employment opportunities that resulted from the women's movement would also bring an increase in opportunities to commit crime (such as embezzlement from employers). Adler linked the apparent increase of women in crime statistics to the influence of the women's movement and suggested that a "new female criminal" was emerging: women were becoming more violent and aggressive, just like their male counterparts.

The women's liberation thesis "captured the imagination of the media and practitioners" (Morris and Gelsthorpe 1981: 53, cited in Gavigan 1993: 221). While law enforcement officials were quick to affirm its tenets, charging that the women's movement was responsible for triggering a massive crime wave, the media had a heyday with its claims, featuring headlines such as "Lib takes the lid off the gun moll" (*Toronto Star* 15 May 1975, cited in Gavigan 1993: 222). Nevertheless, representations of emancipated women running amok in the streets and workplaces did not hold up under closer scrutiny (see, for example, Chesney-Lind 1978; Weiss 1976; Steffensmeier 1980; Naffine 1987). Smart (1976), for one, noted that the women's liberation thesis was premised on a "statistical illusion" in that the supposed increases in women's crime were being reported as percentages. Given the small base number of women charged with criminal offences, it did not take much of a change to show a large percentage increase. Holly Johnson and Karen Rodgers (1993: 104) provided an example of this problem using Canadian data. Between 1970 and 1991, charges against women for homicide increased by 45 percent, but that figure reflected a real increase of only fifteen women charged. As well, while the women's movement was primarily geared toward privileged white women, poor women and women of colour were most likely to appear in police and prison data. These women were not inclined to think of themselves as "liberated" and — far from considering themselves as feminists — were quite conventional in their ideas and beliefs about women's role in society. For many feminist criminologists, the main difficulty with the women's liberation thesis — similar to the chivalry thesis — was that it posed a question that took males to be the norm: were women becoming more liberated and thus more like men, even in their involvement in crime? In Naffine's (1997: 32) judgment, the thesis that women's liberation causes crime by women has been "perhaps the most time-consuming and fruitless exercise" in criminology.

Another effort to attend to the gender-ratio problem was put forward by John Hagan and his colleagues (Hagan, Simpson and Gillis 1979, 1987; Hagan, Gillis and Simpson 1985), who combined elements of feminist theory with Hirschi's control theory to fashion a power-control theory of sex and delinquency. Focusing attention on the gender roles and differential socialization of males and females, power-control theory was designed to explain the sex differences in delinquency by drawing linkages between the variations in parental control and the delinquent behaviour of boys and girls. More specifically, Hagan and his colleagues suggested that parental control and adolescents' subsequent attitudes toward risk-taking behaviour are influenced by family class relations. They distinguished two ideal types of family: the patriarchal family, in which the husband is employed in an authority position in the workforce and the wife is not employed outside the home; and the egalitarian family, in which both husband and wife are employed in authority positions outside the home. Hagan and his colleagues suggested that in the former a traditional gender division exists, whereby fathers and especially mothers are expected to control their daughters more than their sons. Given the presence of a "cult of domesticity," girls will be socialized to focus their futures on domestic labour and consumption activities, while boys will be prepared for their participation in production activities. In the egalitarian family, parents will redistribute their control efforts such that girls are subject to controls that are more like the ones imposed on boys. "In other words, in egalitarian families, as mothers gain power relative to husbands, daughters gain freedom relative to sons" (Hagan, Simpson and Gillis 1987: 792). As such, the authors predicted that these different family forms will produce differing levels of delinquency in girls: "Patriarchal families will be characterized by large gender differences in common delinquent behaviours, while egalitarian families will be characterized by smaller gender differences in delinquency" (Hagan, Simpson and Gillis 1987: 793).

While Hagan and his colleagues endeavoured to place delinquency by girls in a broader structural context (by attending to the labour force participation of parents), they made an important assumption: if a woman is working for wages, there will be "equality" within the household. Their formulation does not pay enough attention to the nature of women's paid work and to other variables that might be in operation (such as how power and control may be exercised between males and females within the household). As well, Chesney-Lind regards power-control theory as a variation on the women's liberation thesis because it links the emergence of the egalitarian family with increasing delinquency among girls. In effect, "mother's liberation causes daughter's crime" (Chesney-Lind 1989: 20, cited in Boritch 1997: 71).

FEMINIST EMPIRICISM: COUNTERING BAD SCIENCE

In their engagement with criminology during the 1970s and 1980s, feminists tended to work within the confines of positivist social science. In other words, they subscribed to the belief that the methods of the natural sciences (measurement and prediction) could be applied to the study of social life. Their critiques of mainstream work in the discipline amounted to the claim that what was being produced was "bad science." In her elaboration of different feminist epistemologies, philosopher Sandra Harding (1990) named this approach "feminist empiricism." Feminist empiricists in criminology held that bringing women into the mix and attending more rigorously to the methodological norms of scientific inquiry could rectify women's omission from the criminological canon. Feminist empiricism is very much reflected in the attempts to reformulate the mainstream theories of crime to include women. It is also reflected in the empirical research conducted to test the chivalry hypothesis and women's liberation thesis.

Yet, given the difficulties encountered in the efforts to respond to the generalizability and gender-ratio problems — in particular, the tendency to take men as the standard or measuring rod — many feminist criminologists saw the need to "bracket" these issues for the time being in order to understand better the social worlds of women and girls (Daly and Chesney-Lind 1988: 121). Maureen Cain (1990) took this suggestion further. She noted that while feminist criminologists needed to understand women's experiences, existing criminological theory offered no tools for doing this. Therefore, feminists needed to transgress the traditional boundaries of criminology, to start from outside the confines of criminological discourse. In carrying out this project, feminist criminologists drew inspiration from the violence against women movement.

TRANSGRESSING CRIMINOLOGY: THE ISSUE OF MALE VIOLENCE AGAINST WOMEN

At the same time as feminists were fashioning their critiques of criminology, the women's movement in Canada and other Western countries was breaking the silence around the issue of male violence against women. This violence was understood as a manifestation of patriarchy — the systemic and individual power that men exercise over women (Brownmiller 1975; Kelly 1988).

As a political movement united around improving the condition and quality of women's lives, feminism in the 1970s took as one of its key issues the provision of support to women who had been victimized by violence. One of the first books ever published on the subject of domestic violence was Erin Pizzey's (1974) *Scream Quietly or the Neighbours Will Hear You*. Pizzey is also credited for opening, in England in 1971, one of the first refuges for battered women and their children. Rape crisis centres and shelters for abused women also began to appear in Canada in the 1970s. With their establishment came the recognition that male violence against women was a widespread and pervasive phenomenon.

In the early 1980s the Canadian Advisory Council on the Status of Women (CACSW) estimated that one in every five Canadian women will be sexually assaulted at some point in her life, and one in every seventeen will be a victim of forced sexual intercourse. In 1981 CACSW released a report, *Wife Battering in Canada: The Vicious Circle*. Linda MacLeod, author of the report, noted, "Women are kicked, punched, beaten, burned, threatened, knifed and shot, not by strangers who break into their houses or who accost them on dark streets, but by husbands and lovers they've spent many years with — years with good times as well as bad" (MacLeod 1980: 6). She estimated that, every year, one in ten Canadian women who is married or in a relationship with a live-in partner is battered.

More recently, in 1993 Statistics Canada released the findings of the Violence

Against Women (VAW) Survey The first national survey of its kind anywhere in the world, the VAW Survey included responses from 12,300 women (see Johnson 1996). Using definitions of physical and sexual assault consistent with the Canadian Criminal Code, the survey found that one-half (51 percent) of Canadian women had experienced at least one incident of physical or sexual violence since the age of sixteen. The survey also confirmed the results of other research in finding that women face the greatest risk of violence from men they know. "Almost half (45%) of all women experienced violence by men known to them (dates, boyfriends, marital partners, friends, family, neighbours, etc.), while 23% of women experienced violence by a stranger (17% reported violence by both strangers and known men)" (Statistics Canada 1993: 2). The VAW Survey also found that 29 percent of ever-married women had been assaulted by a spouse.

A pivotal moment in the violence against women movement occurred on December 6, 1989, when a man entered a classroom at the École Polytechnique in Montreal, separated the men from the women students, proclaimed, "You're all a bunch of feminists," and proceeded to gun them down. He killed fourteen women and wounded thirteen others that day. The gunman's suicide letter explicitly identified his action as politically motivated: he blamed "feminists" for the major disappointments in his life. Police also found a hit list containing the names of prominent women. The "Montreal Massacre" served in a most profound way to reinforce what women's groups across the country had been arguing for two decades: that violence against women is a serious social problem that takes many forms, including sexual harassment in the workplace, date rape, violent sexual assaults and wife abuse.

The violence against women movement had a number of implications for the work of feminist criminologists. First, the movement allowed feminists to break away from the confines of mainstream criminology, which had been complicit in the social silencing around male violence against women. Official statistics suggested that crimes like rape were relatively infrequent in their occurrence. Victim surveys — which asked respondents whether they had been victimized by crime — indicated that the group most at risk of victimization was young males, not women. Most mainstream criminologists took these data sources at face value. They seldom questioned whether (and why) acts like rape might be underreported, undercharged, or underprosecuted, or the extent to which victim surveys had been constructed in ways that excluded the behaviours that women feared most. When criminologists did turn their attention to crimes like rape, the focus was on the small group of men who had been convicted and incarcerated for the offence, and these men were typically understood as an abnormal and pathological group. Much of traditional criminology also tended to mirror widely held cultural myths and misconceptions about male violence against women (such as women "ask for it" by their dress or their behaviour; see Morris 1987; Busby 2014). In his "classic" study of forcible rape, for example, Menachem Amir (1967, 1971) introduced "victim precipitation." This concept states that some women are "rape prone" (because of their "bad" reputation) and others invite rape by their "negligent and reckless" behaviour (by going to bars or hitchhiking) or their failure to react strongly enough to sexual overtures. Amir's work blamed the victim for the violence she encounters. In these terms, the issue of male violence against women pointed to significant knowledge gaps in mainstream criminology and encouraged a host of studies by feminist criminologists intent on rectifying this omission (see Dobash and Dobash 1979; Klein 1982; Stanko 1985; Gunn and Minch 1988).

Second, the violence against women movement brought to the fore the issue of engaging with the state to address the issue — especially in light of law's role historically in condoning the violence, for example, by granting husbands the right to consortium (which legally obligated wives to provide sexual services to their husbands such that there was no such thing as, let alone a crime of, rape in marriage) and the right to chastise their wives (which meant that husbands had the authority to use force in order to ensure that wives fulfilled their marital obligations) (Dobash and Dobash 1979; Edwards 1985; Backhouse 2002). While some feminist criminologists joined with other women's advocates and academics in lobbying the state to reform laws relating to sexual assault and domestic violence, others engaged in critical treatises on the wisdom of engaging the criminal justice system to promote feminist concerns (see Snider 1985, 1991, 1994; Smart 1989; Lös 1990; Faith and Currie 1993; Comack 1993; Martin and Mosher 1995).

Finally, in pointing to the widespread and pervasive nature of male violence against women, the movement raised the issue of the impact that violence has on women who come into conflict with the law. Several quantitative studies in the 1990s began to expose the extent of abuse experienced by women caught up in the criminal justice system. In interviewing women serving federal sentences, Margaret Shaw and her colleagues (1991) found that 68 percent had been physically abused as children or as adults, and 53 percent were sexually abused at some point in their lives. Among Aboriginal women, the figures were considerably higher: 90 percent said that they had been physically abused, and 61 percent reported sexual abuse (Shaw et al. 1991: vii, 31). Another study of women in a provincial jail (Comack 1993) found that 78 percent of the women admitted over a six-year period reported histories of physical and sexual abuse. To address this issue of the relation between victimization and criminalization, several feminist criminologists adopted the position known as "standpoint feminism" (Harding 1990).

STANDPOINT FEMINISM: WOMEN IN TROUBLE

Influenced by Cain's call to transgress the boundaries of criminology and discover more about the lives of the women who were coming into conflict with the law, standpoint feminists began to dig deeper into the lives of women who came into conflict with the law. As Naffine (1997: 46) notes, while standpoint feminism assumed a number of forms — ranging from the assertion that women are the "experts" of their own lives to the proposal that an adequate social science must be capable of grasping the forms of oppression that women experience — the overall intention was "to place women as knowers at the centre of inquiry in order to produce better understandings of women and the world." Central to much of this research were links between women's victimization and their criminal involvement.

In the United States, Mary Gilfus (1992) conducted life history interviews with twenty incarcerated women to understand their entry into street crime. Most of these women had grown up with violence; thirteen of them reported childhood sexual abuse, and fifteen had experienced "severe childhood abuse" (Gilfus 1992: 70). Among the women Gilfus interviewed were eight African-Americans. While there were no race-based differences in reported abuse, the African-American women were more likely than their white counterparts to grow up in economically marginalized families. Violence, loss and neglect were prevalent themes in their narratives about their childhoods. Violence was also a common feature of their relationships with men: sixteen of the twenty women had lived with violent men. Repeated victimization experiences, drug addiction, involvement in the sex trade, relationships with men involved in street crime, and the demands of mothering: these themes marked the women's transitions from childhood to adulthood.

Beth Richie's (1996) study focused on African-American battered women in prison. Richie (1996: 4) developed a theory of "gender entrapment" to explain the "contradictions and complications of the lives of the African-American battered women who commit crimes." According to her, gender entrapment involves understanding the connections between violence against women in their intimate relationships, culturally constructed gender-identity development and women's participation in illegal activities. In these terms, battered Black women were "trapped" in criminal activity in the same way that they were trapped in abusive relationships.

Working in Canada, Ellen Adelberg and Claudia Currie (1987a, 1993) reported on the lives of seven women convicted of indictable offences and sentenced to federal terms of imprisonment. Regularly occurring themes in these women's lives included "poverty, child and wife battering, sexual assault, and women's conditioning to accept positions of submissiveness and dependency upon men," which led Adelberg and Currie to conclude: "The problems suffered by women offenders are similar to the problems suffered by many women in our society, only perhaps more acutely" (Adelberg and Currie 1987b: 68, 98).

My own work, *Women in Trouble* (Comack 1996), was built around the stories of twenty-four incarcerated women. The women's stories revealed complex connections between a woman's law violations and her history of abuse. Sometimes the connections are direct, as in the case of women sent to prison for resisting their abusers. Janice, for instance, was serving a sentence for manslaughter. She talked about how the offence occurred:

> *I was at a party, and this guy, older guy, came, came on to me. He tried telling me, "Why don't you go to bed with me. I'm getting some money, you know." And I said, "No." And then he started hitting me. And then he raped me. And then [pause] I lost it. Like, I just, I went, I got very angry and I snapped. And I started hitting him. I threw a coffee table on top of his head and then I stabbed him.* (Cited in Comack 1996: 96)

Sometimes a woman's law violations are located in the context of her struggle to cope with the abuse and its effects. Merideth, for example, had a long history of abuse, beginning with her father sexually assaulting her as a young child, and extending to several violent relationships with the men in her life. She was imprisoned for bouncing cheques — she said she was writing the cheques to purchase *"new things to keep her mind off the abuse."*

> *I've never had any kind of conflict with the law. [long pause] When I started dealing with all these different things, then I started having problems. And then I took it out in the form of fraud.* (Cited in Comack 1996: 86)

Sometimes the connections are even more entangled, as in the case of women who end up on the street, where abuse and law violation become enmeshed in their ongoing, everyday struggle to survive. Another incarcerated woman, Brenda, described her life on the street:

> *Street life is a, it's a power game, you know? Street life? You have to show you're tough. You have to beat up this broad or you have to shank this person, or, you know, you're always carrying guns, you always have blow on you, you always have drugs on you, and you're always working the streets with the pimps and the bikers, you know? That, that alone, you know, it has so much fucking abuse, it has more abuse than what you were brought up with!... I find living on the street I went through more abuse than I did at home.* (Cited in Comack 1996: 105–106)

This kind of work subsequently became known as "pathways research" — a term that has been applied to a variety of different studies, all of them sharing the effort to better understand the lives of women and girls and the particular features that helped lead to their criminal activity (see, for example, Chesney-Lind and Rodriguez 1983; Miller 1986; Arnold 1995; Heimer 1995; and Chesney-Lind and Shelden 1998; DeHart 2008). In considering this research, Kathleen Daly (1992, 1998) suggests that there is a feminist composite or "leading scenario" of women's lawbreaking:

> Whether they were pushed out or ran away from abusive homes, or became part of a deviant milieu, young women began to engage in petty hustles or prostitution. Life on the streets leads to drug use and addiction, which in turn leads to more frequent lawbreaking to support their drug habit. Meanwhile, young women drop out of school because of pregnancy, boredom or disinterest in school, or both. Their paid employment record is negligible because they lack interest to work in low-paid or unskilled jobs. Having a child may facilitate entry into adult women's networks and allow a woman to support herself in part by state aid. A woman may continue lawbreaking as a result of relationships with men who may also be involved in crime. Women are on a revolving criminal justice door, moving between incarceration and time on the streets. (Daly 1998: 136)

Daly maintains that although this leading scenario draws attention to the gendered contexts that bring girls to the streets, and to the gendered conditions of their survival once they get there, questions continue to linger. In particular, "What lies in the 'black box' between one's experiences of victimization as a child and criminal activities as an adult? Is there something more than economic survival which propels or maintains women in a criminalized status?" (Daly 1998: 136–137). Drawing on pre-sentence investigation reports dealing with the cases of forty women convicted in a New Haven felony court between 1981 and 1986, Daly maps out five different categories: street women, harmed and harming women, battered women, drug-connected women and a final category that she labels "other women." Arguing for a more multidimensional approach to why women get caught up in crime, she proposes three other routes — in addition to the leading scenario of the street woman — that lead women to felony court: 1) abuse or neglect suffered as a child, an "out of control" or violent nature; 2) being (or having been) in a relationship with a violent man; and 3) being around boyfriends, mates, or family members who use or sell drugs, or wanting more money for a more economically secure and conventional life (148).

Overall, these efforts to draw out the connections between women's victimization experiences and their lawbreaking activities had the benefit of locating law violations by women in a broader social context characterized by inequalities of class, race and gender.

INTERSECTIONALITY

While gender was the starting point for analyzing criminalized women's lives, it soon became apparent to feminist criminologists that they needed to somehow capture the multiple, fluid and complex nature of women's identities and their social relations. Much of the impetus for this recognition came from the critiques offered by women of colour and Indigenous women of the tendency for white feminists to theorize "Woman" as a unitary and homogeneous group. As Marcia Rice (1990: 57) noted, while feminist criminologists had succeeded in challenging stereotypical representations of female offenders, Black women and women from developing countries were "noticeably absent in this discourse," and when attempts were made to incorporate Black women's experiences into feminist writings there were few attempts "to develop perspectives which take into account race, gender and class simultaneously." As Mohawk scholar Patricia Monture-Angus (1995: 177–178) tells us, "It is very difficult for me to separate what happens to me because of my gender and what happens to me because of my race and culture. My world is not experienced in a linear and compartmentalized way. I experience the world simultaneously as Mohawk and as woman ... To artificially separate my gender from my race and culture forces me to deny the way I experience the world."

In response to this critique, feminist criminologists embraced "intersectionality," a concept first highlighted by Kimberlé Crenshaw (1989) to theorize the multiple and complex social relations and the diversity of subject positions involved. Crenshaw argues that the experience of oppression is not singular or fixed but derives from the relationship between interlocking systems of power. With regard to the oppression of Black women, Crenshaw explains, "Because the intersectional experience is greater than the sum of racism and sexism, any analysis that does not take intersectionality into account cannot sufficiently address the particular manner in which Black women are subordinated" (1989: 140). Adopting the notion of intersectionality, therefore, means that rather than viewing class, race and gender as additives (that is, race + class + gender), we need to think about these concepts — and the relations and identities they represent — as simultaneous forces (that is, race x class x gender) (Brewer 1997).

In contrast to the women's liberation thesis, which argued that women's involvement in crime was a consequence of their "emancipation," feminist criminologists adopted an intersectionality approach to connect women's involvement in crime to poverty. In recent decades, poverty has increasingly taken on a "female face"

— especially in terms of the number of single parent families headed by women (Gavigan 1999; Little 2003; Chunn and Gavigan 2014). As more and more women are confronted with the task of making ends meet under dire circumstances, the link between poverty and women's lawbreaking has become more obvious. But so too has the move by the state to criminalize those who must rely on social assistance to get by. Using an intersectionality approach, Kiran Mirchandani and Wendy Chan (2007) document the move in British Columbia and Ontario to criminalize welfare recipients through the pursuit of "fraudulent" claimants. In the process, they argue that this "criminalization of poverty" is also racialized and gendered in that women of colour have borne the brunt of this attack.

A focus on the intersections of gender, race and class also helped to explain some forms of prostitution or sex trade work (Brock 1998; Phoenix 2002). According to Holly Johnson and Karen Rodgers (1993: 101), women's involvement in prostitution is a reflection of their subordinate social and economic position in society: "Prostitution thrives in a society which values women more for their sexuality than for their skilled labour, and which puts women in a class of commodity to be bought and sold. Research has shown one of the major causes of prostitution to be the economic plight of women, particularly young, poorly educated women who have limited *legitimate* employment records." Maya Seshia's (2005) research on street sexual exploitation in Winnipeg revealed that poverty and homelessness, colonialism and the legacy of residential schools and gender discrimination and generational sexual exploitation all combined to lead women and transgenders to become involved in the sex trade.

In learning more about the lives of women and the "miles of problems" (Comack 1996: 134) that brought them into conflict with the law — problems with drugs and alcohol use, histories of violence and abuse, lack of education and job skills and struggles to provide and care for their children — feminist criminologists took pains to distance their work from formulations that located the source of women's problems in individual pathologies or personality disturbances. Instead, the intersecting structural inequalities in society — of gender, race and class — that contour and constrain the lives of women provided the backdrop for understanding women's involvement in crime. As British criminologist Pat Carlen (1988: 14) noted, "Women set about making their lives within conditions that have certainly not been of their own choosing."

BLURRED BOUNDARIES: CHALLENGING THE VICTIM/OFFENDER DUALISM

Efforts to draw connections between law violations and women's histories of abuse led to a blurring of the boundaries between "offender" and "victim" and raised questions about the legal logic of individual culpability and law's strict adherence to the victim/offender dualism in the processing of cases (for not only women, but also poor, racialized men). Blurring the boundaries between offender and victim also had a decided influence on advocacy work conducted on behalf of imprisoned women. For instance, *Creating Choices*, the 1990 report of the Canadian Task Force on Federally Sentenced Women, proposed a new prison regime for women that would incorporate feminist principles and attend to women's needs (see TFFSW 1990; Shaw 1993; Hannah-Moffat and Shaw 2000; Hayman 2006). The near-complete absence of counselling services and other resources designed to assist women in overcoming victimization experiences (see Kendall 1993) figured prominently in the Task Force's recommendations.

As Laureen Snider (2003: 364) notes, feminist criminologists at that time succeeded in reconstituting the female prisoner as the "woman in trouble." Less violent and less dangerous than her male counterpart, she needed help, not punishment. When women did engage in violence, it was understood as a self-defensive reaction typically committed in a domestic context (Browne 1987; Jones 1994; Dobash and Dobash 1992; Johnson and Rodgers 1993). Heidensohn (1994) considers this feminist work to be a positive contribution. In comparing her research in the 1960s and 1990s, she argues that the later female prisoners were better equipped to share their standpoints. In the past, not only did women "not easily find voices, there were only limited discourses in which they could express themselves and few places where such expressions could be made" (31). According to Heidensohn, feminist research provided these women "with a particular language, a way of expressing themselves" (32).

Nevertheless, while the concept of blurred boundaries and the construct of the woman in trouble were important feminist contributions to criminology, they were to later have particular ramifications for the ability of feminist criminologists to counter competing knowledge claims — ones founded on representations of women not as victims but as violent and dangerous.

POSTMODERN FEMINISM: CRIMINALIZED WOMEN

In addition to feminist empiricism and standpoint feminism, a third position has informed the work of feminist criminologists over the last decade or so. "Postmodern feminism" emerged largely as a critique of the other two positions. In particular, postmodern feminists reject the claims to "truth" proposed by scientific objectivity. "Reality," they say, is not self-evident, something that can simply be revealed through the application of the scientific method. While the postmodern critique of empiricism does not negate the possibility of doing empirical research — that is, of engaging with women, interviewing them, documenting their oral histories (Smart 1990: 78–79) — postmodernists are sceptical of attempts to challenge male-centred approaches by counterposing them with a more accurate or correct version of women's lives. Given the differences within female perspectives and identities, they question whether such diversity can be formulated or expressed in a single account or standpoint of women.

Feminist empiricism and standpoint feminism are still very much firmly grounded on a modernist terrain. Postmodern feminism, however, "starts in a different place and proceeds in other directions" (Smart 1995: 45). While modernist approaches are characterized by the search for truth, the certainty of progress and the effort to frame grand narratives about the social world, postmodernism draws attention to the importance of "discourse" — "historically specific systems of meaning which form the identities of subjects and objects" (Howarth 2000: 9). Discourses are contingent and historical constructions. As David Howarth (2000: 9) describes it, their construction involves "the exercise of power and a consequent structuring of the relations between different social agents." Through the method of deconstruction — which involves taking apart discourses to show how they achieve their effects — postmodernists endeavour to reveal how certain discourses (and their corresponding discursive practices or ways of acting) come to dominate in society at particular points in history.

Adopting a postmodern epistemology has led feminist criminologists to interrogate the language used to understand women's involvement in crime. Carol Smart (1989, 1995), Danielle Laberge (1991) and Karlene Faith (1993), among others, point out that crime categories (such as "crimes against the person," "crimes against property" or "public order offences") are legal constructions that represent one way of ordering or making sense of social life. In these terms, the offences for which women are deemed to be criminal are the end result of a lengthy process of detection, apprehension, accusation, judgment and conviction; they constitute the official version of women's actions and behaviours. As well, crime categories are premised on a dualism between the criminal and the law-abiding, which reinforces the view of women involved in crime as "other" and thereby misses their similarities with non-criminal women. In this respect, women who come into conflict with the law are in very many ways no different from the rest of us. They are mothers, daughters, sisters, girlfriends and wives, and they share many of the experiences of women collectively in society. Given that crime is the outcome of interactions between individuals and the criminal justice system, Laberge (1991) proposed that we think not in terms of criminal women but of criminalized women.

Throughout the 1990s, in addition to the increasing influence of a postmodern epistemology, feminist criminologists also began to draw heavily on the ideas of the French poststructuralist theorist Michel Foucault. Much of Foucault's (1977, 1979) writing was concerned with the relation between power and knowledge. Rejecting the notion that power was a "thing" or commodity that can be owned, Foucault concentrated on the mechanisms of power that came with the development of what he called the "disciplinary society," characterized by the growth of new knowledges or discourses (such as criminology, psychiatry and psychology) that led to new modes of surveillance of the population. For Foucault, knowledge is not objective but political; the production of knowledge has to do with power. A reciprocal relation exists between the two: power is productive of knowledge, and knowledge is productive of power. In his later work, Foucault (1991 [1978]) replaced his notion of power/knowledge with the concept of "governmentality" to address the specific "mentality" of governance — the links between forms of power and domination and the ways in which individuals conduct themselves.

Australian criminologist Kerry Carrington (1993) employed Foucault's notion of power/knowledge to explore how certain girls come to be officially defined as delinquents. Critical of feminist work depicting male power over women as direct, monolithic, coercive and repressive, Carrington emphasized the fragmented, fluid and dispersed nature of disciplinary power. In a similar fashion, British criminologist Anne Worrall (1990) adopted a Foucaultian approach to explore the conditions under which legal agents (judicial, welfare and medical) claim to possess knowledge about the "offending woman" and the processes whereby such claims are translated into practices that classify, define and so domesticate her behaviour. Taking a critical view of feminist studies of women's punishment because of their failure (among other things) to take gender seriously as an explanatory variable, Adrian Howe (1994) argued for the need to consider the gendered characteristics — for both women and men — of disciplinary procedures in advancing the project of a postmodern penal politics.

Feminist postmodernism has had a decided impact on the trajectory of feminist criminology. Not interested so much in the task of explaining *why* women come into conflict with the law, those who work in this area raise important *how* questions, such as how women and girls are constituted or defined by professional discourses, and how particular techniques of governance (in a number of different sites) work to contain, control, or exclude those who are marginalized in society. The postmodern attention to discourse has also opened the way to a questioning of the kinds of language used by criminologists and criminal justice officials. Under the tutelage of postmodernists, terms such as offenders, inmates, clients and correctional institutions — although still widely disseminated — are no longer uncontested.

Nevertheless, at the same time as feminist criminologists were being influenced by the epistemological and theoretical shifts occurring within academia during the 1990s, shifts in the socio-political context and a series of notable events relating to the issue of women and crime were having a significant impact on the work of feminist criminologists. More specifically, as the century drew to a close, neo-liberal and neo-conservative political rationalities had begun to take hold and were readily put to work in the construction of women and girls as violent, dangerous — and downright "nasty."

THE SHIFTING SOCIO-POLITICAL CONTEXT: NEO-LIBERALISM AND NEO-CONSERVATISM

In the initial phases, the efforts of the women's movement to address women's inequality in society were fed by a sense of optimism. Given the expressed commitment by the Canadian state to the ideals of social citizenship (what came to be called the Keynesian welfare state) — that all citizens had a right to a basic standard of living, with the state accepting responsibility for the provision of social welfare for its citizenry — the prospects of realizing substantive change on issues like violence against women and women's treatment by the criminal justice system seemed bright. This change was made all the more possible with the entrenchment of the *Canadian Charter of Rights and Freedoms* in 1982, and especially the invoking of section 15 (the equality section) in 1985, which prohibited discrimination on the basis of sex. In a climate that appeared to be favourable to hearing women's issues, feminists and women's advocates organized and lobbied throughout the 1980s to bring about a number of changes (including reforms to rape legislation and the provision of resources for women in abusive relationships) and launched human rights and Charter challenges to address the unfair treatment of imprisoned women. With regard to women in prison, many observers took the government's acceptance of the "Creating Choices" report in 1990 as a sign that a sea change was underway, that substantive reform was possible.

Yet, the 1980s also saw a distinct shift in the socio-political terrain. Under the sway of globalization, the state's expressed commitment to social welfare was being eroded. In its place, neo-liberalism became the new wisdom of governing. "Neo-liberalism" is a political rationality founded on the values of individualism, freedom of choice, market dominance and minimal state involvement in the economy. Under neo-liberalism, the ideals of social citizenship are replaced by the market-based, self-reliance and privatizing ideals of the new order. As political scientist Janine Brodie (1995: 57) explains it:

> The rights and securities guaranteed to all citizens of the Keynesian welfare state are no longer rights, universal, or secure. The new ideal of

the common good rests on market-oriented values such as self-reliance, efficiency, and competition. The new good citizen is one that recognizes the limits and liabilities of state provision and embraces her or his obligation to work longer and harder in order to become more self-reliant.

In this era of restructuring, government talk of the need for deficit reduction translated into cutbacks to social programs (McQuaig 1993), and gains that the women's movement had realized in the previous decade were now under serious attack (Brodie 1995; Bashevkin 1998; Rebick 2005).

In the criminal justice arena, these economic and political developments ushered in an extraordinary expansion in the scope and scale of penalization. Rising crime rates and a growing economic recession in the 1980s gave way to a crime-control strategy that rejected rehabilitation and correction as the goals of the criminal justice system and replaced them with a concern for "risk management": the policing and minimization of risk that offenders pose to the wider community. Under this neo-liberal responsibilization model of crime control (Hannah-Moffat 2002), criminals are to be made responsible for the choices they make: "Rather than clients in need of support, they are seen as risks that must be managed" (Garland 2001: 175).

But neo-liberalism was not the only ideology to inform criminal justice practices. Subjecting the economy to market forces and cutting back on social welfare meant that increasing numbers of people were left to fend for themselves, without the benefit of a social safety net. As well, the precariousness of middle-income families engendered a social anxiety that easily translated into fear of crime — especially of those groups and individuals left less fortunate by virtue of the economic transformations. Calls for more law and order became louder. In tandem with neo-liberalism, therefore, a "neo-conservative rationality," premised on a concern for tradition, order, hierarchy and authority, fostered crime-control policies aimed at "getting tough" on crime. Zero-tolerance for domestic violence, "super max" prisons, parole-release restrictions, community notification laws and boot camps for young offenders increasingly became the order of the day (Comack and Balfour 2004: 42–43).

This broader neo-liberal and neo-conservative socio-political context proved to be significant in framing how a number of events that occurred in the 1990s came to be understood. These events — and the ways in which they were being framed in the public discourse — were instrumental in assertions about women and girls that had much in common with constructions that had prevailed in earlier times.

VIOLENT WOMEN AND NASTY GIRLS

One decisive event was the Karla Homolka case. In July 1993 Karla Homolka was sentenced to twelve years in prison for her part in the deaths of two teenaged girls, Kristen French and Leslie Mahaffy. Homolka's sentence was part of a plea bargain reached with the Crown in exchange for her testimony against her husband, Paul Bernardo. The Crown had entered into this plea bargain prior to the discovery of six homemade videotapes that documented the sexual abuse and torture of the pair's victims — including Homolka's younger sister, Tammy. Bernardo was subsequently convicted of first-degree murder, kidnapping, aggravated sexual assault, forcible confinement and offering an indignity to a dead body. He was sentenced to life imprisonment in September 1995 (McGillivray 1998: 257).

During Bernardo's trial the real challenge came in trying to explain the role of Homolka, the prosecution's key witness. As Helen Boritch (1997: 2) notes, "Among the various professionals who commented on the case, there was a general agreement that, as far as serial murderers go, there was little that was unusual or mysterious about Bernardo. We have grown used to hearing about male serial murderers." Homolka, however, was the central enigma of the drama that unfolded, transforming the trial into an international, high-profile media event.

The legal documents and media accounts of the case offered two primary readings of Homolka. The first reading constructed her as a battered wife, one of Bernardo's many victims (he had also been exposed as "the Scarborough rapist"). A girlish 17-year-old when she first met the 23-year-old Bernardo, Homolka had entered into a relationship that progressed to a fairytale wedding (complete with horse-drawn carriage) and ended with a severe battering (complete with darkened and bruised raccoon eyes). According to this first reading, Homolka was under the control of her husband, having no agency of her own. Like other women who find themselves in abusive relationships, she was cast as a victim and diagnosed as suffering from the Battered Woman Syndrome, a psychological condition of "learned helplessness" that ostensibly prevents abused women from leaving the relationship (see Walker 1979, 1987). The representation of Homolka as a battered wife and "compliant victim" of her sexually sadistic husband (Hazelwood, Warren and Dietz 1993) was meant to bolster her credibility as a prosecution witness and validate her plea bargain.

This first reading was met with strong resistance in the media and public discourse, leading to the second reading. Journalist Patricia Pearson (1995), for one, vigorously countered the picture of "Homolka as victim" and instead demonized her as a "competitive narcissist" willing to offer up innocent victims (including her own sister) to appease the sexual desires of her sociopathic husband. In a similar fashion, other writers offered diagnoses such as "malignant narcissism": "This personality cannot tolerate humiliation. It is capable of destroying others in the service of meeting its ego needs" (Skrapec, cited in Wood 2001: 60).

Despite their divergent viewpoints, both of these readings relied on the discourse of the "psy-professions" (psychology, psychotherapy and psychiatry) to make sense of Homolka. Feminist criminologists offered competing knowledge claims, for instance, by pointing out that women are seldom charged with the offence of murder and, when they do kill, women are most likely to kill their male partners — or that while Homolka's middle-class background and lifestyle set her apart from the vast majority of women charged with criminal offences, her efforts to conform to the standard feminine script (dyed blond hair, fairytale wedding) put her in company with a host of other women. But these claims were seldom heard. Instead, the cry that "Women are violent, too!" grew louder, even to the point of arguing that women's violence was quantitatively and qualitatively equal to that of men's.

In a widely publicized book, *When She Was Bad: Violent Women and the Myth of Innocence*, Pearson (1997; see also Dutton 1994; Laframboise 1996) argued not only that "women are violent, too," but also that their violence can be just as nasty as men's. Following on the footsteps of the 1950s criminologist Otto Pollak, Pearson (1997: 20–21) suggested that women's violence was more masked and underhanded than men's: women kill their babies, arrange for their husbands' murders, beat up on their lovers and commit serial murders in hospitals and boarding houses. Nevertheless, argued Pearson (1997: 61), when their crimes are discovered, women are more likely to receive lenient treatment from a chivalrous criminal justice system. In a fashion that hearkened back to other early criminologists, Pearson (1997: 210) also stated: "Female prisoners are not peace activists or nuns who were kidnapped off the street and stuck in jail. They are miscreants, intemperate, willful and rough."

Pearson drew support for her position from studies that utilize the Conflict Tactics Scale (CTS) to measure abuse in intimate relationships. Most criminologists who use this scale have found equivalent rates of violence by women and men (Straus 1979; Straus and Gelles 1986; Straus, Gelles and Steinmetz 1980; Steinmetz 1981; Brinkerhoff and Lupri 1988; Kennedy and Dutton 1989). Despite the scale's popularity, however, it has been subject to extensive critiques (DeKeseredy and MacLean 1998; DeKeseredy and Hinch 1991; Dobash et al. 1992; Johnson 1996). Nevertheless, Pearson argued that such critiques amounted to unwarranted attacks by feminists and their supporters, who were invested in a gender dichotomy of men as evil/women as good. In this regard, unlike earlier conservative-minded criminologists, Pearson asserted that women were no different than men. While feminists were intent on gendering violence by drawing its connections to patriarchy, Pearson (1997: 232) was adamant that violence be de-gendered: violence was simply a "human, rather than gendered, phenomena."

Framing the issue in neo-liberal terms, violence was a conscious choice, a means of solving problems or releasing frustration by a "responsible actor imposing her will upon the world" (23).

While the Homolka case generated extensive media attention on the issue of women's violence, the spectre of the "nasty girl" was added into the mix with the killing of fourteen-year-old Reena Virk by a group of mostly teenaged girls in November 1997. Early on, in 1998, six girls were convicted of assault for their part in Virk's death. In 1999 Warren Glowaski was convicted of second-degree murder. In April 2005, after three trials, Kelly Ellard was convicted of second-degree murder.

According to the court documents, Virk was confronted by a group of girls under a bridge in Victoria, B.C., and accused of stealing one of their boyfriends. When she tried to leave she was punched and kicked, and one of the girls stubbed out a cigarette on her forehead. Glowaski testified at his trial that he and Ellard had followed Virk across the bridge and confronted her a second time. The pair kicked and stomped her until she was unconscious and then dragged her body to the water's edge, where she subsequently drowned. While Ellard admitted to being an active participant in the initial attack on Virk, she denied any involvement in the second attack. Asked in court whether the thought of seeing Reena left crumpled in the mud made her upset, Ellard replied, "*Obviously — I am not a monster*" (Armstrong 2004: A7).

Ellard's statement notwithstanding, events like the beating and murder of Reena Virk generated a series of media exposés on the "problem" of girl violence. As one CBC documentary, *Nasty Girls* (airing on March 5, 1997), put it: "In the late 1990s almost everything your mother taught you about polite society has disappeared from popular culture, and nowhere is this more apparent than in what is happening to our teenage girls. Welcome to the age of the nasty girls!" (cited in Barron 2000: 81). Girls, so we were told, were not "sugar and spice" after all — but "often violent and ruthless monsters" (McGovern 1998: 24).

These depictions of women and girls as violent, dangerous and downright nasty were also playing out in relation to what was then the only federal prison for women in Canada — the P4W.

LOMBROSO REVISITED? FRAMING THE P4W INCIDENT

In February 1995 CBC-TV's *Fifth Estate* aired a video of an all-male Institutional Emergency Response Team (IERT) entering the solitary confinement unit at the Prison for Women (P4W) in Kingston, Ontario, and proceeding to extract women from their cells, one by one. The video showed the women's clothing being removed (in some cases the men forcibly cut it off) and the women being shackled and taken to the shower room, where they were subjected to body cavity searches.

The program reported that after the segregation cells were completely emptied (including beds and mattresses), the women were placed back in the cells with only security blankets for clothing.

Some of the women were kept in segregation for up to eight months afterward. They were given no hygiene products, no daily exercise, no writing materials and no contact with family. Their blankets were not cleaned for at least a month. As part of the program, reporter Ann Rauhala also interviewed several of the women, who recounted their feelings of violation and degradation and drew similarities to their past experiences of being raped and sexually victimized.

When the report of Justice Louise Arbour (1996) into the events of April 1994 was released two years later, the CBC's news program *The National* re-televised segments of the program, including the IERT video. Emails posted on *The National's* discussion site in response to the segments revealed pieces of the public discourse that prevailed around women prisoners:

> While I can see how some of the pictures shown could be disturbing to some viewers, I am more disturbed at your handling of the story ... These women were not ordinary citizens ... They are in a correctional facility because they are CONVICTED FELONS, not Sunday School Teachers.
>
> Myself, I would see nothing wrong with a guard beating these inmates every once in a while! After all they lost their rights when they committed their crimes in the first place.
>
> Don't give me the bleeding heart crap. This is what has screwed up society. These women created their own situation — let them deal with the fallout.
>
> The women involved in this incident were the creators of their own misfortune — both in the short term and the long term ... In recent years, it seems that the courts and government have become too lenient with the likes of these women, and men for that matter. The special interest groups and the "politically correct" that are constantly fighting for the rights of prisoners only undermine the rights of law-abiding citizens.

Clearly, the neo-conservative calls to "get tough on crime" — especially in relation to women — were finding supporters in the public at large. Much like the early criminological constructions of women involved in crime, these CBC viewers rejected the depiction of the women as victims and instead saw them as "other," roundly deserving of the brutal treatment they received.

Such law and order populism was no doubt instrumental in bolstering a neo-liberal realignment by the Correctional Service of Canada when it came to implementing the "Creating Choices" recommendations (TFFSW 1990). "Creating

Choices" had been silent around the issue of women's violence. According to Shaw (2000: 62), "Overall, the report portrayed women as victims of violence and abuse, more likely to injure themselves than others as a result of those experiences." The April 1994 event, however, was held out as evidence to the contrary. The CSC maintained that calling the male IERT to the women's prison had become necessary to contain "unruly women" after a fight had broken out between six of the prisoners and their guards. In 1996, in a move that marked an about-turn from the Task Force's women-centred approach and the attendant focus on addressing women's needs, CSC adopted a new scheme for managing women prisoners, the Offender Intake Assessment Scheme, designed for male prisoners. Now, women's needs — including the need to recover from experiences of victimization — were to be redefined (in neo-liberal terms) as risk factors in predicting a woman's likelihood of reoffending. That same year the CSC announced that all women classified as maximum security would not be allowed at the new regional centres (including the Aboriginal healing lodge) that had been constructed on the basis of the "Creating Choices" recommendations. Instead, the women were to be housed in maximum-security facilities located inside men's prisons. As well, CSC implemented a new mental health policy for women thought to be experiencing psychological and behavioural problems. In contrast to its initial endorsement of the "Creating Choices" report, therefore, the government was clearly moving in a different direction.

FEMINIST CRIMINOLOGISTS RESPOND TO THE BACKLASH

The apparent ease with which the neo-conservative and neo-liberal readings of events like the Homolka case, the Virk killing and the P4W incident took hold in the public discourse was emblematic of the dramatic shifts in the socio-political context that were occurring in the 1990s. For the most part, these readings can be interpreted as part of a powerful backlash against feminist knowledge claims, especially the efforts by feminist criminologists to blur the boundaries between offender and victim. In what Snider (2004: 240) refers to as the "smaller meaner gaze of neo-liberalism," the sightlines were closely fixed. "'Victims' were those who suffered from crime, not those who committed it — and the higher their social class, the more traditional their sexual habits and lifestyles, and the lighter their color, the more legitimate their victim status became." Feminist criminologists would respond to this backlash on a number of fronts.

Committed to the view of criminalized women as victims in need of help rather than punishment, feminist criminologists were initially caught off guard by the Homolka case. To be sure, the woman in trouble envisioned by feminist criminologists was not a privileged young woman who engaged in sadistic sex crimes. But repeating the refrain "Homolka is an anomaly, Homolka is an anomaly" did little to prevent her from becoming the public icon for women caught up in the criminal justice system — women who are likely to be racialized, poor and convicted of property crimes rather than of violent sex offences.

With Pearson's assertions about women and violence continuing to hold sway in the popular press, feminist criminologists countered by offering up pointed critiques of her work. In her review of *When She Was Bad*, for instance, Meda Chesney-Lind (1999) took Pearson to task for her routine conflation of aggression and violence. "This is either very sloppy or very smart, since anyone familiar with the literature on aggression ... knows that when one includes verbal and indirect forms of aggression (like gossip), the gender difference largely disappears" (114). Similar to those who claim merit in the women's liberation thesis, Pearson also based her argument on percentage increases in women's arrests for violence, "without any mention of the relatively small and stable proportion of violent crime accounted for by women or the fact that small base numbers make huge increases easy to achieve" (115). Pearson's misuse of research findings, which Chesney-Lind saw as rampant throughout the book, included citing a study that found women's prison infractions to be higher than men's to support her claim that women in prison are "miscreants, intemperate, willful and rough" (Pearson 1997: 210). What Pearson neglected to mention was that these women were being charged with extremely trivial forms of misconduct, such as having "excessive artwork" on the walls of their cells (that is, too many family photos on display). Chesney-Lind concluded her review by acknowledging that feminist criminologists must theorize women's aggression and women's violence, but that "we need a nuanced, sophisticated, and data driven treatment — and most importantly — one that begins by placing women's aggression and violence in its social context of patriarchy" (118).

Jennifer Kilty and Sylvie Frigon (2006) offer such a nuanced account in their analysis of the Homolka case. Reinterpreting the two readings of Homolka — battered wife versus competitive narcissist — as depictions of her as either "in danger" or "dangerous," they argue that these constructions are interrelated rather than mutually exclusive. While emphasizing that the abuse Homolka endured at the hands of Bernardo does not excuse her criminality, they maintain that it did constrain her choices. As such, she was *both* a "woman in danger" *and* a "dangerous woman." Kilty and Frigon (2006: 58) argue, therefore, "Rather than constructing these two concepts as dialectically opposed one must understand them as being interdependent, or more accurately, as along a continuum."

Other feminist criminologists intent on understanding the interconnections between women's experiences of violence and their own use of violence have adopted this shift away from dualistic (victim/offender) thinking and toward the use of a continuum metaphor. Introduced by Karlene Faith (1993) in her book *Unruly Women*, the "victimization-criminalization continuum" is used to signify the myriad of ways in which women's experiences of victimization — including not only violence but also social and economic marginalization — constrain or narrow their social supports and available options and leave them susceptible to criminalization. The continuum, therefore, draws on insights from intersectionality theory to showcase how systemic factors (relating to patriarchy, poverty and colonialism) contribute to women's vulnerability to victimization, thereby restricting their agency or capacity to make choices. Unlike the more linear imagery of the pathways approach, Elspeth Kaiser-Derrick (2012: 63) suggests that the continuum can be envisioned as a web, "with many incursions and redirections from external forces (broad, structural issues like poverty and discrimination, as well as events within women's lives often stemming from those structural issues such as relationship dissolution or the removal of children by the state)."

Gillian Balfour (2008) adopts the victimization-criminalization continuum to explore the relationship between the inordinate amounts of violence experienced by Aboriginal women and the increase in their coercive punishment by the criminal justice system. Balfour argues that — despite the introduction in 1996 of sentencing reforms to encourage alternatives to incarceration (specifically, the provision for conditional sentences to be served in the community and the addition of section 718.2[e] to the Criminal Code, which encourages judges to consider alternatives to imprisonment for Aboriginal peoples) — women's narratives of violence and social isolation have been excluded in the practice of Canadian sentencing law, leading to spiralling rates of imprisonment for Aboriginal women. Kaiser-Derrick (2012) also utilizes the victimization-criminalization continuum to inform her analysis of cases involving Aboriginal women in light of the *Gladue* (1999) and *Ipeelee* (2012) decisions of the Supreme Court of Canada relating to how judges are to undertake a sentencing analysis when Aboriginal defendants come before the court. Focusing on cases for which conditional sentences are or were previously an available sanction, Kaiser-Derrick found that judges translate discourses about victimization and criminalization into a judicial approach that frames sentences for Aboriginal women as "healing oriented"; in essence, Aboriginal women's victimization experiences are interpreted by the courts as precipitating a need for treatment in prison (see also Williams 2009).

Feminist criminologists also responded to the backlash against feminist knowledge claims by undertaking research to evaluate the claim that women are "men's equals" in violence. To explore qualitative differences in men's and women's violence, for example, Vanessa Chopyk, Linda Wood, and I drew a random sample of 1,002 cases from police incident reports involving men and women charged with violent crime in the city of Winnipeg over a five-year period at the beginning of the 1990s. While studies that utilize the Conflict Tactics Scale have concluded that a sexual symmetry exists in intimate violence (men are as likely as women to be victims of abuse, and women are as likely as men to be perpetrators of both minor and serious acts of violence), we found a different picture in the police incident reports (Comack, Chopyk and Wood 2000, 2002). First, the violence tactics used by men and women differed in their seriousness. Men were more likely to use their physical strength or force against their female partners, while women were more likely to resort to throwing objects (such as TV remote controls) during the course of a violent event. Second, female partners of men accused of violence used violence themselves in only 23 percent of the cases, while male partners of women accused of violence used violence in 65 percent of the cases. This suggests that the violence that occurs between intimate partners is not "mutual combat." Third, almost one half (48 percent) of the women accused — as opposed to only 7 percent of the men accused — in partner events were injured during the course of the event. Finally, in incidents involving partners, it was the accused woman who called the police in 35 percent of the cases involving a female accused (compared with only 7 percent in those involving a male accused). Interpreting calls to the police as "help-seeking behaviour" on the part of someone in trouble suggests that in more than one-third of the cases involving a woman accused, she was the one who perceived the need for help. Nevertheless, the woman ended up being charged with a criminal offence.

These findings are supported by data from the General Social Survey conducted by Statistics Canada, which show the scope and severity of spousal violence to be more severe for women than for men. Female victims of spousal violence were more than twice as likely to be injured as were male victims (42 percent versus 18 percent). Women were almost seven times more likely to fear for their lives (33 percent versus 5 percent), and almost three times as likely to be the targets of more than ten violent episodes (20 percent versus 7 percent) (Mahony 2011: 10). In countering the arguments made by writers like Pearson, then, the feminist agenda placed the issue of women's violence and aggression in a prominent position (see also Renzetti 1998, 1999; Marleau 1999; Chan 2001; Mann 2003; Morrisey 2003; Comack and Balfour 2004).

In the wake of the moral panic generated by media reports of a violent crime wave by girls (Schissel 1997, 2001), feminists also set out to counter the claim that girls were becoming "gun-toting robbers" (Pate 1999: 42; see also Artz 1998; Barron 2000; Chesney-Lind and Paramore 2001; Bell 2002; Burman, Batchelor and Brown 2003; Alder and Worrall 2003). In her analysis of official statistics on youth crime, Heather Schramm (1998) warned that any arguments about a dramatic increase in the rate of girls' offending should be interpreted with caution. The theme here was similar to the critique of the women's liberation thesis: because only a small number of girls are charged with violent offences, changes in the rates of girls' violent crime inflate drastically when expressed as a percentage. Marge Reitsma-Street (1999) pointed out that the majority of the increase in the rate of girls' violent crime could be accounted for by an increase in the charges of common or level-one assault (for example, for pushing, slapping and threatening). Anthony Doob and Jane Sprott (1998: 185) concluded that the rising rate of girls (and youths in general) being charged with violent crimes did not indicate an increase in the nastiness of girls; rather, the change "relates more to the response of adult criminal justice officials to crime than it does to the behaviour of young offenders."

As well, feminist criminologists drew on postmodern insights to counter the legal and media representations of the Virk killing. Specifically, by framing the murder in terms of the "empty concept" of "girl violence" (Kadi, cited in Batacharya 2004: 77), dominant approaches rarely addressed the issues of "racism, sexism, pressures of assimilation, and the social construction of Reena Virk as an outcast," and "when they were addressed, it was always in the language of appearance" (Jiwani 2002: 441). In Yasmin Jiwani's view, the erasure of race/racism in judicial decision-making and in the media coverage of the case was "symbolic of the denial of racism as a systemic phenomenon in Canada" (42; see also Batacharya 2004; Jiwani 2006).

Feminist criminologists also engaged in extensive critiques of the use of male-centred risk scales for managing women prisoners (Stanko 1997; Hannah-Moffat and Shaw 2001; Chan and Rigakos 2002). They provided critical commentaries on the apparent transformation of the original feminist vision of *Creating Choices* to fit neo-liberal and neo-conservative correctional agendas (Hannah-Moffat and Shaw 2000), and they reflected on the lessons to be learned from efforts to refashion prison regimes (Hannah-Moffat 2002; Hayman 2006). Countering the tendency of the legal establishment and media to revert to individualized and pathologized renderings of women prisoners — an approach placing the spotlight on the personal failings of these women while keeping the political and economic factors that drive prison expansion in the shadows — some feminist criminologists began the work of connecting "the individual and personal with macroeconomic and geopolitical analyses" in the context of the global expansion of women's imprisonment (Sudbury 2005: xvi).

THE POWER AND THE CHALLENGE

From invisibility and the "othering" of women to the emergence of feminist criminology in the 1970s and the particular pathways that feminist criminologists have followed as they put women at the centre of their knowledge production: over the past fifty years we have slowly moved from Heidensohn's "lonely uncharted seas" to reach the point where it has become increasingly difficult to keep abreast of the research and writing on women and crime. In their own ways, the different epistemological positions of feminist empiricism, standpoint feminism and postmodern feminism have enabled an incredible growth in knowledge about women and crime. Because of this work, we now know so much more about the lives of criminalized women — who they are, the social contexts in which they move and the processes by which they are regulated and controlled — far more than we would have thought possible some five short decades ago. Still, feminist criminology has not developed in a vacuum. In the past fifty years feminist criminologists have drawn energy and insights from work in other arenas — particularly the violence against women movement — as well as responding to events and developments occurring within the ever-changing socio-political climate.

As Snider (2003) notes, it is one thing for feminists to produce particular discourses about women and crime, and it is quite another to have those discourses heard:

> Knowledge claims and expertise always work to the advantage of some and the detriment of others, strengthening some parties and interests while weakening others. Those with power to set institutional agendas, with superior economic, political, social and moral capital, are therefore able to reinforce and promote certain sets of knowledges while ignoring, ridiculing or attacking others. (Snider 2003: 355)

But the feminist engagement with criminology is by no means complete. As the chapters in this book demonstrate, it is very much a vibrant, continuing process. And in these neo-liberal times, meeting the challenge of containing — and especially countering — dominant understandings about women and crime is all the more necessary.

References

Adelberg, E., and C. Currie (eds.). 1987a. *Too Few to Count: Canadian Women in Conflict with the Law*. Vancouver: Press Gang.

____. 1987b. "In Their Own Words: Seven Women's Stories." In E. Adelberg and C. Currie (eds.), *Too Few to Count: Canadian Women in Conflict with the Law*. Vancouver: Press Gang.

____. 1993. *In Conflict with the Law: Women and the Canadian Justice System*. Vancouver: Press Gang.

Adler, F. 1975. *Sisters in Crime*. New York: McGraw-Hill.

Alder, C., and A. Worrall. 2003. *Girls' Violence: Myths and Realities*. Albany: State University of New York Press.

Amir, M. 1967. "Victim Precipitated Forcible Rape." *Journal of Criminal Law and Criminology*, 58, 4.

____. 1971. *The Patterns of Forcible Rape*. Chicago: University of Chicago Press.

Arbour, The Honourable Justice Louise (Commissioner). 1996. *Commission of Inquiry into Certain Events at the Prison for Women in Kingston*. Ottawa: Solicitor General.

Armstrong, J. 2004. "'I am Not a Monster,' Ellard Says." *Globe and Mail*, July 8: A7.

Arnold, R. 1995. "The Processes of Victimization and Criminalization of Black Women." In B.R. Price and N. Sokoloff (eds.), *The Criminal Justice System and Women*. New York: McGraw Hill.

Artz, S. 1998. *Sex, Power, and the Violent School Girl*. Toronto: Trifolium Books.

Australian Institute of Criminology. 2011. "Australian Crime: Facts & Figures: 2011." <aic.gov.au/publications/current%20series/facts/1-20/2011/4_offender.html>.

Backhouse, Constance B. 2002. "A Measure of Women's Credibility: The Doctrine of Corroboration in Sexual Assault Trials in Early Twentieth Century Canada and Australia." *York Occasional Working Papers in Law and Society*. Paper #1.

Balfour, G. 2008. "Falling Between the Cracks of Retributive and Restorative Justice: The Victimization and Punishment of Aboriginal Women." *Feminist Criminology*, 3.

Barron, C. 2000. *Giving Youth a Voice: A Basis for Rethinking Adolescent Violence*. Halifax: Fernwood Publishing.

Bashevkin, S. 1998. *Women on the Defensive: Living Through Conservative Times*. Toronto: University of Toronto Press.

Batacharya, S. 2004. "Racism, 'Girl Violence,' and the Murder of Reena Virk." In C. Alder and A. Worrall (eds.), *Girls' Violence: Myths and Realities*. Albany: State University of New York Press.

Becker, H. 1963. *The Outsiders*. New York: Free Press.

Bell, S. 2002. "Girls in Trouble." In B. Schissel and C. Brooks (eds.), *Marginality and Condemnation: An Introduction to Critical Criminology*. Halifax: Fernwood Publishing.

Bertrand, M-A. 1967. "The Myth of Sexual Equality Before the Law." Fifth Research Conference on Delinquency and Criminality. Montreal, Centre de Psychologies et de Pédagogie.

Boritch, H. 1997. *Fallen Women: Female Crime and Criminal Justice in Canada*. Toronto: Nelson.

Brennan, S. 2012. "Police-Reported Crime Statistics in Canada, 2011." *Juristat*, July 24.

Brewer, Rose M. 1997. "Theorizing Race, Class, and Gender: The New Scholarship of Black Feminist Intellectuals and Black Women's Labour." In R. Hennessy and C. Ingraham (eds.), *Materialist Feminism*. London: Routledge.

Brinkerhoff, M., and E. Lupri. 1988. "Interspousal Violence." *Canadian Journal of Sociology*, 13, 4.

Brock, D. 1998. *Making Work, Making Trouble: Prostitution as a Social Problem*. Toronto: University of Toronto Press.

Brodie, J. 1995. *Politics on the Margins: Restructuring and the Canadian Women's Movement*. Halifax: Fernwood Publishing.

Browne, A. 1987. *When Battered Women Kill*. New York: Free Press.

Brownmiller, S. 1975. *Against Our Will: Men, Women and Rape*. New York: Simon and Schuster.

Burman, M., S. Batchelor, and J. Brown. 2003. "Girls and the Meaning of Violence." In E. Stanko (ed.), *The Meanings of Violence*. London: Routledge.

Busby, K. 2014. "'Sex Was in the Air': Pernicious Myths and Other Problems with Sexual Violence Prosecutions." In E. Comack (ed.), *Locating Law: Race/Class/Gender/Sexuality Connections*, 3rd edition. Halifax and Winnipeg: Fernwood Publishing.

Cain, M. 1990. "Towards Transgression: New Directions in Feminist Criminology."

International Journal of the Sociology of Law, 18.
Carlen, P. 1988. *Women, Crime and Poverty*. Milton Keynes: Open University Press.
Carrington, K. 1993. *Offending Girls: Sex, Youth and Justice*. Sydney: Allen and Unwin.
Chan, W. 2001. *Women, Murder and Justice*. London: Palgrave.
Chan, W., and G. Rigakos. 2002. "Risk, Crime and Gender." *British Journal of Criminology*, 42.
Chesney-Lind, M. 1978. "Chivalry Re-Examined." In L. Bowker (ed.), *Women, Crime and the Criminal Justice System*. Lexington, MA: Lexington Books.
____. 1988. "Doing Feminist Criminology." *The Criminologist*, 13, 1.
____. 1999. "Review of 'When She Was Bad: Violent Women and the Myth of Innocence.'" *Women and Criminal Justice*.
Chesney-Lind, M., and V. Paramore. 2001. "Are Girls Getting More Violent? Exploring Juvenile Robbery Trends." *Journal of Contemporary Criminal Justice*, 17, 2.
Chesney-Lind, M., and N. Rodriguez. 1983. "Women Under Lock and Key." *The Prison Journal*, 63.
Chesney-Lind, M., and R. Sheldon. 1998. *Girls, Delinquency and Juvenile Justice*. California: Wadsworth.
Chunn, D., and S.A.M. Gavigan. 2014. "From Welfare Fraud to Welfare as Fraud: The Criminalization of Poverty." In G. Balfour and E. Comack (eds.), *Criminalizing Women: Gender and (In)Justice in Neoliberal Times*, 2nd edition. Halifax: Fernwood Publishing.
Comack, E. 1993. *Women Offenders' Experiences with Physical and Sexual Abuse: A Preliminary Report*. Winnipeg: Criminology Research Centre, University of Manitoba.
____. 1996. *Women in Trouble*. Halifax: Fernwood Publishing.
Comack, E., and G. Balfour. 2004. *The Power to Criminalize: Violence, Inequality and the Law*. Halifax: Fernwood.
Comack, E., V. Chopyk, and L. Wood. 2000. *Mean Streets? The Social Locations, Gender Dynamics, and Patterns of Violent Crime in Winnipeg*. Winnipeg: Canadian Centre for Policy Alternatives-Manitoba (December).
____. 2002. "Aren't Women Violent Too? The Gendered Nature of Violence." In B. Schissel and C. Brooks (eds.), *Marginality and Condemnation: An Introduction to Critical Criminology*. Halifax: Fernwood Publishing.
Cowie, J., V. Cowie, and E. Slater. 1968. *Delinquency in Girls*. London: Heinemann.
Crenshaw, K. 1989. "Demarginalizing the Intersection of Race and Sex: A Black Feminist Critique of Antidiscrimination Doctrine, Feminist Theory and Antiracist Politics." *The University of Chicago Legal Forum*, 140.
Daly, K. 1987. "Discrimination in the Criminal Courts: Family, Gender, and the Problem of Equal Treatment." *Social Forces*, 66, 1.
____. 1989. "Rethinking Judicial Paternalism: Gender, Work-Family Relations, and Sentencing." *Gender and Society*, 3, 1.
____. 1992. "Women's Pathways to Felony Court: Feminist Theories of Lawbreaking and Problems of Representation." *Southern California Review of Law and Women's Studies*, 2.
____. 1998. "Women's Pathways to Felony Court: Feminist Theories of Lawbreaking and Problems of Representation." In K. Daly and L. Maher (eds.), *Criminology at the Crossroads: Feminist Readings in Crime and Justice*. New York: Oxford.
Daly, K., and M. Chesney-Lind. 1988. "Feminism and Criminology." *Justice Quarterly*, 5, 4.
DeHart, D. 2006. "Pathways to Prison: Impact of Victimization in the Lives of Incarcerated

Women." *Violence Against Women,* 14, 12.

DeKeseredy, W., and R. Hinch. 1991. *Woman Abuse: Sociological Perspectives.* Toronto: Thompson.

DeKeseredy, W., and B. MacLean. 1998. "'But Women Do It Too': The Contexts and Nature of Female-to-Male Violence in Canadian Heterosexual Dating Relationships." In K. Bonnycastle and G. Rigakos (eds.), *Unsettling Truths: Battered Women, Policy, Politics, and Contemporary Research in Canada.* Vancouver: Collective Press.

Dobash, R., R.E. Dobash, M. Wilson, and M. Daly. 1992. "The Myth of Sexual Symmetry in Marital Violence." *Social Problems,* 39, 1 (February).

Dobash, R.E., and R. Dobash. 1979. *Violence Against Wives: A Case Against the Patriarchy.* New York: Free Press.

Doob, A., and J. Sprott. 1998. "Is the 'Quality' of Youth Violence Becoming More Serious?" *Canadian Journal of Criminology,* 40, 2.

Dutton, D. 1994. "Patriarchy and Wife Assault: The Ecological Fallacy." *Violence and Victims,* 9.

Edwards, S. 1985. "Gender Justice? Defending Defendants and Mitigating Sentence." In S. Edwards (ed.), *Gender, Sex and the Law.* London: Croom Helm.

Faith, K. 1993. *Unruly Women: The Politics of Confinement and Resistance.* Vancouver: Press Gang Publishers.

Faith, K., and D. Currie. 1993. *Seeking Shelter: A State of Battered Women.* Vancouver: Collective Press.

Foucault, M. 1977. *Discipline and Punish: The Birth of the Prison.* New York: Vintage.

____. 1979. *History of Sexuality: An Introduction* (Vol. 1). London: Penguin.

____. 1991 [1978]. "Governmentality." In G. Burchell, C. Gordon, and P. Miller (eds.), *The Foucault Effect: Studies in Governmentality.* Chicago: University of Chicago Press.

Garland, D. 2001. *The Culture of Control: Crime and Social Order in Contemporary Society.* Chicago: University of Chicago Press.

Gavigan, S.A.M. 1993. "Women's Crime: New Perspectives and Old Theories." In E. Adelberg and C. Currie (eds.), *In Conflict with the Law: Women and the Canadian Justice System.* Vancouver: Press Gang Publishers.

____. 1999. "Poverty Law, Theory and Practice: The Place of Class and Gender in Access to Justice." In E. Comack (ed.), *Locating Law: Race/Class/Gender Connections.* Halifax: Fernwood Publishing.

Gelsthorpe, L., and A. Morris. 1988. "Feminism and Criminology in Britain." *British Journal of Criminology,* 23.

Gilfus, M. 1992. "From Victims to Survivors to Offenders: Women's Routes of Entry and Immersion into Street Crime." *Women and Criminal Justice,* 4, 1.

Glueck, S., and E. Glueck. 1934. *Five Hundred Delinquent Women.* New York: Alfred A. Knopf.

Gunn, R., and C. Minch. 1988. *Sexual Assault: The Dilemma of Disclosure, The Question of Conviction.* Winnipeg: University of Manitoba Press.

Hagan, J., A.R. Gillis, and J. Simpson. 1985. "The Class Structure of Gender and Delinquency: Toward a Power-Control Theory of Common Delinquent Behavior." *American Journal of Sociology,* 90.

Hagan, J., J. Simpson, and A.R. Gillis. 1979. "The Sexual Stratification of Social Control: A

Gender-Based Perspective on Crime and Delinquency." *British Journal of Sociology,* 30.

———. 1987. "Class in the Household: A Power-Control Theory of Gender and Delinquency." *American Journal of Sociology,* 92, 4 (January).

Hannah-Moffat, K. 2002. "Creating Choices: Reflecting on Choices." In P. Carlen (ed.), *Women and Punishment: The Struggle for Justice.* Cullompton: Willan Publishing.

Hannah-Moffat, K., and M. Shaw (eds.). 2000. *An Ideal Prison? Critical Essays on Women's Imprisonment in Canada.* Halifax: Fernwood Publishing.

———. 2001. *Taking Risks: Incorporating Gender and Culture into the Assessment and Classification of Federally Sentenced Women in Canada.* Ottawa: Status of Women Canada.

Harding, S. 1990. "Feminism, Science, and the Anti-Enlightenment Critiques." In L. Nicholson (ed.), *Feminism/Postmodernism.* London: Routledge.

Hayman, S. 2006. *Imprisoning Our Sisters: The New Federal Women's Prisons in Canada.* Montreal and Kingston: McGill-Queen's University Press.

Hazelwood, R., J. Warren, and P. Dietz. 1993. "Compliant Victims of the Sexual Sadist." *Australian Family Physician,* 22, 4 (April).

Heidensohn, F. 1968. "The Deviance of Women: A Critique and an Enquiry." *British Journal of Sociology,* 19, 2.

Heimer, K. 1995. "Gender, Race and Pathways to Delinquency." In J. Hagan and R. Peterson (eds.), *Crime and Inequality.* Stanford: Stanford University Press.

Hirschi, T. 1969. *Causes of Delinquency.* Berkeley: University of California Press.

Howarth, D. 2000. *Discourse.* Buckingham: Open University Press.

Howe, A. 1994. *Punish and Critique: Towards a Feminist Analysis of Penality.* London: Routledge.

Jiwani, Y. 2002. "Erasing Race: The Story of Reena Virk." In K. McKenna and J. Larkin (eds.), *Violence Against Women: New Canadian Perspectives.* Toronto: Inanna Publications.

Johnson, H. 1996. *Dangerous Domains.* Toronto: Nelson.

Johnson, H., and K. Rodgers. 1993. "A Statistical Overview of Women and Crime in Canada." In E. Adelberg and C. Currie (eds.), *In Conflict with the Law: Women and the Canadian Justice System.* Vancouver: Press Gang Publishers.

Jones, A. 1994. *Next Time She'll Be Dead: Battering and How to Stop It.* Boston: Beacon Press.

Kaiser-Derrick, E. 2012. "Listening to What the Criminal Justice System Hears and the Stories it Tells: Judicial Sentencing Discourses about the Victimization and Criminalization of Aboriginal Women." Master of Laws thesis, University of British Columbia.

Kelly, L. 1988. *Surviving Sexual Violence.* Minneapolis: University of Minnesota Press.

Kendall, K. 1991. "The Politics of Premenstrual Syndrome: Implications for Feminist Justice." *Journal of Human Justice,* 2, 2 (Spring).

———. 1992. "Dangerous Bodies." In D. Farrington and S. Walklate (eds.), *Offenders and Victims: Theory and Policy.* London: British Society of Criminology.

Kennedy, L., and D. Dutton. 1989. "The Incidence of Wife Assault in Alberta." *Canadian Journal of Behavioural Science,* 21.

Kilty, J.M., and S. Frigon. 2006. "From a Woman in Danger to a Dangerous Woman, the Case of Karla Homolka: Chronicling the Shifts." *Women and Criminal Justice,* 17, 4.

Klein, D. 1973. "The Etiology of Female Crime: A Review of the Literature." *Issues in Criminology,* 8, 3.

____. 1982. "The Dark Side of Marriage: Battered Wives and the Domination of Women." In N. Rafter and E. Stanko (eds.), *Judge, Lawyer, Victim, Thief: Women, Gender Roles and Criminal Justice*. Boston: Northeastern University Press.
Konopka, G. 1966. *The Adolescent Girl in Conflict*. Englewood Cliffs: Prentice Hall.
Kruttschnitt, C. 1980–81. "Social Status and Sentences of Female Offenders." *Law and Society Review*, 15, 2.
____. 1982. "Women, Crime and Dependency." *Criminology*, 19, 4.
Laberge, D. 1991. "Women's Criminality, Criminal Women, Criminalized Women? Questions in and for a Feminist Perspective." *Journal of Human Justice*, 2, 2.
Laframboise, D. 1996. *The Princess at the Window*. Toronto: Penguin.
Leonard, E.D. 1982. *Women, Crime and Society: A Critique of Theoretical Criminology*. New York: Longman.
Little, M. 2003. "The Leaner, Meaner Welfare Machine: The Ontario Conservative Government's Ideological and Material Attack on Single Mothers." In D. Brock (ed.), *Making Normal: Social Regulation in Canada*. Scarborough: Nelson Thompson Learning.
Lombroso, C., and E. Ferrero. 1985 [1885]. *The Female Offender*. New York: Appleton.
Lös, M. 1990. "Feminism and Rape Law Reform." In L. Gelsthorpe and A. Morris (eds.), *Feminist Perspectives in Criminology*. Milton Keynes: Open University Press.
Luckhaus, L. 1985. "A Plea for PMT in the Criminal Law." In S. Edwards (ed.), *Gender, Sex and the Law*. Kent: Croom Helm.
MacLeod, L. 1980. *Wife Battering in Canada: The Vicious Circle*. Ottawa: CACSW.
Mahony, T. 2011. *Women in Canada: A Gender-Based Statistical Report Women and the Criminal Justice System*. Ottawa: Statistics Canada. <statcan.gc.ca/pub/89-503-x/2010001/article/11416-eng.pdf>.
Mann, R. 2003. "Violence Against Women or Family Violence? The 'Problem' of Female Perpetration in Domestic Violence." In L. Samuelson and W. Antony (eds.), *Power and Resistance: Critical Thinking About Canadian Social Issues*, 3rd edition. Halifax: Fernwood Publishing.
Marleau, J. 1999. "Demanding to Be Heard: Women's Use of Violence." *Humanity and Society*, 23, 4.
Martin, D., and J. Mosher. 1995. "Unkept Promises: Experiences of Immigrant Women with the Neo-Criminalization of Wife Abuse." *Canadian Journal of Women and the Law*, 8.
McGillivray, A. 1998. "'A Moral Vacuity in Her Which Is Difficult if Not Impossible to Explain': Law, Psychiatry and the Remaking of Karla Homolka." *International Journal of the Legal Profession*, 5, 2/3.
McGovern, C. 1998. "Sugar and Spice and Cold as Ice: Teenage Girls Are Closing the Gender Gap in Violent Crime with Astonishing Speed." *Alberta Report*, 25.
McQuaig, L. 1993. *The Wealthy Banker's Wife: The Assault on Equality in Canada*. Toronto: Penguin.
Merton, R. 1938. "Social Structure and Anomie." *American Sociological Review*, 3 (October).
Miller, E. 1986. *Street Woman*. Philadelphia: Temple University Press.
Mirchandani, K., and W. Chan. 2007. *Criminalizing Race, Criminalizing Poverty*. Halifax: Fernwood Publishing.
Monture-Angus, P. 1995. *Thunder in My Soul: A Mohawk Woman Speaks*. Halifax: Fernwood Publishing.

Morris, A. 1987. *Women, Crime and Criminal Justice.* London: Blackwell.
Morrisey, B. 2003. *When Women Kill: Questions of Agency and Subjectivity.* London: Routledge.
Naffine, N. 1987. *Female Crime: The Construction of Women in Criminology.* Sydney: Allen and Unwin.
Osborne, J. 1989. "Perspectives on Premenstrual Syndrome: Women, Law and Medicine." *Canadian Journal of Family Law,* 8.
Pate, K. 1999. "Young Women and Violent Offences." *Canadian Women's Studies,* 19.
Pearson, P. 1995. "Behind Every Successful Psychopath." *Saturday Night,* 110 (October).
____. 1997. *When She Was Bad: Women's Violence and the Myth of Innocence.* Toronto: Random House.
Phoenix, J. 2002. "Youth Prostitution Police Reform: New Discourse, Same Old Story." In P. Carlen (ed.), *Women and Punishment: The Struggle for Social Justice.* Portland: Willan Publishing.
Pizzey, E. 1974. *Scream Quietly or the Neighbours Will Hear You.* London: Penguin.
Pollak, O. 1950. *The Criminality of Women.* Philadelphia: University of Philadelphia Press.
R v. *Gladue,* [1999] 1 SCR 699.
R v. *Ipeelee,* [2012] SCC 13.
Raftner, N.H., and E.M. Natalazia. 1981. "Marxist Feminism: Implications for Criminal Justice." *Crime and Delinquency,* 27.
Rebick, J. 2005. *Ten Thousand Roses: The Making of a Feminist Revolution.* Toronto: Penguin.
Reitsma-Street, M. 1999. "Justice for Canadian Girls: A 1990s Update." *Canadian Journal of Criminology,* 41, 3.
Renzetti, C. 1998. "Violence and Abuse in Lesbian Relationships: Theoretical and Empirical Issues." In R. Bergen (ed.), *Issues in Intimate Violence.* Thousand Oaks: Sage.
____. 1999. "The Challenge to Feminism Posed by Women's Use of Violence in Intimate Relationships." In S. Lamb (ed.), *New Versions of Victims: Feminists Struggle with the Concept.* New York: New York University Press.
Rice, M. 1989. "Challenging Orthodoxies in Feminist Theory: A Black Feminist Critique." In L. Gelsthorpe and A. Morris (eds.), *Feminist Perspectives in Criminology.* Milton Keynes: Open University Press.
Richie, B. 1996. *Compelled to Crime: The Gender Entrapment of Battered Black Women.* New York: Routledge.
Schissel, B. 1997. *Blaming Children: Youth Crime, Moral Panics and the Politics of Hate.* Halifax: Fernwood Publishing.
____. 2001. "Youth Crime, Moral Panics and the News: The Conspiracy Against the Marginalized in Canada." In R. Smandych (ed.), *Youth Crime: History, Legislation, and Reform.* Toronto: Harcourt Canada.
Schramm, H. 1998. *Young Women Who Use Violence — Myths and Facts.* Calgary: Elizabeth Fry Society of Alberta.
Scutt, J. 1979. "The Myth of the 'Chivalry Factor' in Female Crime." *Australian Journal of Social Issues,* 14, 1.
Seshia, Maya. 2005. *The Unheard Speak Out.* Winnipeg: Canadian Centre for Policy Alternatives–Manitoba.
Shaw, M. 2000. "Women, Violence, and Disorder in Prisons." In K. Hannah-Moffat and

M. Shaw (eds.), *An Ideal Prison? Critical Essays on Women's Imprisonment in Canada*. Halifax: Fernwood Publishing.
Shaw, M., K. Rodgers, J. Blanchette, T. Hattem, L.S. Thomas, and L.Tamarack. 1991. *Survey of Federally Sentenced Women: Report of the Task Force on Federally Sentenced Women*. User Report 1991-4. Ottawa: Corrections Branch, Ministry of Solicitor General of Canada.
Simon, R. 1975. *Women and Crime*. Lexington: D.C. Heath.
Smart, C. 1976. *Women, Crime and Criminology: A Feminist Critique*. London: Routledge and Kegan Paul.
____. 1977. "Criminological Theory: Its Ideology and Implications Concerning Women." *British Journal of Sociology*, 28, 1.
____. 1989. *Feminism and the Power of the Law: Essays in Feminism*. London: Routledge.
____. 1990. "Feminist Approaches to Criminology or Postmodern Woman Meets Atavistic Man." In L. Gelsthorpe and A. Morris (eds.), *Feminist Perspectives in Criminology*. Milton Keynes: Open University Press.
____. 1995. *Law, Crime and Sexuality*. London: Sage.
Snider, L. 1985. "Legal Reform and Social Control: The Dangers of Abolishing Rape." *International Journal of the Sociology of Law*, 13, 4.
____. 1991. "The Potential of the Criminal Justice System to Promote Feminist Concerns." In E. Comack and S. Brickey (eds.), *The Social Bias of Law: Critical Readings in the Sociology of Law*, 2nd edition. Halifax: Fernwood Publishing.
____. 1994. "Feminism, Punishment and the Potential of Empowerment." *Canadian Journal of Law and Society*, 9, 1.
____. 2003. "Constituting the Punishable Woman: Atavistic Man Incarcerates Postmodern Woman." *British Journal of Criminology*, 43, 2.
____. 2004. "Female Punishment: From Patriarchy to Backlash?" In C. Sumner (ed.), *The Blackwell Companion to Criminology*. Oxford: Blackwell.
Snyder, H. 2012. *Arrest in the United States, 1990-2010*. Washington: Bureau of Justice Statistics. <bjs.gov/content/pub/pdf/aus9010.pdf>.
Stanko, E. 1985. *Intimate Intrusions: Women's Experience of Male Violence*. London: Routledge and Kegan Paul.
____. 1997. "Conceptualizing Women's Risk: Assessment as a Technology of the Soul." *Theoretical Criminology*, 1, 4.
Statistics Canada. 1993. "The Violence Against Women Survey." *The Daily*, 18 November.
Steffensmeier, D., and J. Kramer. 1982. "Sex-Based Differences in the Sentencing of Adult Criminal Defendants." *Sociology and Social Research*, 663.
Steinmetz, S. 1981. "A Cross-Cultural Comparison of Marital Abuse." *Journal of Sociology and Social Welfare*, 8.
Straus, M. 1979. "Measuring Intrafamily Conflict and Violence: The Conflict Tactics (CT) Scales." *Journal of Marriage and the Family*, 41, 1.
Straus, M., and R. Gelles. 1986. "Societal Changes and Change in Family Violence from 1975 to 1985 as Revealed by Two National Surveys." *Journal of Marriage and the Family*, 48.
Straus, M., R. Gelles, and S. Steinmetz. 1980. *Behind Closed Doors: Violence in the American Family*. New York: Doubleday.
Subury, J. 2005. "Introduction: Feminist Critiques, Transnational Landscapes, Abolitionist Visions." In J. Sudbury (ed.), *Global Lockdown: Race, Gender, and the Prison-Industrial*

Complex. New York: Routledge.
Sutherland, E. 1949. *Principles of Criminology, 4th edition*. Philadelphia: J.B. Lippincott.
Taylor, I., P. Walton, and J. Young. 1973. *The New Criminology*. London: Routledge and Kegan Paul.
TFFSW (Task Force on Federally Sentenced Women). 1990. *Creating Choices: The Task Force Report of the Task Force on Federally Sentenced Women*. Ottawa: Correctional Service of Canada.
Thomas, W.I. 1967 [1923]. *The Unadjusted Girl*. New York: Harper and Row.
Walker, L. 1979. *The Battered Woman*. New York: Harper and Row.
____. 1987. *Terrifying Love: Why Battered Women Kill and How Society Responds*. New York: Harper Collins.
Weiss, J. 1976. "Liberation and Crime: The Invention of the New Female Criminal." *Crime and Social Justice*, 6.
Williams, T. 2009. "Intersectionality Analysis in the Sentencing of Aboriginal Women in Canada: What Difference Does It Make?" In E. Grabham, D. Cooper, J. Krishnadas, and D. Herman (eds.), *Intersectionality and Beyond: Law, Power and the Politics of Location*. New York: Routledge-Cavendish.
Wood, T. 2001. "The Case Against Karla." *Elm Street Magazine*, April.
Worrall, A. 1990. *Offending Women: Female Lawbreakers and the Criminal Justice System*. New York: Rutledge and Keagan Paul.
Zingraff, M., and R. Thomson. 1984. "Differential Sentencing of Women and Men in the U.S.A." International Journal of the Sociology of Law, 12.

Chapter 8

CRIME IN THE CONTEXT OF ORGANIZATIONS AND INSTITUTIONS

William O'Grady

From: *Crime in Canadian Context: Debates and Controversies*, 3rd edition, Chapter 7 (reprinted with permission).

INTRODUCTION

To this point in our study, it might appear that most crime is generated by lower-class males who are not properly bonded to society, have bleak futures or else face insupportable emotional strains. In fact, a number of criminological theories were developed to explain male street crime. But how do criminologists explain why a group of people who appear to have a great stake in conformity commit more crime than impoverished inner-city youth? These individuals may have homes in more than one country, may hold positions as CEOs of large business enterprises, or may even have their own airlines, television shows, clothing lines, or very profitable home-decorating chains of stores. It is unlikely that these individuals suffer from atavism, low intelligence, or are economically disenfranchised, but they break the law nonetheless. This chapter will focus on white-collar or corporate, transnational, environmental and political crime before turning to an analysis of wrong-doing committed by police, religious leaders and others in positions of trust. The point of addressing crimes that are committed by these groups is to demonstrate that sometimes citizens presumed responsible are involved in crime. The protective immunity of their affiliations — from which such people benefited in the past — has begun to weaken only relatively recently.

WHITE-COLLAR AND CORPORATE CRIME

American sociologist Edwin Sutherland was the first scholar to draw attention to crime committed by groups in society who occupied positions of power and influence. In 1939, Sutherland introduced the term "white-collar crime" to the American Sociological Association. In drawing attention to "crime that is committed by a person of respectability and high social status in the course of his [*sic*] occupation" (Sutherland 1939: 2) Sutherland was calling for criminologists to bring an end to the practice of exclusively focusing on crimes committed by the socially disadvantaged. Not only was Sutherland interested in broadening the definition of crime, but he also wanted to draw attention to the issue because of the respectable social status and power held by white-collar criminals. Because these types of rule-breakers lived in prosperous neighbourhoods and were held in high regard, society in general — even criminology — was turning a blind eye to massive harm being inflicted on society by such individuals. What sorts of harm was Sutherland speaking of? Consider the following list that he compiled on the brink of the Second World War:

- Misrepresentation in financial statements of corporations
- Manipulation in the stock exchange
- Commercial bribery
- Bribery of public officials directly or indirectly to secure favourable contracts and legislation
- Misrepresentation in advertising and salesmanship
- Embezzlement and misappropriation of funds
- Misapplication of funds in receiverships and bankruptcies

Anyone who follows the news could be under the impression that this inventory was put together only recently. For example, the first item, the "misrepresentation in financial statements of a corporation," might refer to the scandal surrounding WorldCom, the large American telecommunications company that filed for bankruptcy protection in 2002 because it was $41 billion in debt and had to lay off 17,000 employees. Due to a series of "accounting irregularities" (that is, by inflating profits in financial statements, the company appeared to be more profitable than it really was), the CEO of the company, Bernie Ebbers, was found guilty of fraud and for filing false documents to regulators and was sent to prison for twenty-five years (CBC News Online 2006).

Another well-publicized example of corporate fraud involves the once huge American energy company Enron. Like WorldCom, Enron Corporation was billions of dollars in debt, and to conceal the corporation's financial problems from shareholders, earnings reports were exaggerated. After Enron filed for bankruptcy, numerous Enron employees lost billions of dollars in retirement savings invested in Enron stock. Even though they knew that Enron stocks were losing value, Enron executives prohibited employees from withdrawing their retirement funds while at the same time, allegedly, selling their overvalued stocks at enormous profit. Kenneth Lay, one of the central figures of the scandal, was reported to have made $146 million from options trades (Beirne and Messerschmitt 2006: 210). Both Lay and Jeffrey Skilling, another Enron executive implicated in the corporate swindle, were convicted of multiple counts of conspiracy and fraud.

While Sutherland focused almost exclusively on one type of white-collar crime — corporate crime — not all white-collar criminals are corporate criminals. The two types of activity are similar in the sense that both white-collar crime and corporate crime take place within the context of the business world. However, the difference between the two comes down, in part, to who benefits from the illegal activity. If the beneficiary is an individual, then we are talking about white-collar crime. On the other hand, if the offences benefit the corporation, than it is a corporate crime. Of course, the two types of offences are not always mutually exclusive because individual and corporate gain can occur simultaneously. For example, if a corporate executive "cooks the books" so that his or her company appears to investors to be worth more than it actually is, then, if the accounting fabrications are not detected, in the short term at least, the individual may make money from profit-sharing or from stock price increases. This appears to be what occurred in both the Enron and the WorldCom cases.

Crime committed within the context of the workplace is not confined to white-collar and corporate wrong-doing. Individuals who commit crime within the course of their employment roles are engaging in occupational crime. The two most common forms of occupational crime are theft and fraud. Examples of occupational thefts are the removal by employees of job-related items from the workplace. While there are obviously various degrees of employee theft — from stealing a pencil to stealing furnishings or a car — most employees do steal, and if such costs are multiplied by the numbers who do, the expense is high. In the United States, "inventory shrinkage," which not only includes employee theft but also shoplifting, is estimated to add 15 percent to the cost that consumers pay for goods and services (Coleman 2002).

An example of occupational fraud is insider trading. This illegal activity occurs when an employee uses information not available to the public to gain personal advantage over others in the buying and selling of stock. Such information is obtained simply because a person's job happens to have given her or him access to privileged information. But stocks are supposed to be open to the public with equal opportunities for those with money to access their purchase through the stock market.

The profile of insider trading in the United States and elsewhere was raised in the public view by the misfortune of Martha Stewart, the well-known American entrepreneur and "lifestyle diva" who has amassed considerable wealth from her work in the mass media and in the retail sector. In 2001 Stewart sold shares she had invested in ImClone — a pharmaceutical company that manufactured a cancer drug — earning about $40,000 from the sale. Regulatory officials were concerned about Stewart's profit, and possible insider trading, because she was a friend of Sam Waksal, founder of ImClone. Stewart was initially charged with insider trading, but was later convicted only of lying to investigators and was sentenced to five months in prison and fined $4,000 — the maximum fine for this offence. Even though Martha Stewart's profit was

minuscule in the financial world she inhabited, and a case might be made for her having been pursued for her "misdemeanor" because she is a successful woman with an abrasive personality in what is essentially a man's world, her case is nevertheless an example of a situation where a powerful person was found guilty of breaking the law.

More recently, in 2009, Bernie Madoff, a New York investor who reportedly enjoyed a lavish lifestyle, was sentenced to prison for 150 years after pleading guilty to 11 charges for bilking investors worldwide of more than $60 billion dollars (MacDonald 2009). Madoff had organized a wide-reaching Ponzi scheme, which is a form of fraudulent investment. Named after Charles Ponzi, who was notorious for using the technique in the United States during the 1920s, the illegal scheme pays returns to investors from their own money or money from other investors rather than from profits earned. The Ponzi scheme attracts new investors by offering returns far higher and more consistent than other — normally legal — investments. The perpetuation of the returns that a Ponzi scheme advertises and pays requires an ever-increasing flow of money from investors to keep the scheme going. Similar to a Ponzi scheme is a pyramid scheme. The difference between the two is that Ponzi schemes actually appear to investors as a real investment opportunity, whereas pyramid schemes normally require that participants make a payment for the right to recruit other people into the scheme, at which point they will receive money.

Canadians are not immune to these types of illegal financial activities, of course. In 2009, after a long and well-publicized trial, Canadians Garth Drabinsky and Myron Gottlieb were found guilty of fraud and forgery and were later sentenced to prison for seven and six years, respectively. Drabinsky and Gottlieb were the founders of Livent, a company from Toronto that produced elaborate musical theatre shows such as *Phantom of the Opera* and *Ragtime*. Their scheme consisted of altering the accounting books to inflate the profits of the public company, thus artificially rising share prices and asset values. The end result was that banks and other investors were deceived into paying more than $500 million to Livent in the form of stock purchases and loans. Ex-Canadian Conrad Black, who rescinded his Canadian citizenship to become a British Lord (Lord of Crossharbour), was sentenced in 2007 to 6.5 years in a Florida prison for his role in the misappropriation of millions of dollars from the Hollinger newspaper empire he once headed. He was released from prison in 2012 and returned to his home in Toronto. Interestingly, Black once was on the board of Livent.

LIMITED DATA ON WHITE-COLLAR AND CORPORATE CRIME

It is important to be aware that the information criminologists use to study corporate crime is rather limited. By and large, the data used to study corporate offending are produced by the criminal justice system or other regulatory bodies. In other words, only "official" information is available about those who are charged or convicted of corporate wrong-doing to researchers or anybody else interested in studying this phenomenon. There are no reliable, large-scale, self-report surveys, for instance, that contain information about the prevalence of this type of crime throughout society. So there is really no way of knowing if the types of offences that come to the attention of the authorities, and the people who are identified in this type of law-breaking, are actually representative of corporate offending more generally.

THE PUBLIC AS VICTIM

A common misconception about corporate crime is that its effects are mainly financial. This idea cannot be further from the truth. The harm that comes to the general public, workers and consumers from illegal corporate activity is significant. The public is exposed to the noxious effects of corporate antisocial behaviour in a number of ways.

Corporations are deemed persons under the law, but they are not subject to laws pertaining to persons, a circumstance that gives them great power with few controls regarding responsibility to the societies in which they flourish. The legal status of corporations has allowed them to wreak havoc on some people's lives (for example, mistakes or false claims made by some pharmaceutical companies about their products, the dumping of toxic wastes by mining and chemical companies) and on the planet (engineering travesties on the environment through mining, drilling and open-pit mineral extraction, for example). Persons as individuals and through class action suits make attempts to sue companies for criminal sorts of activities to bring their behaviours under some kind of control. For years the odds weighed heavily on the side of the corporations, not only because of their wealth but because of their status under the law. It has therefore been difficult for the courts to successfully prosecute corporations for breaking the criminal law because it was difficult to prove that a corporation was of a requisite guilty state of mind. However, with the changes made to Canada's corporate criminal liability laws in 2012, the law now makes reference to *organizations* rather than corporations. While the motivation for these changes was arguably made to make it easier for authorities to prosecute terrorist organizations, they do have implications for making it less onerous on the Crown to prosecute white collar criminals. Only time will tell if these changes will lead to more prosecutions for while-collar offenders.

One infamous example of corporate irresponsibility is the Love Canal tragedy. For years the Hooker Chemical Company dumped tons of toxic waste into the abandoned Love Canal, located at Niagara Falls, New York. In the mid-1950s a school board purchased this dump site for a nominal fee and then sold it to a private housing developer. The canal had been covered with landfill so that houses could be built on top of this toxic storage container. In the 1970s many families who had moved to this housing development were experiencing major health problems, including miscarriages and birth defects in their infants. According to Simon (1996: 9), "There is evidence that Hooker Chemical knew of the problem as far back as 1958 but chose not to warn local health officials of any potential problems because the cleanup costs would have increased from $4 million to $50 million."

A toxic waste site of an even larger scale can be found in a city on Canada's east coast. For nearly a century, the operation of a steel plant in Sydney, Nova Scotia, has created what has been called "the largest toxic waste site in eastern Canada" (McMullan and Smith 1997: 61). Several thousand tons of poisonous by-products from the coking operation lie in an area known as the "tar ponds." According to McMullan and Smith, scientists from Environment Canada have reported that the contaminants contained in the tar ponds pose a serious threat to the workers and families who live near the site.

Corporate pollution is a problem not limited to the Canadian steel industry. For years, pulp and paper manufacturers have been dumping toxic waste into Canadian waterways at levels far above government standards. For example, in 2004 Irving Pulp and Paper pleaded guilty to a violation of Canada's Fisheries Act and was fined $30,000. The company had dumped untreated paper mill effluent into a river near Saint John, New Brunswick (Environment Canada 2004).

In May of 2000, seven people died and 2,300 became ill after drinking E. coli-contaminated water in Walkerton, Ontario, a town of just under 5,000 people about 250 kilometres northwest of Toronto (Snider 2004). The tragedy in this small Ontario town made front-page news across the country, and after a public inquiry and nine months of hearings, the O'Connor Report was released, which was highly critical of the provincial government's role in the deregulation of municipal drinking water. According to an analysis of the tragedy undertaken by Snider, the privatization of water-testing, along with the closure of public laboratories in 1996, played an important role in why the E. coli in the Walkerton drinking water was not detected until it was too late. In fact, this line of thinking was clearly expressed in the report prepared by Dennis O'Connor, an Ontario Court of Appeal judge who was appointed to lead the public inquiry. Snider views the incident at Walkerton as the "culmination of a series of deliberate decisions that put business, and business interests, ahead of people" (Snider 2004: 283).

CRIME AGAINST CONSUMERS

Consumers are also subject to victimization from corporations. A primary concern pertains to consumers who have been harmed by using unsafe products. While figures are difficult to assemble for Canada, in the United States it is estimated that some 20 million people have been injured as the result of using unsafe products (Simon 2001). Over the years a countless number of products have been found to be injurious to consumers. An appalling example of an unsafe product that killed as many as 900 people (Dowie 1977) during the 1970s was the Ford Pinto, an economy-sized vehicle that was also popular on Canadian roads at that time. Because the Ford Pinto was manufactured with a defective fuel system, the gas tank had a tendency to rupture upon rear impact (Simon 1996: 124). Even though the Ford Motor Company was
 aware of the problem, executives decided against a recall or to retool assembly line machinery because of the unwanted costs that would be incurred. During his detailed analysis of the case, Simon learned that Ford carried out a cost–benefit analysis that estimated that 180 burn deaths, 180 burn injuries and 2,100 burned vehicles would cost $49.5 million (each death was estimated at $200,000). Ford also estimated that it would cost $11 per vehicle to remedy the problem, but undertaking a recall of all Pintos and doing the $11 repair would cost the company $137 million. Simon describes such a decision as a "profits-over-human consideration" (Simon 1996: 125). In 1978, nearly a decade after the federal government first investigated the carnage caused by the Pinto, and despite Ford Motor Company's lobbying efforts to keep the cars on the road, tests undertaken by the Department of Transportation deemed the car to be unsafe and ordered a recall on all 1971–76 models (126).

An example of a case that has been considered to have negatively affected the health of thousands of Canadian women concerns silicone gel breast implants that were on the market in the early 1990s. Many women reported ill health after having breast implant surgery. A class action suit was filed against Dow Corning, one of the largest manufacturers of breast implants at that time. A civil settlement was reached in 1999 where $25 million was awarded to those women who survived who had received implants (Schwartz et al. 2005).

Another realm where consumers are affected by corporate wrong-doing concerns a practice known as "price fixing." This term refers to a situation where companies get together and agree to set or fix prices on goods or services, which they then sell on the open market. In Canada in the latter part of the nineteenth century, formal rules and regulations were first put in place designed to protect competition in the marketplace. In 1889 the Combines Investigation Act was introduced to regulate business activities. Today the Competition Bureau is responsible for the administration and enforcement of:

- the Competition Act;
- the Consumer Packaging and Labelling Act;
- the Textile Labelling Act; and
- the Precious Metals Marketing Act.

A recent example of a case of price fixing involved a graphite electrodes cartel that lessened competition for the product on the world market. In 2005, Nippon Carbon Co., Ltd pleaded guilty and was fined $100,000 by the Federal Court of Canada for aiding and abetting an international conspiracy to fix the price of graphite electrodes used in steel production. The company was the seventh party to be convicted in Canada for being involved in the cartel. Two former executives of UCAR, another company involved in the price-fixing scheme, were fined $25 million for their roles in the worldwide conspiracy.

While consumers of products are the ultimate victims of such illegal business practices, corporations can also be adversely affected by the unscrupulous practices of other corporations. Take, for example, a case that occurred in the Canadian airline industry when Air Canada waged a $220 million lawsuit against rival WestJet Airlines. WestJet agreed to settle with Air Canada by offering to pay $5.5 million of Air Canada's legal expenses and promised to donate "$10 million in the name of both airlines to children's charities across Canada" (Westhead 2006). A statement released jointly by WestJet and Air Canada declared that "in 2003–4, certain members of WestJet management engaged in an extensive practice of covertly accessing a password protected proprietary website to download detailed and commercially sensitive information without authorization or consent from Air Canada" (ibid.). Moreover, WestJet admitted that the activity took place "with the knowledge and direction of the highest management levels of WestJet and was not halted until discovered by Air Canada" (ibid.). Air Canada alleged that WestJet used the information to schedule its own flights on Air Canada's most profitable routes and times.

WORKERS AS VICTIMS

Since Canada first began to industrialize in the middle of the nineteenth century, countless numbers of workers have lost their lives while on the job. Conventional wisdom might have us believe that workers who die or who get injured on the job do so as a result of their own fault (worker carelessness or accident proneness). But some criminologists — most notably critical criminologists — suggest otherwise. Reiman (2004), for one, believes that the conditions under which many workers must labour cannot be overlooked as a key factor in accounting for "accidents" that take place within the workplace.

In Canada, researchers who share Reiman's perspective suggest that the organization of the workplace plays a fundamental role in understanding the mayhem that occurs in the lives of many Canadian workers and their families. Considering statistics measuring the major causes of Canadian death rates, it is not surprising that heart disease and cancer are at the top of the list. However, what would be surprising to most Canadians is that occupational death is the third leading cause of death in Canada — even greater than motor vehicle accidents and considerably greater than homicide (Reasons et al. 1981). In fact, in 2003 there were 6.1 work-related deaths per 100,000 workers in Canada. In that same year, the homicide rate in Canada was 1.72 per 100,000 population (Krahn et al. 2007). Since that time, the work-related death rate has remained about the same and the work-related death rate in Canada continues to be much greater than the homicide rate.

A case study that meticulously documented the anguish experienced by a group of fluorspar miners from a small community in rural Newfoundland has been carried out by Elliott Leyton (1975). Fluorspar is a mineral used in the manufacture of products such as aluminum, gasoline and insulating foam. Leyton's study vividly describes the slow and agonizing deaths of miners whose lungs had been contaminated by high levels of radon gas. Moreover, the study also points a finger at both the company and the government for its knowledge that these miners were working in an extremely dangerous environment, yet little action was taken to protect these workers. In total, approximately 200 workers lost their lives as the result of industrial disease between the 1930s and the 1970s (Rennie 2005). An analysis of the period from 1933 to 1945 reveals that well before it was confirmed that radon gas was a health hazard, the alleged conditions in the mines in St. Lawrence, Newfoundland, were having a severe impact on miners' health, and the miners fought to have those fears recognized and addressed. During this period, workers continually demanded that action be taken about their health concerns. However, according to Rennie (2005: 3):

In all instances, however, their concerns were ignored or downplayed by government and corporate interests who did not wish to have the issue placed on the labour relations agenda. The actions of the Trade Dispute Board stand out as an especially striking instance among a series of neglected opportunities to curtail somewhat the impending disaster. Perhaps most importantly, a study of the origins of this industrial disaster demonstrates that while workers at St Lawrence were victims, they were neither passive nor unknowing. Rather, their knowledge was ignored and devalued and their actions undermined by corporate and political interests whose goals were widely divergent from and even contradictory to those of the workers.

This idea that harm to workers that occurs during the process of resource extraction, which are the collective result of the interplay between the federal and provincial government agencies and the private sector who own and operate the mining of the resource, has been captured in a phrase coined by Kramer and Michalowski as "state–corporate crime." They define this term as "illegal or socially injurious actions that occur when one or more institutions of political governance pursue a goal in direct co-operation with one or more institutions of economic production and distribution" (cited in McMullan and Smith 1997: 63). This position has also been applied to the situation in Sydney, Nova Scotia, where the health both of workers and of the community at large was jeopardized as the result of being exposed to large quantities of industrial pollution.

CAUSES OF WHITE-COLLAR CRIME

Understanding the nature of white-collar crime and white-collar criminality is complex, and over the years a number of different theoretical approaches have been used to explain "elite deviance," ranging from differential association theory to conflict theory. Generally speaking, the literature on the causes of corporate crime can be broken down into two perspectives: macro and micro explanations. Macro explanations (structural/large scale) tend to focus on the
sorts of issues in which it is argued that the criminal law reflects the concerns and interests of the dominant class. And since in a capitalist society it is mainly economic and business elites which are the dominant class, they control the state and subsequently the legal system will primarily reflect their interests. Therefore, laws which regulate corporate malfeasance remain weak and their enforcement ineffective. While this macro explanation, conflict perspective, is useful for drawing attention to the class based nature of law-making, the fact remains that some laws do exist which are meant to control corporate crime, and people have been sent to jail in Canada for violating such laws. Moreover, it is also true that not all

"capitalists" engage in corporate wrong-doing. Partly in response to these issues, more micro explanations of corporate offending have emerged which focus on the kinds of people and the more immediate environments in which corporate offending occurs. A useful framework for understanding this type of offending at a micro level (where individual opportunities and behaviour is explored) has been put forward by Shover and Wright (2001), who have approached this issue by considering three sets of

factors: (1) white-collar criminal opportunities; (2) white-collar decision making; and (3) the characteristics of white-collar offenders.

Opportunity plays a role in corporate crime. With the use of high-speed electronic information networks, money from banks and business accounts can now be controlled almost instantaneously and over long distances. This technology, along with the developments in finance capitalism — a relatively new form of economic activity where profits are made possible through the management of financial accounts — is a feature of the new economy and of globalization, which also enhances opportunities to make money illegally. This, of course, is very much unlike the old, non-digital economy that was dominated by the manufacturing of goods and the production of services. The emergence of new communication technologies has basically changed the ways people relate to one another in organizations. An unintended consequence of these developments has been an increase in the availability of white-collar criminal opportunities.

The second factor that criminologists examine in attempting to explain corporate crime involves decision making. Many opportunities to offend present themselves within the corporate world, but this does not mean that all individuals or organizations do so. One perspective explains the particularities of decisions around offending as rational choice theory. Rational choice theory alerts us to the observation that organizational crimes are the result of real-life decisions made by managers and executives. Decisions to commit accounting fraud, for example, are seen to be based, in part, on the actor's ability to weigh and calculate the potential consequences of rule-breaking. Paternoster and Simpson (2001: 205), rational choice proponents, have proposed a social psychology model of corporate offending based on the costs and benefits of illegal behaviour. They contend that it's important to consider the following factors when attempting to understand the choices that managers and executives make:

- Perceived certainty/severity of formal legal sanctions (external legal system: criminal, civil, or regulatory);
- Perceived certainty/severity of informal sanctions (loss of job, demotion, loss of status);
- Perceived certainty/severity of loss of self-respect (self-image of a "re-

spectable person" could be jeopardized);
- Perceived cost of rule compliance (loss of profits and competitiveness);
- Perceived benefits of non-compliance (promotion);
- Moral inhibitions (how wrong is it, for example, to price-fix?);
- Perceived sense of legitimacy/fairness (reasonableness of rules, evaluation of experience of judicial or regulatory process);
- Characteristics of criminal event (cultural conduciveness, environmental factors); and
- Prior offending by person.

The final set of factors that criminologists examine when attempting to understand corporate crime are the characteristics of those who have been implicated and identified by the authorities. Like street crime, gender is by far the best predictor of white-collar criminal activity. While there are certainly exceptions to this general tendency (such as the case involving Martha Stewart), males continue to fill the roles of corporate criminals. These gender differences reflect the number of males who continue to dominate positions of power in large corporations in North America. Even though almost as many women as men participate in today's labour market, and women now outnumber men in Canadian universities, women continue to lack access to positions of power and authority in the corporate work world, so they lack the opportunities that would be necessary for them to engage in corporate crime.

This is not to say that women are uninvolved in crime in the workplace. According to Daly (1989), there is such a thing as "his and hers white-collar crime." While the numbers of females who are involved in crimes such as antitrust violations, bribery and security fraud are very low (less than 5 percent of the total), it is not unusual for women to be involved in credit card and postal frauds, and women comprise 45 percent of convicted bank embezzlers. However, according to Daly (1989), most women who are implicated in embezzlement in the banking industry are tellers, while males involved in this crime tend to occupy more senior positions, such as financial officers. Women's motives for occupational theft are more likely than men's to be based on financial need for themselves or their families. Men, on the other hand, were more likely to report that they were influenced by others, and some steal because they want to advance their careers or obtain desired status symbols — that is, money to buy a sports car (Bartol 2001).

While corporate crime has likely been around since the dawn of the corporation, more and more of these types of wrong-doings — especially more serious violations — are making their way to the courts and drawing the attention of the mass media. However, given the difficulties involved in collecting information on white-collar crime that does not come to the attention of authorities, there is really no way of knowing the true extent of such crime. If recent incidents that have appeared in the media represent a shift in enforcement practices aimed at such offending, such crime is likely to continue to increase.

Criminologists are increasingly expressing an interest in a field that is closely related to the study of corporate crime. This is an area known as green (or environmental/conservation) criminology. "Green criminology" is the study of environmental damage, caused by human activity, viewed through a criminological lens. A growing number of criminologists have come to recognize that a wide range of crime and criminal justice activity takes place that is directly related to environmental issues. In sync with the social-reaction perspective, the study of environmental harm is part of a tradition that critically questions the definition and meaning of crime in society. Until recently a great deal of human-made environmental damage that took place on the planet went unquestioned in society. However, in the aftermath of the Exxon Valdez oil spill off the coast of Alaska, the Union Carbide gas tragedy in Bhopal, India and the BP fire and massive oil spill in the Gulf of Mexico in 2010 where eleven men died, more and more attention is being given to such human-made damage. Not only does green criminology draw attention to the human costs associated with such damage but it also attempts to understand these events within the context of corporate power and political influence. Green criminology draws attention to environmental issues such as the illegal disposal of hazardous waste (for eample, E-waste), wildlife violations (for example, trade in endangered species or animal parts such as elephant and rhinoceros tusks), the illegal extraction of natural resources (for example, illegal logging, fishing, mining and plant removal) and illegal land management (for example, illegal filling of wetlands, endangered species habitat removal) (Gibbs et al. 2010: 133). Similar to the general field of criminology, in theoretical and methodological terms, green criminology is very much a multidisciplinary framework integrating insights acquired from the social and natural resource sciences.

POLITICAL CRIME

Another area of wrongful activity among revered people is political crime. Historically, like corporate crime, these types of crimes often were not recognized by society. Even within the criminological community, until recently, the study of political crime has not been paid much attention. Political crime has two principal dimensions: crimes committed against the state and crimes committed by the state.

One example of a crime committed against the state is when a social group resorts to violence in an effort to transform the social order. There are several examples of this type of violence throughout Canadian history, beginning in the 1830s with the Upper and Lower Canada rebellions led in what today is Ontario by William Lyon

Mackenzie and in what today is Quebec by Louis-Joseph Papineau. These violent conflicts were fought against the established order of the time to gain "responsible government." A more recent series of incidents marked by such violence occurred during the 1970 October Crisis, which involved the activities of a small group of Quebec terrorists known as the Front de Libération du Québec (FLQ), who were devoted to bringing about a sovereign, socialist Quebec. In their quest for recognition, members of the FLQ kidnapped the British Trade Commissioner, James Cross, and later kidnapped and killed a Quebec cabinet minister, Pierre Laporte. Prime Minister Pierre Trudeau responded to these terrorist tactics by invoking the War Measures Act. This was a controversial piece of legislation in its own right as it allowed the police to arrest and detain people without a warrant. In fact, more than four hundred people were arrested and detained in Quebec at that time merely for being sympathetic to the cause of Quebec separation. Today in Quebec there is a provincial party (Parti Québécois) and a federal party (Bloc Québécois) both committed to the cause of Quebec independence. While most Canadians were relieved that the FLQ crisis was over, many wondered if Trudeau's use of the War Measures Act was an overreaction to the political situation in Quebec.

Activities of groups labelled as "terrorists" have been in the spotlight in many countries throughout world, especially since the destruction of the World Trade Center in New York on 11 September 2001. In Canada, for example, in May 2006 a group of eighteen young men, mainly from the Greater Toronto Area, were accused by Canadian authorities of plotting to storm the House of Commons and take hostage several members of Parliament. The investigators found evidence that the group of Islamic fundamentalists was intending to behead the prime minister, blow up the Toronto Stock Exchange, and destroy with a homemade bomb the Toronto facility of the Canadian Broadcasting Corporation. Of the eighteen males who were charged by the police, seven had their charges dropped or stayed, four were found guilty and seven pleaded guilty (Gazze 2013).

Not all protest activity committed against the state is violent, however. In fact, most political crime directed against the state is deliberately non-violent. Protestors usually commit acts like blocking roads or highways, carrying placards and singing or chanting, pasting advertisements of their opinions on public property or setting small fires to keep themselves warm in winter but also using them to burn effigies of opponents, slogans, or other symbolic items. The environmental movement has been involved in such actions in British Columbia. Aboriginal protestors have also blocked roads (Caledonia, Ontario) and occupied parks (Ipperwash, Ontario) to express discontent over issues of disputed land rights. On the east coast, groups of people from fishing communities have blocked highways to protest government mismanagement of the cod fishery.

Political crimes also can be committed by the state in conjunction with the private sector. The sponsorship scandal that played a prominent role in the 2005–6 Canadian federal election campaign, and likely was a key factor for the Canadian electorate's ousting of the Liberals and electing a minority Conservative government led by Stephen Harper, can be seen as an example of such activity. The sponsorship program was initially set up by the federal government to oppose the separatist movement in Quebec after the 1995 Quebec referendum was narrowly won by federalists. Allegations were made that a fraudulent scheme was linked to the program. More specifically, $155 million in federal funding allegedly was given to Liberal-friendly advertising agencies in Quebec where little or no work was done for the money. Moreover, "part of the money was siphoned back to the Quebec wing of the federal Liberal Party, with $800,000 in official donations and more than $1 million in kick-backs" (CTV News 2006). A public inquiry was struck to investigate matters, and after a lengthy series of hearings that included the testimony of former prime minister Jean Chrétien, the Gomery Commission determined that there had indeed been a misappropriation of public funds, which later resulted in fraud charges being laid against Chuck Guité, a senior bureaucrat closely involved with the sponsorship program, along with Jean Brault and Paul Coffin, two senior advertising executives from Montreal who had been given contracts by the federal government. Coffin, the first person to be charged with fraud, originally received a conditional sentence of two years less a day, which was to be served in the community. Later, however, as a result of the case being appealed to the Quebec Court of Appeal, Coffin was given an 18-month prison term for defrauding the federal government of $1.5 million in sponsorship funds. Brault was also found guilty of five fraud-connected charges and was sentenced to 30 months in prison (CTV News 2006). Chuck Guité, the federal bureaucrat who ran the sponsorship program, was also found guilty in the case.

As with corporate crime, there are not many examples that have implicated women in political corruption cases in Canada. This fact is no doubt associated with the same reasons that were given in the earlier discussion regarding gender and corporate crime. Only relatively recently have women become actively involved in institutional politics in Canada. Men continue to outnumber women in the House of Commons and in provincial legislatures.

State political repression occurs when the state uses its power to remove or suspend the rights and liberties of targeted groups within the population for fear that these groups represent a threat to the social order. While some may regard the use of the War Measures Act in 1970 as an example of state repression, others felt the invocation of that measure was reasonable. In the past in Canada, state police and the military have been used violently on numerous occasions in support of corporate Canada to break up strikes, worker movements, and Aboriginal protests — the Winnipeg General Strike (1919), the On-to-Ottawa Trek (1935),

> **Terrorism**
>
> Following the terrorist attacks of September 11, 2001, the United States enacted "homeland security" legislation such as the Patriot Act and the Maritime Security Act. These laws have extended the powers of government to surveillance of public transportation facilities such as airports, bus and train stations, and ferry terminals.
>
> Shortly after these anti-terrorist laws were enacted in the United States, similar legislation was introduced in Canada. In December 2001, Canada's Anti-Terrorism Act became law. This legislation provided measures to identify, prosecute, convict, and punish terrorists by:
>
> - defining and designating terrorist groups and activities to make it easier to prosecute terrorists and those who support them;
> - making it an offence to knowingly participate in, contribute to, or facilitate the activities of a terrorist group or to instruct anyone to carry out a terrorist activity or an activity on behalf of a terrorist group;
> - making it an offence to knowingly harbour a terrorist;
> - creating tougher sentences and parole provisions for terrorist offences;
> - cutting off financial support for terrorists by making it a crime to knowingly collect or give funds, either directly or indirectly, to carry out terrorism, denying or removing charitable status from those who support terrorist groups, and by making it easier to freeze and seize their assets.
>
> The police have also been granted new powers so that it is easier to use electronic surveillance to monitor suspected terrorist groups. The Anti-Terrorism Act allows the police to arrest and detain suspected terrorists without actually having to press charges. As long as the authorities suspect that an individual is a terrorist, he or she can be detained indefinitely.
>
> This act however, has not been without its critics. This legislation gives police the right to incarcerate people merely on the suspicion they may be a terrorist and are believed to be about to commit a crime. The authorities also have the power to force testimony from anyone they believe has information associated with a terrorism investigation. The act also allows for closed trials and can deny an accused and his/her counsel full knowledge of the evidence against them (Department of Justice Canada 2003). This website has more information about this issue <http://ccla.org/2011/04/04/op-ed-anti-terror-laws-must-uphold-canadian-values/>.

the Asbestos, Quebec, strike (1949) and the Oka, Quebec (1990) and Ipperwash, Ontario (1995), confrontations are only a few of many such instances.

The internment of the Japanese community in British Columbia during the Second World War is also an example of state repression. Not long after the bombing of Pearl Harbor and the declaration of war on Japan in 1941, persons of Japanese descent were rounded up by government authorities and taken away from their homes and livelihoods. Approximately 22,000 members of the British Columbia Japanese community — many of whom were born in Canada — were relocated away from coastal areas of the province because they were regarded by the government as posing a threat to national security. Many families were not kept together. Men were usually sent to camps in the interior of British Columbia, or ended up in camps in Ontario and Saskatchewan, while most women and children were relocated to inland areas of British Columbia.

There is evidence to suggest that the living conditions for the Japanese were so harsh in these camps that the Red Cross responded by providing the evacuees with additional food. It was not until four years after the war that the Japanese were permitted to return to their homes. By that time, however, many decided not to return as they had established roots elsewhere. Those who did try to return found most of their property had been confiscated by the government and sold for only a fraction of its worth. In 1988 the Canadian government formally apologized for the internment and offered all surviving evacuees $21,000 in compensation. Canadian scientist and award-winning environmentalist David Suzuki was, with his family, among those interned during that period in a British Columbia internment camp.

Given the broad set of circumstances that can be involved in political crime, there is no one explanation that has been developed to account for these activities. However, in situations where politicians misappropriate public money using fraudulent means, the motivations and rewards suggested in the previous section to explain corporate crime would also be appropriate to political wrong-doing.

ORGANIZED TRANSNATIONAL CRIME

Organized transnational crime is organized criminal activity that takes place across national jurisdictions. With advances in transportation and information technology, law enforcement officials and policy makers have needed to respond to this form of crime on a global scale. There are several different types of organized transnational crime. These include human trafficking, money laundering, drug smuggling, illegal arms dealing, cybercrime and terrorism. While it is impossible to precisely measure the extent of this type of criminal activity, in 2009 the Millennium Project, an international think tank, assembled statistics on several aspects of transnational crime. Below is a summary of this information (all on an annual basis):

- World illicit trade of almost $730 billion
- Counterfeiting and piracy of $300 billion to $1 trillion
- Global drug trade of $321 billion
- Trade in environmental goods of $69 billion
- Human trafficking of $44 billion
- Weapons trade of $10 billion
- McAfee estimates that theft and breaches from cybercrime may have cost businesses as much as $1 trillion in 2008.

(For more information on the Millennium Project, visit <www.unmillenniumproject.org>.)

It has only been relatively recently that criminologists have begun to study this phenomenon. For example, the Australian Institute of Criminology has released a series of policy papers that have taken some important steps in defining and providing case studies of transnational crime within an Australian context.

While criminologists have made advances in defining and measuring transnational organized crime, the discipline is still far from developing a parsimonious explanation of transnational crime. This is largely because of the wide range of crimes that fall under this rather broad umbrella term and the lack of information about opportunities and motives of those involved in such activities. However, since transnational crime is organized illegal activity, the phenomenon logically lends itself to explanations offered earlier about corporate crime (opportunities, decision making and backgrounds of offenders). In addition, questions asked about transnational crime have generally been informed by issues related to policing. For example, Beare (2003) notes that countries are expected to react to and police organized crime and corruption in a uniform manner based upon international agreements, conventions and accords. Yet until more empirical research is carried out in this area, Beare contends that the costs and effectiveness of these enforcement measures remain clear.

POLICE MISCONDUCT

Like politicians, the police are a public institution whose mandate is not only to serve the public but to offer protection as well. Yet police officers become involved in wrong-doing from time to time. Police misconduct is defined as situations when the actions of police officers are "inconsistent with the officer's legal authority, organizational authority and standards of ethical conduct" (Barker and Carter 1986, cited in Goff 2004: 144). This may include acts such as tampering with evidence or raiding a suspect's home without a valid search warrant, or abuses of authority that involve intimidation — physical or verbal — when apprehending or interrogating suspects.

The United States has a well-documented history of police corruption and provides criminologists with a range of examples of what can go wrong in that social group. The issue of police wrong-doing came to a head in the United States after a report was released by the Knapp Commission in 1970. The Commission looked into allegations of police corruption in New York City, and the findings were attention-catching. The Commission found that police corruption was extensive. It ranged from officers collecting small gratuities (for example, accepting free meals at restaurants) to more serious actions, such as receiving payoffs from construction companies, illegal gambling outlets and drug dealers (Knapp Commission 1973). As a result of the Commission's findings, police departments throughout the country were placed under greater public scrutiny and efforts were made to ensure more accountability from the police.

However, police wrong-doing in the United States continues to flourish. For example, in the late 1990s an investigation discovered several corrupt acts had been committed by officers of the Los Angeles Police Department (LAPD). Several officers of the anti-gang unit were caught up in bribery, making false arrests and framing innocent people (Coleman 2002). Besides the fact that dozens of criminal convictions were overturned as a result of these findings, the federal government was given responsibility to reform the LAPD. This is the same police force that was in the spotlight in 1991 over the Rodney King beating. Commonly referred to as the best-known case of abuse of force by the police in American history, four members of the LAPD were caught on amateur videotape as they beat and tasered (an electronic shocking device used by police to subdue suspects) King after he had been asked to pull his vehicle over to the side of the road. Portions of the incident that were captured on the tape were telecast by major news networks across the United States and around the world. Since King was a Black man, and because the LAPD had a reputation for being tolerant to rough treatment of suspects, especially when dealing with Blacks and Hispanics, millions of viewers were watching when the four police officers who were involved in the incident were facing charges in a jury trial (Martin 2005). Not long after the officers were acquitted on all charges, a massive three-day riot broke out on the streets of south central Los Angeles that killed several people and caused extensive damage to property. Subsequent to a successful appeal by the state, two of the four officers were later found guilty of charges related to the King incident and were sent to jail (ibid.).

As one might suspect, Canada is not immune from police corruption. One instance related to the FLQ crisis in Quebec, mentioned above, and involved an RCMP plot to steal Parti Québécois membership files in 1973. The intent of accessing this information was to determine whether any members of the federal civil service were separatist supporters. If civil servants' names did appear on the list, then these individuals could be monitored by the RCMP Security Service — which was later disbanded when the Canadian Security Intelligence Service (CSIS) was formed in 1984.

Not only was the RCMP implicated in the theft of Parti Québécois membership lists but they were also found to be involved in an illegal barn-burning incident in Quebec. This time federal civil servants were not the target, but two alleged terrorist groups were: the FLQ and the Black Panthers — a revolutionary group from the United States that was committed to ethnic and working-class emancipation. On a tip from the FBI, the RCMP Security Service burned a barn near Montreal that was thought to be the clandestine meeting place for the two groups. While no one was injured in the incident, an act of arson was nevertheless committed (Mann and Lee

1979). No arrests, or even reprimands, were given to the officers involved in the incident. Quite a different outcome, however, happened in 2010 to Sheldon Cook, a nineteen-year veteran of the Peel Regional Police Service. After being convicted for stealing what he believed were packages of cocaine (they were in fact bags of flour) from a botched RCMP drug sting, Cook was sentenced to five years in prison.

A number of explanations have been offered to explain police wrong-doing. The most popular but least accepted by the criminological community is the "bad-apple theory." The adage is "one rotten apple spoils the whole barrel." The theory is that a little police corruption spreads like rot among apples. The counterclaim by the police is that one rotten apple can be removed and the rest of the organization protected. The underlying assumption of this view is that police wrong-doing is due to individual shortcomings in a small number of "bad-apple" police officers who break the law while on the job. While senior police officials will agree that there may be a few rotten apples within any police force, they claim that these can be monitored and removed and that, overall, the barrel (that is, the organization as a whole) remains trustworthy.

Explanations such as this are regularly used by police departments to account for wrong-doing within their rank and file. In fact, this was the reasoning used by the lapd when allegations were made about corruption within that particular police force (Martin 2005). Claims are made to suggest that the actions of a small number of officers are not to be seen as indicative of the standards and behaviour within the broader organization. This perspective, however, was not used to account for police wrong-doing in the Knapp investigation noted earlier. According to Knapp's thorough and systematic investigation of the New York Police Department (NYPD), individual corruption was found to be a symptom of organizational pathology. Because Knapp found that corruption within the New York City police force at that time was so extensive, and senior staff did so little to deal with these problems, he could not accept the proposition that wrong-doing could be understood simply on an individual basis. Indeed, corruption was found in every plainclothes gambling enforcement squad, in addition to squads that enforced drugs and criminal investigations. Moreover, according to Henry (1994), "a system of internal corruption was revealed where managerial discretion and favour were bought and sold in a marketplace of payoffs" (cited in Newburn 1999: 15).

Partly in recognition of the findings of the Knapp Commission, sociological accounts of police wrong-doing that focused on systemic and organization factors became much more prevalent during the 1970s and afterwards. A new centre of attention on police corruption steered away from looking simply at the characteristics of deviant officers and examined more broadly how policing is organized and how subcultures emerge that foster a corrupt environment.

An excellent model of police corruption has been put together by Sherman

(1974). He draws attention to two sets of causes of police wrong-doing: constant and variable. Constant factors begin by identifying the role played by discretion. The reason why police discretion is linked to wrong-doing relates very much to material gain, as opposed to professional judgment. Consider a hypothetical situation where a police officer stops a person who has been speeding. When the officer asks the occupant of the speeding vehicle for her licence and insurance, a $100 bill is put into the hand of the officer. While taking bribes is a criminal offence, there is no doubt that there are occasions when an event such as this would invoke some degree of temptation in the mind of the officer to take the monetary bribe and simply let the speeder go without charging her.

Another organizational factor in police wrong-doing relates to police officers' actions taking place in situations of low visibility to their supervisors. Returning to the above example, it would be very unlikely that the police officer who took the bribe in such a situation would actually be seen doing this by one or more of his or her supervisors. Similarly, there are also very low levels of public visibility for police officers in such situations.

A constant factor in much police work concerns the high levels of police secrecy; police culture is characterized by solidarity and secrecy. For instance, if an officer observes an impropriety of another officer, it would be unlikely that such an event would come to the attention of superior authorities. Even if the event did come to the attention of police management, since most police officers in management positions have worked their way up through the rank and file, they share many of the same values as those they manage and supervise.

Sherman had also identified, as noted above, a second set of variable factors that play an important role in predicting police wrong-doing. This set of factors pertains to both the culture of the police organization and to the culture of the community being policed. One of the more important of these variable factors is the level of moral cynicism in a community. In short, if the citizenry who are being policed are cynical of the legal system, then the police may also adopt similar attitudes, especially if there is close and daily contact with lawbreakers. A second feature of variability concerns the opportunities for corruption — the greater the number of opportunities for corruption, the greater the likelihood that corruption will occur. For example, vice squad work can often provide police with temptations to break the law. Consider a supposed situation when officers who are working in a drug enforcement squad happen to confiscate two kilos of cocaine in a raid of a drug dealer's home. Who would ever know if the officer(s) involved in the raid were to keep half of the amount of the drug that was originally confiscated for his or her personal use? As the street saying suggests, "Cops always have the best drugs."

While these are just a few of the causal factors that have been identified by Sherman as affecting the development of corrupt police practices, the point has been made through his model that to effectively understand police wrong-doing one must move beyond the study of bad apples and study the environment in which policing occurs.

CRIME IN TRUSTED SOCIAL ORGANIZATIONS

Several examples could be given illustrating cases where individuals have betrayed public trust within their occupational roles. Teachers, lawyers, university professors, medical doctors and clergy — from several different religious denominations — have been implicated in various forms of wrong-doing.

For example, during the late 1980s and early 1990s several cases came to media attention in the United States that involved the dubious activities of several high-profile religious figures. Jim Bakker, a fundamentalist evangelist known through his PTL (Praise the Lord) Club television program, was convicted in 1989 of fraud and conspiring to commit fraud. Bakker was later sentenced to forty-five years in federal prison for diverting donations from his followers' organization for his own personal use. There have been several more recent cases where Roman Catholic clergy have been prosecuted for sexual abuse. There is, of course, a terrible irony in spokespersons for the conversion from a life of wrong-doing to a life of holiness being found guilty of criminal behaviour.

In Canada, there have also been cases where clergy have been prosecuted for sexual assault. One case that drew national attention and led to a public inquiry involved Mount Cashel, an orphanage in St John's, Newfoundland, that was operated by the Roman Catholic Christian Brothers from 1898 to 1991. Investigations of child sexual abuse in the orphanage had been reported to the police as far back as the mid-1970s. Two police investigations, one in 1975 and a second in 1982, resulted in one charge of a sexual offence where one Christian Brother was sentenced to four months in jail and three years probation (Harris 1990). However, as a result of a 1989 open-line radio show in St. John's to which a caller had suggested that a government cover-up of abuse had occurred at Mount Cashel, a judge who heard the allegation was successful in opening the case again. This time, after a more thorough investigation and a number of victims who had grown up at the orphanage had come forward, fourteen people (nine brothers and five civilians) were arrested on 88 counts of physical and sexual abuse (ibid.). Furthermore, the Department of Justice was found to have indeed interfered with earlier police investigations. The authorities were well aware that abuse was taking place at the orphanage, but nothing was done to protect the young boys from further neglect and assault. Not long after the report of the Hughes Commission was released to the public, the Mount Cashel Orphanage was destroyed, the property sold and the proceeds were used to compensate victims who took civil action against the Christian Brothers.

In Ontario, twenty-five ex-employees from St. Joseph's Training School for Boys, a reform school that was also run by the Christian Brothers from 1933 to 1974, were charged with a total of 182 offences of physical and sexual abuse (Native Women's Association of Canada 1992). The charges stemmed from incidents alleged by approximately 400 former students of the training school. Although criminal charges were not laid in this case, a $16-million compensation package was agreed on by the Ontario government and the Roman Catholic Church for the victims of said abuse in 1999. Another parallel to the Mount Cashel case was that cabinet ministers, cardinals and archbishops had been made aware of the abuse that was taking place in St Joseph's yet had failed to act (ibid.).

In recent years information has been uncovered, mostly in western Canada, concerning the experiences of Aboriginal youth within the residential school system. The residential school system dates back to 1874 when, under the Indian Act, the federal government began to provide educational services for Aboriginal children. The residential school system was composed of a variety of institutions (that is, industrial, boarding and residential schools) that were located in most Canadian provinces and were run mainly by religious organizations, such as the Anglican Church. According to the federal government, approximately 100,000 children attended these schools between the latter part of the nineteenth century and most of the twentieth century. The original idea behind the schools was to assimilate Aboriginal children into mainstream Canadian society, thereby "solving" the Aboriginal problem by phasing out Aboriginal culture altogether. Given the large Aboriginal presence in western Canada, many of these schools were located in Saskatchewan and British Columbia. Mainly during the 1990s, many Aboriginal peoples who had attended these schools came forward with agonizing stories of sexual and physical abuse that occurred while they attended these schools. In fact, in 1996 the Royal Commission on Aboriginal Peoples revealed many such accounts of abuse. As a result of the abuses that took place over the years at these residential schools, in 1998 the federal government committed $350 million for a community-based healing strategy to assist Aboriginal communities where physical abuse, sexual abuse and drug and alcohol problems remain problematic.

There is no specific, agreed-on theory to explain situations in which members of the clergy become involved in sexual or physical wrong-doing. Explanations similar to those that have been presented to explain wrong-doing by those who hold positions of power or privilege in society (for example, police deviance) may have some relevance. The fact that some religious bodies require sexual abstinence from their members may create interior pressures beyond the ability of some individuals to contain within their vows. No doubt individual and psychological factors are involved in such offending, but these behaviours need to be understood within the context of the broader social organizations in which they occur. Belonging to an authoritative organization where one is granted a high level of trust opens up opportunities to offend that are unavailable to those who do not hold such positions. Moreover, historically, society has associated these positions of power with behaviour that has been beyond reproach, which indeed some of the individuals holding these offices have demonstrated. However, when expectations become rigid and human abilities to meet these expectations falter, there need to be fail-safe measures in place in institutions. Children are always vulnerable — a fact that was not recognized by most social institutions until the mid-twentieth century.

Some institutions have addressed the problem. The Anglican Church of Canada publicly apologized on behalf of its former representatives to those of the residential schools who had been hurt, not only by sexual assaults but by the traumatic removal from their homes and societies. The Roman Catholic and Anglican churches in negotiations with Aboriginal peoples and the federal government, have made substantial monetary reparations as signs of their regret for the abuses that had occurred (Anglican Church of Canada 2008). In the Anglican Church, every individual congregation shared proportionally in that monetary expression of regret.

In November 2002, the government and the Anglican Church of Canada reached an agreement that detailed the payment of compensation to residential school survivors. Under the agreement, the federal government agreed to pay 70 percent of the compensation and the Anglican Church committed to pay 30 percent, to a maximum of $25 million. In March 2003, the agreement was ratified. In November 2005, the federal government and legal counsel for former students, legal counsel for churches, the Assembly of First Nations and other Aboriginal organizations signed an agreement-in-principle to all outstanding residential schools issues. The agreement stipulates five major issues to be addressed:

- a "common experience payment" to be made to all former students;
- an "independent assessment process" (IAP);
- a "truth and reconciliation process";
- commemoration; and
- ongoing healing.

Accusing members of the clergy of misconduct takes courage, especially if one is a committed follower and believer of a religious faith. Since the legitimacy of the organization would be seriously undermined if the public were to lose confidence in its members, it is not surprising that church officials, having been made aware of wrong-doing, are reticent to take action against clerics. Like police deviance, wrong-doing within religious organizations tends to be accounted for on the basis of the bad-apple theory. The religious institution, however, considers that it provides an opportunity for change (through confession, repentance, forgiveness and reformation) and may be prone not to reject or prosecute the perpetrator of a crime but to offer that opportunity for reformation as an alternative to prosecution under the law. Prosecutions, such as those we have described, may have the effect in the future of bringing crimes committed within the context of the religious institutions into the public judicial system.

CONCLUSION

The crimes discussed in this chapter take place among people who occupy positions of power or privilege. Sutherland's (1939) initial work on defining white-collar crime and raising the profile of corporate wrong-doing within the criminological community was introduced. Recent examples of corporate crime were presented that drew on cases from the United States and Canada. Contrasting the types of crime that have been discussed earlier, information about crime committed by those with high social standing is usually only revealed when it comes to the attention of the authorities. There are not any large-scale self-report surveys available that measure these types of rule-breaking.

The harms resulting from "elite deviance" were acknowledged, beginning with those felt by the public, which include environmental pollution. This was followed by examples of corporate wrong-doing that adversely affect consumers and workers. There is no doubt that the damage caused to society by white-collar crime is massive. Explanations for the causes of these types of crime were also suggested.

Political crime, police deviance and crime committed by religious leaders were also introduced to show how those in society who hold positions of power and have public trust are not immune from criminal behaviour, but may be provided with unique opportunities to commit crime in addition to organizational protection from criminal prosecution.

References

Beare, M. 2003. *Critical Reflections on Transnational Organized Crime, Money Laundering, and Corruption.* Toronto, ON: University of Toronto Press.
Beirne, P., and J. Messerschmitt. 2006. *Criminology, 4th edition.* Los Angeles, CA: Roxbury.
CBC News Online. 2006. "The WorldCom Story." <http://www.cbc.ca/news/background/worldcom>.
Coleman, J. 2002. *The Criminal Elite: Understanding White-Collar Crime.* New York: Worth.
CTV News. 2006. "Harper Considers Legal Action Over Adscam Funds." <http://www.ctv.ca/CTVNews/Canada/20060511/tories_adscam_060511/>.
Daly, K. 1989. "Gender and Varieties of White-Collar Crime." *Criminology,* 27: 769–793.
Department of Justice Canada. 2003. "Antiterrorism Act." <http://lawslois.justice.gc.ca/PDF/A-11.7.pdf>.
Environment Canada. 2004. Atlantic region news release, 13 December.
Gazze, M. 2013. "16-year sentence for Toronto 18 terror ringleader." *Globe*

and Mail, 28 February. <https://www.theglobeandmail.com/news/national/16-year-sentence-for-toronto-18-terror-ringleader/article4262949/>.
Gibbs, C., M. Gore, E.F. McGarrell, and L. Rivers. 2010. "Introducing Conservation Criminology: Towards Interdisciplinary Scholarship on Environmental Crimes and Risks." *British Journal of Criminology*, 50, 1: 124–144.
Goff, C. 2004. *Criminal Justice in Canada*, 3rd edition. Toronto, ON: Thompson.
Harris, M. 1990. *Unholy Order: Tragedy at Mount Cashel*. Markham, ON: Penguin.
Knapp Commission. 1973. *Knapp Commission Report on Police Corruption*. New York: Braziller.
Krahn, H., G. Lowe, and K. Hughes. 2007. *Work, Industry and Canadian Society*, 5th edition. Toronto, ON: Thompson.
Leyton, E. 1975. *Dying Hard: The Ravages of Industrial Carnage*. Toronto, ON: McClelland & Stewart.
MacDonald, N. 2009. "Look Out Victims, the Government Wants Its Share Now." CBC *News*, 12 March. <http://www.cbc.ca/world/story/2009/03/12/>.
Mann, E., and J.A. Lee. 1979. *RCMP vs the People*. Don Mills, ON: General Publishing.
Martin, B. 2005. "Hold a Cover-Up in the Open." *Sydney Morning Herald*, June 23: 15.
McMullan, J., and S. Smith. 1997. "Toxic Steel: State Corporate Crime and the Contamination of the Environment." In J. McMullan, D. Perrier, S. Smith, and P. Sawn (eds.), *Crimes, Laws and Communities*. Halifax, NS: Fernwood Publishing.
Native Women's Association of Canada. 1992. "The Canadian Human Rights Act: Changes Required by Behalf of the NWAC." 25 February.
Newburn, T. 1999. *Understanding and Preventing Police Corruption: Lessons from the Literature*. London, UK: Home Office, Research Development and Statistics Directorate.
Paternoster, R., and S. Simpson. 2001. "A Rational Choice Theory of Corporate Crime." In N. Shover and J. Wright (eds.), *Crimes of Privilege: Readings in White-Collar Crime*. New York: Oxford University Press.
Reasons, C., L. Ross, and C. Patterson. 1981. *Assault on the Worker: Occupational Health and Safety in Canada*. Toronto, ON: Butterworths.
Reiman, J. 2004. *The Rich Get Richer and the Poor Get Prison: Ideology, Class and Criminal Justice*, 5th edition. Boston, MA: Allyn and Bacon.
Rennie, R. 2005. "The Historical Origins of an Industrial Disaster: Occupational Health and Labour Relations at the Fluorspar Mines, St. Lawrence, Newfoundland, 1933–1945." *Labour/Le Travail*, 55: 107–142.
Schwartz, M., T. Dunfee, and M. Kline. 2005. "Tone at the Top: Ethics Code for Directors?" *Journal of Business Ethics*, 58: 79–100.
Sherman, L. 1974. "Becoming Bent: Moral Careers of Corrupt Policemen." In L.W. Sherman (ed.), *Police Corruption: A Sociological Perspective*. Garden City, NY: Anchor Books.
Shover, N., and J. Wright. 2001. *Crimes of Privilege: Readings in White-Collar Crime*. New York: Oxford University Press.
Simon, D. 1996. *Elite Deviance*, 5th edition. Boston, MA: Allyn and Bacon.
____. 2001. *Elite Deviance*, 7th edition. Boston, MA: Allyn and Bacon.
Snider, L. 2004. "Resisting Neo-Liberalism: The Poisoned Water Disaster in Walkerton, Ontario." *Social & Legal Studies*, 13, 2 (June): 265–289.
Sutherland, E. 1939. *Principles of Criminology*. Philadelphia, PA: Lippincott.

Chapter 9

RACIALIZATION, RACIAL PROFILING AND RACIALIZED POLICING

Elizabeth Comack

From: *Racialized Policing: Aboriginal People's Encounters with the Police*, pp. 23–26; 27–35; 56–65; 219–234 (reprinted with permission of the author).

RACIALIZATION AND POLICING

Attending to the notions of race and racism — and racialization, everyday racism and racial formation — sensitizes us to some of the dynamics involved in uncovering the complicated and complex ways in which these conditions have come to pervade the practice of policing in Canada. One of the key ways in which this issue has been examined is in the racial-profiling debate, especially as it has played out in Ontario in relation to the claim that police use race as a primary variable in their decisions to stop and search, arrest and charge people of colour. The offence known as "driving while Black" epitomizes these practices. While this debate has had the benefit of drawing attention to issues relating to racialized policing, the notion of racial profiling individualizes the problem. The idea slips too easily into arguments that rest on simplistic claims such as "police are racist bigots" or that the problem is one of "a few bad apples." Shifting the focus to racialized policing calls attention to the role of the police in the "reproduction of order" (Ericson

1982) — for instance, to how race and racism inform the cultural frames or stocks of knowledge adopted by police in their work. Moreover, in reproducing order, police work involves not just the policing of individuals but the policing of spaces. When police concentrate their attention and activity on spaces deemed to be "disorderly" and "dangerous," they contribute to the process of racialization and the construction of racial hierarchies. In short, "place becomes race" (Razack 2000, 2002). When we apply racialized policing to the matter of Aboriginal–police relations, we are led to investigate the role that it has played in the colonial project of constructing a white settler society.

Situating Aboriginal–police relations in a historical context involves challenging the "foundational narrative" of the nation's history to map out the role of policing in the colonial project of creating Canada as a white settler society. Specifically, the North West Mounted Police (NWMP) occupied a central role in managing and containing the Aboriginal population as white settlement advanced. Colonialism, however, has not disappeared but has taken on new forms in contemporary times. Poverty and social exclusion, violence and alcohol use, becoming tangled up in the net of the criminal justice system: these experiences have come to dominate the lives of too many Aboriginal people. Similar to the role played by the NWMP in the colonial project of creating the white settler society, contemporary police forces have been assigned a central role in the management and containment of Aboriginal peoples. As a consequence, relations between Aboriginal peoples and the police have been rife with conflict and controversy.

One event that has come to symbolize the strained relationship between Aboriginal peoples and the police is the shooting death of Aboriginal leader John Joseph Harper on a Winnipeg street in March 1988. Harper's tragic death became one of two incidents — the other being the murder of Helen Betty Osborne in The Pas, Manitoba in 1971 — that led to the establishment of the Aboriginal Justice Inquiry of Manitoba (AJI) in April 1989. The AJI was headed by Justice Alvin Hamilton and Judge Murray Sinclair. At the time, Hamilton was an associate chief justice of the Manitoba Court of Queen's Bench and Sinclair was a newly appointed associate chief justice of the provincial court who had the distinction of being the first Aboriginal judge to be appointed in Manitoba since Confederation.

Given its stated purpose of examining the relationship between Aboriginal peoples and the justice system in Manitoba, the AJI covered a broad scope. Intent on learning directly from Aboriginal peoples, the two commissioners visited over thirty-six Aboriginal communities (some of which were only accessible by air travel and winter roads) and held hearings in seven other Manitoba communities and five provincial jails. Some one thousand people made presentations at the community hearings. In addition, the inquiry conducted research projects on a range of subjects and commissioned a number of background papers. It also made trips to the United States to observe the operation of tribal courts there (Hamilton and Sinclair 1991a: 5–6).

The AJI released its two-volume report in the summer of 1991 (Hamilton and Sinclair 1991a, 1991b). The report stands as an indictment of the criminal justice system's treatment of Aboriginal people — in all of its stages. The commission's findings with respect to Harper's death and its aftermath, along with other sources, reveal the ways in which race and racism played out in the case.

More recently, the freezing deaths of three Aboriginal men — Neil Stonechild, Rodney Naistus and Lawrence Wegner — and the experience of Darrel Night in Saskatoon set off a tidal wave of controversy revolving around the issue of Starlight Tours: the police practice of picking up people and taking them to some remote location and dropping them off, leaving them to find their own way home. Aboriginal activists and organizations declared the practice to be evidence of the racism that was rampant on the Saskatoon police force. Meanwhile, the police and their supporters denied any wrong-doing and posited that Starlight Tours were a myth perpetrated by "special interest groups." Unfortunately, in the broader context of racialized policing, Starlight Tours may well have become normalized as a strategy that police use to reproduce order when dealing with troubled and troublesome people.

Saskatoon is not the only Prairie city in Canada where troubling relations between Aboriginal people and the police prevail. Manitoba's largest urban centre, Winnipeg, has garnered a reputation as crime- and violence-ridden, especially in its inner-city communities where levels of poverty are high and a large proportion of the province's Aboriginal people reside. Just as AJI commissioners Hamilton and Sinclair (1991a: 594) concluded two decades ago, reports of Aboriginal peoples about their experiences with police provide a collective narrative that documents "a problem of considerable magnitude." When interviewed, Aboriginal men report being regularly stopped by the police because they "fit the description." While Aboriginal men are assumed by police to be involved in the drug trade and/or affiliated with a street gang, Aboriginal women found in the racialized space of the inner city are regularly assumed to be involved in the street sex trade. Racialized frames contour police interactions with Aboriginal people. So too does the use of racist, sexist, and other forms of disrespectful language.

Just as concerning are the troublesome police practices reported by Aboriginal peoples. The improper uses of the drunk tank, beatings and physical violence in the form of the "phone book treatment," banishment and "red zoning," and Starlight Tours figure prominently in the interviews about encounters with police that I carried out with Aboriginal residents of Winnipeg's inner city. Not surprisingly, mistrust and animosity readily flow from such practices.

These forays into the historical and contemporary manifestations of Aboriginal peoples' experiences with the police provide the necessary context for an understanding of the death of Matthew Dumas in January 2005. The official version that emerged from the inquest into Dumas's death was premised on the claim that "race had nothing to do with this." Moving beyond the immediate event and bringing into view the broader dynamics of encounters between Aboriginal peoples and the police lead to the opposite conclusion. The issue is not simply about how the police behave, however problematic that may be on some occasions. Rather, the issue is much broader. It has to do with how race and racism are embedded in everyday experiences and institutional practices and implicated in our society's prevailing patterns of marginalization and social exclusion.

RACIAL PROFILING VERSUS RACIALIZED POLICING

Police encounters with racialized groups — especially members of the African-Canadian community in Toronto — have been a subject of considerable discussion and debate in recent years. African-Canadian residents of Toronto claim that police engage in discriminatory practices against members of their community. The form of discrimination known as "driving while Black" became the experience of Toronto Raptors basketball star, Dee Brown, who reported being pulled over by police in 1999 simply for being a Black man at the wheel of an expensive vehicle. Brown was arrested after blowing over the legal alcohol limit in a breath test. In his defence he argued that police had no reasonable cause for stopping his vehicle in the first place, and that his arrest was the result of racial profiling. A judge agreed with him. In April 2003, the Ontario Court of Appeal took judicial notice of the existence of racial profiling and ordered a new trial in the case. In its ruling, the court said: "Racial profiling provides its own motivation — a belief by a police officer that a person's colour, combined with other circumstances, makes him or her more likely to be involved in criminal activity" (cited in Makin 2003).

Other incidents involving police shootings of Black people and the alleged mistreatment of Black youth led members of the African-Canadian community in Ontario to argue: "We have two systems of justice within the criminal justice system. One is for the majority group in our society — people who have money, connections, etc. — and the other is for the racial minorities" (Commission on Systemic Racism in the Ontario Justice System 1998: 200). In response, government-sponsored task forces and inquiries, journalistic reporting and research by criminologists have all endeavoured to assess the issue of whether discrimination is perpetrated by the police in particular and the criminal justice system in general against Black people. Much of this focus has been on the issue of racial profiling; that is, the issue of whether police officers utilize race as a primary variable in their stop and search, arrest, and charging practices.

Racial profiling by police has received considerable attention in the United States (Harris 2002; Fridell et al. 2001) and Britain (Solomos 1988; Gilroy 1991; Holdaway 2003). When the issue finally emerged in Canada it was, in the words of William Closs and Paul McKenna (2006: 146), "explosive," generating lively debate. On the one side are those who maintain that racial profiling by police is indeed a practice that occurs (and with some regularity) among Black people, especially young males. On the other side are those who argue that the police have been falsely accused of racial profiling and that the evidence presented to support the charges is so unreliable that it constitutes "junk science."

While some scholars suggest that racial profiling by police has been proven to the point at which there is no need for any further discussion as to its existence (Tator and Henry 2006; Tanovich 2006), I propose that the focus of the debate produces a frame that is too narrow or confined for understanding the complex ways in which race and racialization play out in relation to policing. Instead, I argue that the notion of "racialized policing" broadens the focus to encompass the role of police in the wider society; specifically, as "reproducers of order." Poverty and social exclusion are logical outcomes of the way in which our society is organized. So too are related problems, such as certain forms of crime and violence. The police have been assigned the daunting task of responding to the "disorder" that results from these social conditions. In the process, policing itself has become a racial project. In surveilling the social spaces that police are assigned to govern, race and racialization are put into everyday policing practices as officers bring to bear the cultural frames of reference or stocks of knowledge that inform their work.

GOVERNMENT INQUIRIES

In the last few decades a number of government-initiated inquiries have investigated the issue of race and policing in Ontario. In 1988, for instance, in response to public protests spawned by the fatal police shooting of two Black men, the Solicitor General of Ontario appointed Clare Lewis as chair of the Race Relations and Policing Task Force. The task force's report, released in 1989, affirmed the perception of racialized groups: "They do not believe that they are policed fairly and they made a strong case for their view which cannot be ignored" (Ontario 1989: 14). The report, extremely critical of the state of race relations in Ontario, made fifty-seven recommendations for improvement, including the creation of the Special Investigations Unit (siu), initiatives aimed at increasing the representation of visible minorities in Ontario police services, improved community relations, and the collection of use of force statistics. As a result of this report, Ontario introduced a new Police Services Act in 1990. The Act represented a major overhaul in the approach to policing in the province.

The police killing of teenager Raymond Lawrence in May 1992 — which coincided with the acquittal of U.S. police officers in the beating of Rodney King, an event that had been captured on a civilian's video camera and sparked riots in Los Angeles — again generated public protests in Toronto and prompted the New Democratic Party government to take further action. Ontario Premier Bob Rae appointed a special adviser on race relations, Stephen Lewis, to develop a comprehensive action plan. After consulting extensively with African-Canadian and other racialized communities in the province, Lewis released a report in June 1992 that contained three key elements. First, the report recognized "the reality of systemic discrimination" as a pervasive feature of Ontario society. As Toni Williams (2001: 204) notes, "This recognition marked a departure from reliance on the language of 'multiculturalism' and 'race relations' to name and frame the experiences and concerns of people from racialized communities." Second, while Lewis acknowledged that other racialized groups were subject to systemic racism, his report identified Black people as especially vulnerable. According to Williams (2001: 205), "With this move, Lewis made it more difficult to marginalize black people's complaints about systemic racism by pitting their negative experiences against the allegedly more positive experiences, or perhaps more muted complaints, of people from other racialized communities." The third element of the Lewis report was to broaden the focus on policing to include a comprehensive investigation of the other stages of the criminal justice system (see Ontario 1992).

Some four months later the Ontario government established the Commission on Systemic Racism in the Ontario Criminal Justice System. The six-person inquiry had the mandate to examine the extent to which systemic racism affects the administration of justice in Ontario, with a specific focus on "anti-Black" racism (Ontario 1995). In carrying out its mandate, the Commission undertook an extensive program that involved consultations with community members and criminal justice professionals and research to examine the practices, procedures, and policies in three major components of the criminal justice system: the police, courts, and correctional institutions.

SYSTEMIC RACISM AND RACIALIZATION

The work of the Commission was framed by a particular construction of "systemic racism": as "patterns and practices ... which, although they may not be intended to disadvantage any group, can have the effect of disadvantaging or permitting discrimination against ... racial minorities" (Ontario 1995: Appendix A). In their report, the commissioners maintain that the starting point of their analysis of systemic racism is racialization. Acknowledging that the notion of race is itself an idea or a myth, they explain racialization as "the process by which societies construct races as real, different and unequal in ways that matter to economic, political and social life" (Ontario 1995: 40). The commissioners go on to note that racialization can be either explicit, official, and supported by law or an implicit and unofficial feature of a social system; either way, "The process of adopting and perpetuating racialization within these social systems constitutes systemic racism" (Ontario 1995: 56).

From the commissioners' standpoint, racialization is "instilled" into social systems by the personnel working within them. This action can take one of two forms: overt racism; and covert, subtle, or implicit racism. While overt racism involves acting in ways that are personally hostile towards members of racialized groups, the covert, subtle, or implicit brand does not involve specific racist motives or intentions but has the same effect. For instance, the use of racially abusive language can be motivated by a desire to intimidate or control (and not by racist beliefs per se), but will have the effect of reflecting "society's judgments about the superiority of white people and inferiority of others" (Ontario 1995: 47).

Racialization can also be inserted into systems "when the standards or criteria for making decisions reflect or permit bias against racialized people" (Ontario 1995: 50). These standards or criteria can be either formal and explicit in laws, policies, and procedures or informal, arising from accepted ways of doing things. Bias in one part of the system can affect other parts. In the case of the criminal justice system:

> Each stage of the process depends on choices made in other parts of the system. Judges, for example, can impose penalties only on people who come before them for sentencing. People who appear before judges are neither a comprehensive sample of Canadians who commit crimes, nor a random sample of offenders. Who appears before a judge for sentencing depends on earlier decisions of members of the public, police officers, lawyers, justices of the peace, and sometimes other judges. (Ontario 1995: 51)

In addition to personnel and decision-making criteria, the organization or delivery of services can also encourage racialization. As the commissioners note, if the personnel within the criminal justice system (police, lawyers, judges) are mainly white, but large proportions of accused persons are from Aboriginal, Black or other racialized communities, there may be a perception that the system supports racialization.

Finally, the commissioners state that systems manage personnel, decision making and service delivery through operating norms that include not only formal rules, procedures and policies but also informal rules that are "the often unspoken understandings about how the day-to-day work of the institution is conducted."

These operating norms contribute to "a complex and dynamic culture" that influences and is influenced by the individuals who work within the system. Operating norms may tolerate racialization in three different ways: passive toleration (lack of awareness of biases); disregard (awareness of racism but it is ignored); and collusive toleration (differential treatment is explicit and promoted by the system) (Ontario 1995: 54–56).

THE COMMISSION'S FINDINGS

The Commission released its 445-page report at the end of 1995. In their report the commissioners observed that, compared to white people, Black people stand a disproportionate chance of being charged and imprisoned in Ontario, and that this overrepresentation had skyrocketed within a period of six years, with 204 percent more Blacks jailed in 1994 than in 1986 (from 4,205 to 12,765 admissions), compared to an increase of 23 percent for whites (from 49,555 to 60,929 admissions) (Ontario 1995). Based on a survey of the general population, the Commission found a widespread perception among Black (58 percent), Chinese (31 percent) and white (36 percent) Torontonians that judges do not treat Black people the same as white people (Ontario 1995: i). While many judges and lawyers interviewed flatly rejected the possibility that systemic racism was a problem in the Ontario criminal justice system, others acknowledged differential treatment based on race as well as class or poverty: "Four in ten defence counsel (40%) and three in ten (33%) provincial division judges appointed since 1989 perceived differential treatment of white and racial minority people in the criminal justice system" (Ontario 1995: i–ii).

Police Stops: Use of Discretionary Power

With regard to the police, a survey of 1,657 Metropolitan Toronto residents about their experiences of being stopped by police in the previous two years found that more Black (28 percent) than white (18 percent) or Chinese (15 percent) residents reported being stopped by the police in the last two years (Ontario 1995: 352). More Black (17 percent) than white (8 percent) or Chinese (5 percent) residents reported being stopped more than once in the past two years. Many more Black respondents (39 percent) than white (9 percent) or Chinese (14 percent) respondents believed that the officers who stopped them did not treat them fairly (Ontario 1995: 352).

When broken down by sex and race, the data showed that Black men were particularly vulnerable to being stopped by police. About 43 percent of Black male respondents, but only 25 percent of white male and 19 percent of Chinese male respondents, reported being stopped by the police in the past two years. Also, significantly more Black (29 percent) than white (12 percent) or Chinese

(5 percent) men reported being stopped by the police two or more times in the past two years (Ontario 1995: 352).

Analysis of the male sample by age as well as race revealed distinctive patterns. Among men aged eighteen to twenty-four, Black (50 percent) and white (48 percent) men were equally likely to report being stopped by police in the past two years, while Chinese men (22 percent) were less likely to report being stopped. However, Black men (50 percent) aged eighteen to twenty-four were much more likely than both their white (24 percent) and Chinese (11 percent) counterparts to report two or more stops in the past two years. Every Black man aged eighteen to twenty-four who reported being stopped by the police said he was stopped more than once. By contrast, about half of the white or Chinese men in this age group who reported being stopped had experienced tat act on more than one occasion (Ontario 1995: 355). Similar patterns existed for older age groups, with Black men being most likely to have experienced a police stop in the past two years.

When the data on police stops were analyzed in a subsample of male university graduates, Black males (48 percent) with a university degree were much more likely than white (19 percent) or Chinese (11 percent) male university graduates to report being stopped by the police in the past two years. Black male graduates (39 percent) were also much more likely than white (11 percent) or Chinese (7 percent) male graduates to report two or more stops (Ontario 1995: 355).

Perceived Fairness of Police Stops
The Commission's report also noted that many of the Black respondents strongly believed that police stopped them partly or wholly because of their race. Reflecting the notion that police target African Canadians simply for "driving while Black," some of these respondents believed that they were stopped because they were driving an expensive car. One respondent, for example, said that police stopped him "because they saw a Lexus with a black driver. We were not speeding or anything. They had no real reason to stop us." Others believed that police suspected them of selling drugs. One man said he was stopped because "if you are black and you drive something good, the police pull you over to ask about drugs." In some cases, respondents believed they were stopped because they were accompanied by a white woman. Interestingly, some white people mentioned race as the reason for the police stopping them, but it was the race of their companion that was the factor. One young white male said that he was stopped "because my friend was driving my Mercedes and he's black" (Ontario 1995: 356).

In interpreting these findings, the commissioners rejected the individualistic explanation that "all Metro Toronto Police officers are overt racists who consciously stop black people simply because they are black" (Ontario 1995: 357). If that were indeed the case, according to the commissioners, then one would expect more Black people — including women — to report police stops and the differential between Black and white respondents to be much higher. As the commissioners noted, "The racial difference in the number and perception of reported stops suggests that the cause is not 'a few bad apples' among the police" (Ontario 1995: 357; see also Tator and Henry 2006). Rather, they suggest that racialized characteristics, especially those of Black people, in combination with other factors — such as sex (male), age (youth), make and condition of a vehicle (if driving), location, dress and perceived lifestyle — provoke police suspicion. One of the outcomes of this racialization, according to the commissioners, is that "these stops (particularly if unpleasant and also if frequent) breed distrust and suspicion of the police among black and other racialized people" (Ontario 1995: 358). In sum, the commissioners concluded:

> Systemic racism, the social process that produces racial inequality in how people are treated, is at work in the Ontario criminal justice system. Commission findings leave no doubt that the system is experienced as unfair by racialized people and, at key points in the administration of justice, the exercise of discretion has a harsher impact on black than white people. The conclusion is inescapable: the criminal justice system tolerates racialization in its practices. (Ontario 1995: 106)

The Exercise of Discretionary Power

While the Commission should be credited for its efforts to address the systemic nature of racism in the criminal justice system, much of the research undertaken for the Commission — particularly with regard to the police — focused on the exercise of discretionary power. This individualized focus derived very much from the commissioners' view that "system personnel [are] the means by which a social system applies and transmits racialization" (Ontario 1995: 56).

In this regard, Williams (2001) notes that the Commission succeeded in producing "formal knowledge of how discretionary power may be abused in ways that produce racial inequality, and it showed how the abuse of power may become embedded in routine practices." Nevertheless, she also suggests that the difficulty with the empirical studies carried out for the Commission is that they were founded on a "formal equality model" that relies on demonstrating differential treatment by focusing on the outcomes of discretionary power and the practices of those who exercise it. In the process, this approach explains systemic racism in terms of attitudes, beliefs, and assumptions that decision-makers hold (either explicitly or subconsciously), and it sees solutions to the problem as resting in education and consciousness-raising — as opposed to necessitating more substantive, systemic change. Williams also makes the point that, given broader observations that law enforcement processes treat most people badly, realizing formal equality — that is, treating all individuals alike, regardless of their race — may not be the desired end: "To put the point bluntly, equality may be a hollow goal if it means nothing more than a criminal justice system that (mis)treats poor black people no worse than it (mis)treats poor white people" (Williams 2001: 213).

This tendency to focus on the use of discretionary power by criminal justice personnel became even more pronounced in debates generated by a series of *Toronto Star* articles alleging racial profiling of Black people by the Toronto police.

FROM RACIAL PROFILING TO RACIALIZED POLICING

Encounters between racialized groups and the police in Ontario, then, have often been framed within the context of racial profiling. Moreover, much of the focus of the racial profiling debate has concentrated on the "driving while Black" practice — on the police decision to stop and search racialized individuals.

The issue of "driving while Black" has been raised in other provinces. On June 4, 2008, Robert Wilson, a 35-year-old African-Canadian minister and rapper known as "Fresh I.E.," was in his Chrysler 300 with a passenger — a Black youth protégé he mentors — and used a Starbucks drive-through to get a coffee. Apparently, he forgot part of this order and returned for a second time. That was when an officer, spotting him, became suspicious and decided to run a licence plate check. Either the wrong licence plate was entered or the results from the check were misinterpreted; the result was that the vehicle was reported as stolen.

Several police cruisers converged on Wilson's car, boxing it in at a red-light intersection. Approaching the vehicle with weapons drawn, police removed Wilson and his passenger from the car. The officers forced Wilson to the ground, emptied his pockets, handcuffed him and placed him in the back of a police cruiser. Meanwhile Wilson was telling them that he owned the vehicle. The officers apparently laughed at him when he told them he was a minister. Some fifteen minutes elapsed before the officers checked Wilson's identification and found that he was, in fact, the registered owner of the vehicle. Wilson and his young passenger were released and the officers offered an apology.

Feeling humiliated and wronged by the incident, Wilson reported it to the media. The following day, in response, Winnipeg Police Chief Keith McCaskill issued a statement admitting that his officers had made a mistake. Still, the Police Chief was adamant that the incident was not a case of racial profiling, but rather of "human error." Although Wilson accepted the apology he maintained that racism was the underlying issue. This was not the first time that he had been targeted by police. In the previous year, he had been stopped by police officers five times. Wilson said he was making his story public in an attempt to "let the public know that this is happening" and "to be a voice for people who regularly experience racial stereotyping" (CBC News 2008a).

The decision by police to define an expensive vehicle with two Black occupants as "suspicious" raises concerns about the police practice of profiling. Nevertheless, the practice is only part of the puzzle of racialized groups' encounters with police. While some writers have maintained that racial profiling is "another word for racism or racialization" (Tator and Henry 2006: 8) and "a manifestation of systemic racism" (Tanovich 2003–4), the use of the term has a decidedly individualized focus; specifically, on the exercise of discretion by individual police officers. What is missing is the need to set the issue within the broader dynamics involved in the encounters between racialized groups and the police as an institution. "Racialized policing" implicates that broader context.

Policing and police work do not occur in a social vacuum. Given that race and racialization — defined earlier as the production of difference, the process of constructing racial categories, identities, and meanings — exist in the wider society, it is unreasonable to presume that the practice of policing will be an exception. We need to uncover, therefore, the ways in which race and racialization are implicated in what Holdaway (1997: 384) calls the "mundane processes and related ideas that are part of organizational life." To do so involves situating policing within its broader societal context.

Drawing upon the work of Richard Ericson (1982), I argue that a primary purpose of policing is the "reproduction of order." Moreover, given the existing dynamics of race and racialization, the "order" that the police are charged with reproducing is decidedly "raced" (as well as gendered and classed). It is in the process of surveilling the social spaces that they are assigned to govern that race and racialization are put into everyday policing practices as officers bring to bear the cultural frames of reference or stocks of knowledge that inform their work.

Policing and the Reproduction of Order

In both the public imagination and official discourse, the images of police as "crime fighters" and "law enforcers" dominate. Media portrayals (such as the popular television shows *Cops* and *Law and Order*) regularly feature these images. Police departments use them to justify more personnel, more equipment, and more enabling legislation. In the minds of most police officers, "real" police work is crime work, a view that is also endorsed by their organizations. In commenting on police culture, Eugene Paoline (2003: 202) states, "Traditionally, police training, the creation of specialized divisions, the focus on crime statistics, and most importantly, performance evaluation and promotion, all reinforce the law enforcement orientation."

Of the different positions within a modern police department, patrol work is "by far the biggest assignment in policing" (Bayley 2005: 141). Police officers, working alone or in pairs, and either in cruisers or on foot (and sometimes bicycles), patrol the various districts of an urban area. In his survey of twenty-eight police forces in five different countries, David Bayley found that 65 percent of officers in the United States are assigned to patrol work, with 64 percent in Canada, 56 percent in England and Wales, 54 percent in Australia, and 40 percent in Japan. Much of this work is in response to calls from the public because "over 90 per cent of the work of patrol officers is generated by dispatch" (Bayley 2005: 141, 142). While patrol work makes up the bulk of policing assignments, other tasks include criminal investigation, regulation of motor vehicle traffic and administration. Among the modern police departments that Bayley studied, "About 60 per cent of police personnel patrol and respond to requests for service, 15 per cent investigate crime, 9 per cent regulate traffic and 9 per cent administer" (2005: 148).

Although police officers may view fighting crime as their main purpose, research reveals that very little of the work of patrol officers has to do with crime. In Britain and the United States, as Bayley (2005: 142) shows, only a small percentage of calls to the police — somewhere between 15 and 20 percent — are about crime; and often police who respond to initial reports of crime do not find that a crime has been committed. As Bayley concludes, "The real proportion of requests to the police that involve crime" may be somewhere in the range of 7 to 10 percent. Patrol officers spend little time on making arrests, and most of the crime that they deal with is minor in nature. As John Sewell (2010: 10) notes, "The average Canadian police officer can expect to make seven or eight criminal arrests a year, or one arrest every six or seven weeks. The majority of these crimes involve property, not violence to a person."

Nevertheless, Egon Bittner (2005) maintains that arrest statistics are a poor indicator of the nature of police work. He also takes issue with the view that police officers are simply engaged in the rote application of law. Police, according to Bittner, are not mere "functionaries of the law." They do not simply "walk around, respond to service demands, or intervene in situations, with the provisions of the penal code in mind, matching what they see with some title or another, and deciding whether any particular apparent infraction is serious enough to warrant being referred for further process." While police on occasion do simply apply the appropriate law to a situation, "in their routine work," Bittner says, they are usually using the provisions of the law "as a means for attaining other objectives" (2005: 158). In a similar vein, Ericson suggests that police use the law according to the other forms of social control that are available and can be used effectively.

For the patrol police, this is particularly the case in interpersonal disputes and problems of public order and decorum. When all else fails or is deemed likely to fail, the officer decides he must remove one party in the conflict from the situation, and consequently he arrests someone. A specific infraction with a clearly applicable law does not determine the arrest, but rather *the law is used to make the arrest to handle the situation.* (Ericson 1982: 14; emphasis added)

If, as research has shown, very little of the activity of police patrol work involves fighting crime, and if police are not simply law enforcers or mere "functionaries of the law" in the work they undertake, then what *is* their main purpose?

Given that police regularly make house calls and are available around the clock, they are called upon to attend to all manner of social problems and issues. Research findings suggest that police are more likely to be engaged in "social work" than in crime-fighting or law-enforcement activities; these findings have been taken as evidence that the nature of police work needs to be re-envisioned to better reflect the reality of the police role in contemporary societies. Bittner (2005: 165) argues that equating the work of police officers with that of other social service providers is a mistake because "the service they perform involves the exercise of a unique competence they do not share with anyone else in society." As Bittner notes, police are typically attuned to respond to circumstances that involve "something-that-ought-not-to-be-happening-and-about-which-someone-had-better-do-something-now!" In particular, what separates the police from other service providers is that their work "consists of coping with problems in which force *may have to be used*" (2005: 165). Indeed, as Philip Stenning and his colleagues (2009: 98) remind us, "Police organizations are not commonly called 'police *forces*' for no reason." While police departments may vary in the styles of policing they adopt — including the more recent turn to a community policing model (see, for example, Fielding 1995, 2005; Rosenbaum 1994; and Chaco and Nancoo 1993) — what ultimately distinguishes the police as an organization is the authority to use force.

But to what end is this authority to use force directed? In his now classic study, Ericson develops the argument that "patrol police are essentially a vehicle in the 'reproduction of order.'" Their mandate is "to transform troublesome, fragile situations back into a normal or efficient state whereby the ranks in society are preserved." But as Ericson clarifies, "It is not the mandate of the police to produce a 'new' order." Rather, "their sense of order and the order they seek to reproduce are that of the status quo." As well, Ericson specifies: "The term 'reproduction' implies that order is not simply transmitted in an unproblematic manner but is worked at through processes of conflict, negotiation, and subjection" (1982: 7).

Ericson's formulation has relevance for situating policing within the context of race and racialization, that is, as racialized policing. While the order that police are assigned to reproduce will differ in certain historical periods and between societies, it will nonetheless be an order *of a particular kind*. In other words, the very order that police are consigned to reproduce can be a racialized one. Drawing on Omni and Winant's (1994) notion of racial formation, with its focus on how racial projects work to produce race at the level of cultural representation (that is, as a descriptor of group or individual identity, social issues, and experience) and on how particular institutional arrangements are organized along racial lines, racialized policing can be said to constitute one of the projects through which race is interpreted and given meaning and the means by which the racialized order of a society is reproduced.

But this notion of racialized policing requires more texture. How is race interpreted and given meaning in the everyday, routine practices of policing? Stated differently, what are the cultural frames of reference or stocks of knowledge that police draw upon in the reproduction of a racialized order?

The Culture of Policing

Within the vast literature on policing, the most common way of analyzing police work has been through the lens of "police culture." In this view police work is typically seen as an occupation that, like other occupational groups, has developed a cultural repertoire of formal and informal rules and shared beliefs about how the work of the organization is to be done. It is through the process of socialization into this occupational culture that new recruits are said to learn the elements of the job. As Paoline (2003: 199) notes, however, "If one were to ask about the nature of police culture, one would find that there are many different definitions and interpretations." Paul Manning (1989: 360), for instance, defines police culture as the "accepted practices, rules, and principles of conduct that are situationally applied, and generalized rationales and beliefs." Robert Reiner (1992) equates police culture with the values, norms, perspectives and craft rules that inform police conduct. Despite these variations, the emphasis is on how the work environment of policing produces the distinctive world view of the police officer.

In his classic book *Justice without Trial*, Jerome Skolnick (1975) referred to this world view as the "policeman's working personality." Skolnick (1975: 42) suggested, "The police, as a result of combined features of their social situation, tend to develop ways of looking at the world distinctive to themselves." He saw the police officer's working personality as contoured by two elements associated with the job: danger and authority. While the element of danger makes an officer especially attentive to signs indicating a potential for violence and law-breaking, the element of authority separates the officer from the civilian world. Together, these elements create social isolation, and a corresponding social solidarity among officers.

While police work may involve a distinctive world view, police culture is not "monolithic, universal nor unchanging" (Reiner 1992: 109). Given the hierarchical structure of police organizations, differences will exist — for example, between "street cop" culture and "management cop" culture. As well, officers are not simply "passive or manipulated learners" of police culture (Chan 1996: 111). In attending to these issues, Clifford Shearing and Richard Ericson argue that rather than simply being socialized into and guided by the rules of the police culture, officers are active participants in the construction of the culture in their everyday practices through the constant telling of police stories:

> In their street talk police officers use stories to represent to each other the way things are, not as statements of fact but as cognitive devices used to gain practical insight into how to do the job of policing. For them the appropriate criteria for evaluating stories is not their truth value in a scientific sense but rather whether the knowledge they capture "works." Such stories, be they told in words or in action or via spectacles, capture the sedimented residue of generations of police experience and convey it in a form that police officers can capture and use to construct their actions on an ongoing basis. (Shearing and Ericson 1991: 491–492)

For Shearing and Ericson, then, police culture is more akin to a storybook than a rule book, "a tool kit used in the production of order." These stories enable police officers to make decisions "on a moment-to-moment basis, often without a moment's reflection." They provide a way of seeing by constructing a "vocabulary of precedents" that officers use in their daily work. "Like biblical parables and legends police stories provide directions for being a police officer, guidance as to how officers should experience the world if they are to act as police officers within it" (1991: 485, 487, 490, 491).

Holdaway (1997) notes that while race is not a discrete category in the culture of policing, mundane features of the rank-and-file occupational culture operate to sustain processes of racialization. In this respect, one way in which race invades the culture of policing is in relation to the ever-present concern with danger. While much of police work may be mind-numbingly monotonous, as police spend considerable time waiting around for "something-that-ought-not-to-be-happening" to occur, the *potential* for danger or for violence to break out is always present. As Bittner (2005) notes, in determining whether a situation is, in fact, one where "someone-had-better-do-something," police officers draw upon their stock of knowledge — their storybook — about particular persons, places and past events. Skolnick (1975: 45) suggests that police officers develop "a perpetual shorthand to identify certain kinds of people as symbolic assailants, that is, as persons who use gesture, language, and attire that the policeman has come to recognize as a prelude to violence." Because of the ever-present threat of danger, then, police officers develop a heightened sensitivity towards those individuals who they consider to be the "usual suspects," opening the way to form judgments about, say, particular racialized groups. Skolnick (1975), for instance, found that police officers in the U.S. city he studied came to identify the Black man with danger.

In the same way that racialization enters into constructions of "usual suspects," however, it also informs constructions about particular places and spaces.

Racialized Spaces

Sherene Razack (2002) and her colleagues have explored how "place becomes race," that is, "how the constitution of spaces reproduces racial hierarchies" (Razack 2007: 74). Contrary to familiar, everyday notions, spaces do not simply "evolve, are filled up with things, and exist either prior to or separate from the subjects who imagine and use them" (2007: 76). Rather, spaces are abidingly *social*. They have not only a materiality in that they connect to the social relations that produce and use them but also a symbolic meaning attached to them. Spaces can variously come to represent places of home, work, or leisure, sites of comfort and the familiar, or places of danger and disorder. Together, the material and the symbolic "work through each other to constitute a space" (2007: 77). From this standpoint, racialization processes can be directly experienced as spatial:

> When police drop Aboriginal people outside the city limits leaving them to freeze to death, or stop young Black men on the streets or in malls, when the eyes of shop clerks follow bodies of colour, presuming them to be illicit, when workplaces remain relentlessly white in the better paid jobs and fully "coloured" at the lower levels, when affluent areas of the city are all white and poorer areas are mostly of colour, we experience the spatiality of the racial order in which we live. (Razack 2007: 75–76)

As such, it is through everyday routines and experiences that space "comes to perform something in the social order, permitting certain actions and prohibiting others. Spatial practices organize social life in specific ways" (2007: 77).

In reporting on his study of the encounters between Black youth and police in six Ontario cities, Carl James commented on the importance of "the street" as a social space for marginalized youth:

> The streets serve many purposes. For the car owner or drivers, the street may be the "public" asphalted path used to drive from one place to another and/or a place to park one's vehicle. For pedestrians, particularly those with no alternatives, the street, or more specifically, the sidewalk, is much more. It is a public path to move about, get from one place to another, and a social space; probably the most available, accessible and relatively non-restrictive social space in which to meet, "hang out," and converse. For some "street users," particularly young, working-class apartment dwellers, because of their limited access and opportunities to alternative leisure and recreational spaces, the sidewalk, the street, the street corner and the mall become an integral part of daily living and a part of cultural life. (James 1998: 162)

Nevertheless, while "the street" constitutes a meaningful part of everyday life for many marginalized youth, their presence and visibility in that space make them ready targets for heightened police surveillance and intervention. From a police perspective, youth who congregate on the streets are considered to be "doing nothing" or "up to no good." As a result, they are regularly stopped and questioned. Many of the Black youth that James interviewed reported that these regular stops emanated from the notion that "all Blacks look alike" (1998: 167). According to James, "In policing Black youth — stopping, questioning and harassing them, and placing the onus on them to prove that they are not the 'suspects' that police seek — law enforcement agents engage in a process of othering which in turn contributes to their criminalization of the youth" (1998: 172).

In reproducing order, then, police work involves not just the policing of individuals but the policing of spaces. Over time, certain spaces come to be identified as places in which crime and violence are most likely to occur. For instance, inner-city communities populated by impoverished Aboriginal people and new immigrants are more likely to be seen as "disordered" and "dangerous" places, whereas suburban white middle-class neighbourhoods — with their tree-lined streets, manicured lawns and spacious homes — become spaces of "civility" and "respectability." In carrying out their task as reproducers of order, then, police concentrate their attention and activity on the former and not on the latter racialized spaces. In the process, they help to constitute and normalize particular spaces — and the people found within them — as "disorderly" and "dangerous."

MOVING FORWARD

Racial profiling has been a contentious issue in Ontario over the past two decades. While attention to the phenomenon does expose some of the ways in which race and racialization enter into the encounters between racialized individuals and police officers, we need to broaden our focus beyond the interpersonal level to include the ways in which race and racism play out in institutional practices and systemic processes. The notion of racialized policing does that. It offers the potential to move us away from arguments that rest on simplistic claims that "police are racist bigots" or the problem is one of "a few bad apples" and enables a better appreciation of the complexity of the matter of encounters between racialized groups and the police.

The debates, government inquiries and criminological research on the issue of racial profiling have focused mainly on the experiences of African Canadians. One notable exception, however, is the report of the Ontario Human Rights Commission (2003), which did include a special section on the impact of racial profiling on the Aboriginal community. As the Commission acknowledged, "Aboriginal peoples in Canada occupy different political, historical and individual realities from other Canadians" (OHRC 2003: 55). Aboriginal peoples are not just another "minority group" or "ethnic group," and characterizing them that way fails to take into account the special place they occupy in the nation's history as the original peoples of the land. The historical treatment of Aboriginal peoples, including their encounters with police, is also unique and has played an important role in the colonial project that is Canada.

RACIALIZED POLICING AND REPRODUCING ORDER

"Crime control is an impossible task for the police alone," Richard Ericson (1982: 11) writes. "They are expected to handle a phenomenon caused by social, political, economic, and cultural forces beyond their control and have to give the *appearance* that things are (more or less) under control."

Indeed, this "impossible task" of responding to a problem has its source in a much broader context, and that context has a historical dimension. Contemporary Aboriginal–police relations are rooted in the colonial relation between the original inhabitants of the land now called Canada and the role occupied by the NWMP in managing and containing the Aboriginal population as the emerging settler society took shape. But the unequal power relations between the colonizers and the colonized continue into the present.

In contemporary times colonialism is evidenced by the desperate living conditions in many First Nations communities, where basic necessities such as potable drinking water and adequate housing have taken on the status of a luxury that seems out of reach for too many Aboriginal families. It is also evidenced by the racialized poverty and a culture of despair that characterizes life in inner-city communities, especially in the Prairie provinces, where well-paid jobs are scarce and young Aboriginal men have a greater likelihood of ending up in jail than they do of finishing high school.

It is within this colonial context that police are assigned to do their job — a challenging job that involves much "dirty work" as officers are called upon to deal with all manner of troubles, including people who are in crisis, hurt, sick, intoxicated, angry and sometimes violent. While crime control has become the leitmotif of modern policing, with the dominating public image of police officers as "crime fighters" and "law enforcers" out to "get the bad guys," at its core policing involves the reproduction of order, the transforming of troublesome situations back to their "normal" state — and the management and containment of troublesome persons — thus preserving the ranks of society. When the social order that the police are reproducing is founded on racism and racial inequality (and other forms of social inequality), policing becomes one of the projects through which race is interpreted and given meaning. It becomes a means by which the racialized order of society is reproduced. In short, policing itself becomes racialized.

While racialized policing emanates from the "impossible task" assigned to police, it also stems from the character of policing itself — for instance, in the cultural frames or stocks of knowledge that police officers draw upon in their everyday work. When particular persons come to be viewed as the "usual suspects," and particular places come to be viewed as spaces of danger and disorder, these frames or stocks of knowledge inform police encounters with Aboriginal peoples. In the racialized space of the inner city, young Aboriginal men are regularly stopped because they "fit the description," while Aboriginal women are assumed to be involved in the street sex trade. Over time, mistrust and animosity grow, especially as police adopt troublesome practices of their own as a way of dealing with troubled and troublesome people.

THE DENIAL OF A FUNDAMENTAL PROBLEM

Making the claim that policing is racialized is sure to generate controversy and opposition. After all, Aboriginal peoples who make public their negative experiences with police, such as in the Saskatoon case of Darrel Night, are readily cast as being unbelievable. As well, Aboriginal organizations and their spokespeople are regularly accused of "playing the race card" to advance their own political agenda when they name racism (see Comack and Bowness 2010). Journalists who write about the issue are chastised for engaging in "political correctness," and criminal justice officials who take action on incidents of racialized policing are criticized for being "too soft on crime" or acceding to the demands of "special interest groups" (McLean 2006). The efforts to address what many perceive to be a fundamental problem with relations between Aboriginal people and the police, then, are more often than not met with denials of the problem even existing.

The police participate in this discourse of denial. When the *Toronto Star* published its findings regarding racial profiling, the Toronto chief of police responded by asserting, "We don't do racial profiling" (Rankin et al. 2002), and the Toronto Police Association launched a $2.7-billion lawsuit against the newspaper for publishing its results. In a similar vein, a few years ago I worked on a project that involved interviews with police officers about safety and security in Winnipeg's inner-city communities (Comack and Silver 2006, 2008). As part of that project I interviewed Chief of Police Jack Ewatski. At one point in the interview I asked him about something that Aboriginal people were saying: that their young people were being targeted by police and they were often treated roughly and disrespectfully by police officers. The police chief suggested that this perception did not match up with reality. He went so far as to say that this standpoint constituted "urban lore":

> I am not going to deny the fact that there have been times that police have treated people in a manner that is not acceptable, and when those incidents occur we deal with them, and if we could prove that that is actually

the case, that that has happened, then those officers are sanctioned; there's consequences to their actions, too. But I'm also aware of some of the urban lore out there and some of the things of, well, "I heard from a friend of a friend who said that the police came by, beat me up for no reason, and then just dropped me off somewhere." Well, how real is that?

Despite the police chief's denial discourse, Aboriginal peoples report that racist, sexist and disrespectful language, physical violence and assaults, and drop-offs and Starlight Tours occur frequently and regularly in their encounters with police — too much so to be disregarded as "myths" or "urban lore."

Similarly, legal professionals and academics who dismiss accounts by Aboriginal people and other racialized groups about their encounters with police as "mere anecdotes" (Gold 2003; Gabor 2004) contribute to this denial discourse. Instead, they privilege official versions and quantitative methodologies as being more valid than qualitative research aimed at gathering individual stories. Nevertheless, as Carol Tator and Frances Henry (2006: 117) comment: "The stories people tell about their lived experiences are more than mere individual communications; they are embedded in a cultural and ideological context. These stories reflect their existing social relations; and while many stories reflect an individual's experiences, taken together they reveal cultural assumptions that transcend the individual."

In his book, *The Truth about Stories: A Native Narrative*, Thomas King (2003: 9) writes, "Stories are wondrous things. And they are dangerous." King is reminding us that the stories Aboriginal peoples tell of their experiences with the police have the power to inform and transform — so long as we are prepared to *listen to* and *hear* what is being said.

Despite the controversy and opposition surrounding the issue, both the argument and the evidence for how race and racism pervade the practice of policing have been mounted many times before. The Ontario Commission on Systemic Racism in the Criminal Justice System (Ontario 1995: 106) concluded that "systemic racism, the social process that produces racial inequality in how people are treated, is at work in the Ontario criminal justice system … The criminal justice system tolerates racialization in its practices." The Ontario Human Rights Commission (2003) found that the experience of being racially profiled by police has become routine for people of colour, and the impact of that experience has been profound, with an impact not only on people's trust of police but also on their everyday activities. In its investigation of the shooting death of J.J. Harper, the Aboriginal Justice Inquiry of Manitoba concluded, "Racism exists within the Winnipeg Police Department" (Hamilton and Sinclair 1991b: 93). Similarly, the Royal Commission on the Donald Marshall, Jr. Prosecution deemed racism to be at work in the Sydney, Nova Scotia, police force, and that it was spawned from the "general sense in Sydney's White community at the time that Indians were not 'worth' as much as Whites" (Nova Scotia 1989: 3).

Government-sponsored commissions and inquiries have named the racism in the criminal justice system. They have also been severely critical of police forces for their failure to mount proper investigations when cases of police mistreatment of Aboriginal peoples come to light. We have seen evidence of this in case after case. AJI commissioners Hamilton and Sinclair deemed the investigation by the Winnipeg Police Department into the death of Harper to be "at best, inadequate. At worst, its primary objective seems to have been to exonerate Const. Robert Cross and to vindicate the Winnipeg Police Department" (1991b: 113). The Royal Commission on the Donald Marshall, Jr. Prosecution called the police investigation into the death of Sandy Seale "entirely inadequate, incompetent and unprofessional" (Nova Scotia 1989: 3). Justice Wright found the police investigation into Neil Stonechild's death to be "insufficient and totally inadequate." According to the commissioner, "the deficiencies in the investigation go beyond incompetence or neglect. They were inexcusable" (Wright 2004: 212, 103). Similarly, Justice Davies was heavily critical of the Vancouver Police Department's treatment of Frank Paul, describing the police investigation into the matter as "fundamentally flawed" (Davies 2008: 18).

Despite the combined weight of all of these pronouncements by government-sponsored commissions and inquiries, the fundamental problem of Aboriginal–police relations persists. At the very least, one would expect public outrage — and not denial — when cases involving racialized policing come to light. But it seems that mainstream society is content to assign the job of ensuring its safety and security to the police. Carsten Stroud (1983: 228) commented years ago on the increasing tendency of society to transfer responsibility for managing social problems to professionals such as the police:

Canadians seem to be increasingly ready to abdicate personal responsibility, to place the burden of society's problems on "professional" shoulders. We leave our grandparents in nursing homes, we let the poor fall into welfare nets, we create "commissions" and "review boards" and "agencies" to do the things any thinking person once felt ethically obliged to take care of personally. And we surrendered the responsibility for our safety and security of our families to the police forces. Having done so, we [that is, those of us with privilege] slapped our collective hands together and walked off to enjoy our peace as something bought and paid for. The fact that the policeman can't do the job alone seems to be viewed as a breach of contract.

In the neo-liberal climate, calls to "get tough" on crime carry the promise of a quick and ready solution to the problems brought on by the increasing divide between rich and poor and the social unease and anxiety these problems generate. Implicit in the public support garnered for these "get-tough" strategies is the assumption that they will *not* be directed at "Us" — the "ordinary citizen" — but only at "Them" — those deemed to be "trouble." So, if police require enhanced powers to arrest, detain, or otherwise control the criminalized "other," then so be it. If zero-tolerance policing leads to more aggressive tactics to manage squeegee kids, welfare recipients, street-gang members, or other "troublesome" members of society, then so be it. If these strategies extend to include whole communities populated by Aboriginal peoples and other racialized groups, then so be it. In these terms, the order that the police are reproducing is a racialized order that privileges certain groups over others.

Expecting that police will do this dirty work enables the continued denial of the fundamental problem of racism and ostensibly absolves the rest of us from social responsibility. But this denial comes at considerable cost. As Joyce Green (2006: 158) notes: "While racism is most violently experienced by Aboriginal people, it also mains the humanity and civility of those who perpetuate it, deny it or ignore it. Racism injures the capacity of the body politic to work collaboratively toward common visions." Surely, as Green points out, if all of us who live in this country are ever to realize the necessary sense of social cohesion that will sustain our everyday lives and growth, we must confront and eliminate racism in its every form and every instance.

WHAT IS TO BE DONE?

One strategy for responding to this fundamental problem of Aboriginal–police relations is to encourage Aboriginal people to make formal complaints about their treatment by police. In Manitoba, complaints can be made to the Law Enforcement Review Agency (LERA), created in 1985 under the authority of the Law Enforcement Review Act. According to the Act, any person "who feels aggrieved by a disciplinary default allegedly committed by any member of a police department may file a complaint" with LERA (cited in Hamilton and Sinclair 1991a: 629). However, data provided by LERA suggests that these complaints are not likely to proceed very far. In 2010, for instance, 274 investigations were conducted involving police officers in the province — down from 321 investigations in 2009, 367 in 2008, 422 in 2007, and 560 in 2006. The Winnipeg Police Service accounted for 83 percent of the complaints received in 2010. Processing these cases can be a lengthy undertaking. Of the 274 investigations started in 2010, 103 (37.5 percent) were still ongoing at the end of the year. Of the 171 completed investigations, the vast majority were either dismissed by the commissioner as not supported by sufficient evidence to support a hearing (57 percent) or abandoned or withdrawn by the complainant (32 percent). According to LERA, "In many cases, when a LERA investigator is unable to locate the complainant, a letter is sent to the complainant's last known address asking the complainant to contact the investigator. If contact is not made within 30 days, the complaint is considered abandoned and a registered letter is sent to that effect" (LERA n.d.: 29). Of the remaining complaints, the commissioner dismissed seven cases (4 percent) as being outside the scope of the Act and one case (.5 percent) as frivolous or vexatious; one case (.5 percent) was resolved informally, and eleven cases (6 percent) resulted in a public hearing before a provincial court judge.

None of the seventy-eight inner-city residents in Winnipeg who we interviewed about their experiences with police had been successful in launching a LERA complaint. Many of those interviewed believed that there was no point in lodging a formal complaint. As one woman remarked, "You could try, you could do it, but you're not going to get anywhere because you're fighting a whole system." When we asked people why they chose not to report an incident, a typical response was "who's going to believe me?" For people lacking the social capital and acutely aware of their position of disempowerment relative to the power and public support accorded the police, making a formal complaint is often seen as too risky an endeavour. But even when people do try to take action, they can be thwarted. In one of our interviews we had this exchange:

[When the cops stop you, do you ever try to get their badge numbers or anything?]
I tried to do that. The cops just walked away.
[They just walked away?]
Yeah.
[And you said, "What's your badge number. I want to write it down." And they just walked away?]
Yeah. Then they threaten to put you in the cop car if you find out the badge number.

The government-sponsored inquiries and commissions often recommend another strategy: increase the diversity of police forces by recruiting more Aboriginal peoples (as well as other racialized groups). Manitoba's AJI, for example, argued that increasing the representation of Aboriginal people on the Winnipeg Police Department would have the benefit of providing positive role models for Aboriginal youth and enabling the force to be more culturally sensitive to the communities it serves.

When J.J. Harper was killed in 1988, the Winnipeg police force included only eight Aboriginal police officers. In December 1990 that number had increased to 18 Aboriginal officers (out of a total of 1,125). Since Aboriginal peoples made up 11.8 percent of Manitoba's population at that time, the AJI commissioners recommended that the department hire an additional 115 Aboriginal officers to reach a more equitable number of 133 (Hamilton and Sinclair 1991b: 107). By 1998 the number of Aboriginal officers had increased to 98 (Sinclair 1999: 385). By 2009 there were 141 Aboriginal officers, representing 10.7 percent of the total complement of 1,411 sworn officers employed by the Winnipeg Police Service. The force described another 91 officers (6.4 percent) as "visible minorities" (WPS 2009: 25).

These figures are encouraging because they suggest a concerted effort on the part of the Winnipeg Police Service to improve the representation of Aboriginal people among its rank and file. Yet this strategy alone will not be enough. As Nicole Lugosi (2011: 308) notes, "Striving for a more proportionate and representative legal system is a good start, but representation alone does not fundamentally challenge the racial hierarchies in the system." Moreover, given that strong internal culture of solidarity in which the identity of police officer overshadows racial or ethnic identities, it is doubtful whether a complement of 10.7 percent can bring about a sea change in the standard operating procedures and everyday practices of policing.

Police forces have also supplemented these efforts to increase diversity by implementing cultural sensitivity training for all of their staff. Typically, these initiatives are aimed more at countering negative stereotypes about Aboriginal peoples and educating officers about Aboriginal cultures and teachings — and less at "the reality and cultures of *whiteness* as a constructed race and position of privilege" (Lugosi 2011: 313). As Green (2006: 520) notes, on their own, cultural awareness activities, such as having police officers participate in a smudge ceremony, "will not bring about a shift in racist practices or institutions." The broader culture of policing will also have to be addressed, especially in relation to its role in perpetuating troublesome police practices.

Given the command structure and the close working relationships that develop with the force, police are doubtless aware of fellow officers carrying out troublesome practices such as Starlight Tours and the phone book treatment. So why don't they take action to stop them? One of the consequences of the blue wall is that it shields those officers who perpetrate such practices and acts as a barrier to change. Given the strong social bonds that develop within the force, and the edict to "stand by your partner," police are motivated to unite in solidarity to protect their own. They do so at great cost because these actions not only reflect badly on the entire police organization, but also engender mistrust and animosity within the communities that the police are delegated to serve.

Our interviews with inner-city residents in Winnipeg produced examples of positive encounters between Aboriginal peoples and the police and the professionalism, kindness and concern that officers can demonstrate as they go about their work. Many more Aboriginal peoples, however, spoke of the disrespect shown to them by police. In the same way that troublesome police practices create a toxic climate for police–community relations, so too does the use of offensive language by police officers in their interactions with Aboriginal peoples. The word "fuck" (and its variants) should never be part of a police officer's vocabulary, nor should "squaw," "cunt," or other similarly offensive words. Such abusive language runs counter to the professionalism that police officers are mandated to uphold and should not be tolerated within the force.

Attending to the culture of policing and the language and actions of individual police officers, however, addresses only part of the fundamental problem of Aboriginal–police relations. The structure and organization of police work also needs to be addressed. One recommendation that often flows from government-sponsored inquiries and commissions is for police forces to implement community policing as an organizational philosophy and strategy.

The AJI commissioners advocated for a community policing approach, arguing that this model represents a marked improvement over the traditional crime-fighting model, whereby policing is reactive and incident-driven, where the job of police officers is basically about "driving around the streets in a car, isolated from the citizenry, waiting for a dispatcher to call" (Hamilton and Sinclair 1991a: 598). Community policing, in contrast, is decentralized and prevention oriented. It encourages a partnership between the police and the community; it is flexible and adaptable to Aboriginal cultural standards and accommodating to the wide variation of lifestyles in Aboriginal communities (1991a: 598–599). In the commissioners' view, community policing is "a vital strategy for enabling local residents to have a structured, open relationship with the police" (1991a: 600).

One of the mandates of the Ontario Commission on Systemic Racism in the Criminal Justice System was to investigate and make recommendations on community policing policies and their implementation. The Commission's consultations, however, showed that while community policing had been adopted by local police services, concerns about systemic racism in police practices remained widespread. In particular, community members expressed "fear that racial equality is not on the community policing agenda" (Ontario 1995: 337). Similarly, even though police forces across the country have implemented community policing initiatives, concerns have emerged about the extent to which these initiatives have had an impact on the hierarchical structure and bureaucratic organization of the services. Writers have pointed to difficulties in effectively implementing community policing initiatives in neighbourhoods where the residents are not in a position to participate actively in the kind of ownership and co-operation envisioned by the model. Commentators have also noted that individual police officers have tended to resist efforts to implement community policing because they consider the model to be akin to social work and therefore at odds with the "real" police work of fighting crime (Linden, Clairmont, and Murphy 2000; Greene 2000; Herbert 2001). The advent of more aggressive models, such as zero-tolerance policing, has also shifted the focus of policing away from the more co-operative approach involved in community policing and back to the traditional model of police as "crime fighters."

Government-sponsored commissions and inquiries have also led to another recommendation around the need for improvements in investigation processes and procedures in cases of alleged police wrong-doing. Critical of the state of race relations in the province, the Ontario Race Relations and Policing Task Force (Ontario 1989) made fifty-seven recommendations for its improvement, including the creation of the Special Investigations Unit (SIU). In 1990 Ontario became the first province to establish an independent civilian oversight body responsible for carrying out criminal investigations involving the police. Appointed and funded by the provincial government, the SIU is responsible for investigating allegations of wrong-doing involving serious injury and death caused by police officers.

Ontario's SIU became subject to considerable public scrutiny after its inception, including at least seven reports, one of which was produced by the Ontario Ombudsman in 2008. Entitled *Oversight Unseen* (Marin 2008), the report called the independence of the agency into question, especially given the use of former police officers as investigators. It also noted that the public perception of the SIU was akin to "a toothless tiger and muzzled watchdog" (Marin 2008: 74). David MacAlister, principal researcher for the B.C. Civil Liberties Association, summarizes some of the concerns raised in the report:

In some instances, police refused to cooperate with SIU investigators. Delays in being notified of cases requiring SIU involvement were compounded by delays in interviewing witnesses. Decisions made by the SIU not to charge police officers are not subject to explanation in a public venue, causing further concern. A significant concern was the deference given to the police by SIU investigators during their investigations. There was a reluctance to insist on police cooperation. The internal culture of the SIU was found to have been adversely affected by the large number of ex-police officers on staff. (MacAlister 2010: 16)

Other provinces have also established civilian oversight bodies to deal with allegations of police wrong-doing. In Manitoba, the AJI noted that "Manitoba compares poorly with other western provinces in its regulation of police activities" (Hamilton and Sinclair 1991a: 624) and highlighted "the need for independent investigations of serious incidents involving the police, especially those where possible criminal acts are alleged against the police, or where a person dies or suffers serious injury in an incident involving the police" (Hamilton and Sinclair 1991a: 628). Yet it was almost two decades before the provincial government undertook a revision of its Provincial Police Act. The impetus for this revision came not from a concern to remedy the fractured relations between Aboriginal peoples and the police but from an inquiry into a traffic death caused by an off-duty police officer.

In the early morning of February 25, 2005, a light pickup truck driven by 31-year-old Derek Harvey-Zenk, a constable with the Winnipeg Police Service, crashed into the back of a car driven by 40-year-old Crystal Taman. On her way to work, Taman had been sitting at a controlled intersection on a highway near the perimeter of Winnipeg, waiting for the light to change. She was killed instantly. It was later revealed that Constable Zenk had spent the previous evening at a local bar with a group of fellow officers from his North End police district. Leaving the establishment at around 2:30 a.m., several of the officers continued the party at the residence of a police sergeant. Zenk was on his way home at 7:00 a.m. when the crash occurred (Salhany 2008).

Constable Zenk was initially charged with impaired driving causing death, criminal negligence causing death, refusing a Breathalyzer test and dangerous operation of a motor vehicle causing death. But a plea agreement was struck in which he pleaded guilty to a lesser offence of dangerous driving causing death in exchange for a conditional sentence of two-years-less-a-day to be served at his home (CBC News 2007). Public outcry over the plea bargain and allegations that the police investigation had been botched led the Manitoba justice minister to pass an order-in-council in December 2007 establishing an inquiry into the case. The Taman Inquiry, which overlapped the inquest into the death of Matthew Dumas, ran for eight weeks in 2008.

In his report, Commissioner Roger Salhany, a retired Ontario superior court justice, deemed the initial investigation into the accident by the East St. Paul Police Service to be "riddled with incompetence" (Salhany 2008: 7). Officers were found to have falsified their notes and engaged in a "cover-up" in an effort to protect one of their own (Salhany 2008: 11). The commissioner also deemed the subsequent Winnipeg Police Service investigation to have been conducted "so poorly ... that it cast light on a broader systemic problem. It showed the perils of having police officers investigate, or even interview, other police officers from their own force in criminal cases" (Salhany 2008: 8). The Commissioner therefore recommended that a special investigation unit independent of all police enforcement agencies in Manitoba be established "for the purpose of investigating any alleged criminal activity of a member of the police service" (Salhany 2008: 14).

In March 2009, the Manitoba government introduced changes to the Provincial Police Act. The Act provides for the establishment of a civilian-led Manitoba Police Commission to oversee policing throughout the province. Civilian boards will have the authority to hire and fire police chiefs and set the tone for policing in their respective communities. Police will no longer investigate their own officers in the event of serious criminal allegations, such as a police-involved shooting death. Nevertheless, police officers will still play a role in the investigation. They can be either current or former police officers selected by a civilian director. The current police officers would be seconded from their police service. As Manitoba's justice minister Dave Chomiak noted at the time, the assignment of police officers to the investigative unit has the potential to generate controversy, but "to be logical, that's what it will probably have to be. Investigators don't sort of grow on trees" (Owen 2009).

In August 2011, the province announced the appointment of Inspector Brian Cyncora, a thirty-year-veteran of the Winnipeg Police Service, as the first executive director of the Manitoba Police Commission. The composition of the Commission's board had previously been announced. Criminologist Rick Linden was appointed to head the board; other commissioners included an Aboriginal representative as well as Robert Taman, the husband of Crystal Taman (Owen 2011). While reporter Bruce Owen (2009) opined that Manitoba's new Provincial Police Act will "effectively tear down the 'blue wall' that has separated many Manitobans from their police officers," whether that will in fact be the case remains to be seen.

Strategies such as encouraging Aboriginal peoples to make formal complaints, increasing the racial diversity of police forces, implementing cultural sensitivity training for officers, attending to the disrespect (such as the use of offensive language) shown to Aboriginal peoples by the police and improving investigative processes and procedures when acts of police wrong-doing arise could most likely go a long way towards improving relations between Aboriginal peoples and the police. But those strategies alone will not remedy the fundamental problem; they fail to address its roots. What is required is a dramatic shift in how we frame the problem of Aboriginal–police relations.

REFRAMING THE PROBLEM

How a problem is framed will govern the particular ways of responding to it. For instance, the current trend is to frame the problems confronting inner-city communities in criminal justice terms, as located in the prevalence of crime, violence and street gangs in these communities. With this framing, "law-and-order" strategies such as zero-tolerance policing and heightened surveillance and containment make sense. If, however, the problem is reframed as being rooted in the impoverished social and economic conditions in these communities, then crime, violence and street gangs become symptoms of a deeper problem that requires solutions beyond "fighting crime" to ameliorate them.

One rationale for shifting how the problem is framed is the costs incurred by criminal justice interventions. Crime control is an incredibly expensive venture. According to Sewell (2010: 141), "Police services eat up almost a quarter of the property tax revenues of many municipalities, and those governments find themselves under increasing financial pressure." Despite declining crime rates, spending on police forces rose by 41 percent per capita across the country between 1999 and 2009 (Morrow 2011). While salaries take up some 80 percent of police budgets (Linden, Clairmont and Murphy 2000), the use of expensive technologies only adds to that burden. For instance, the purchase of a helicopter by the Winnipeg Police Service cost the city $3.5 million, while the Province of Manitoba contributes $1.3 million annually in operating costs (CTV Winnipeg 2011). As the first contact point in the criminal justice system, police are also involved in funnelling individuals into what Angela Davis (2000) called the "prison industrial complex." Mass incarceration involves huge financial costs for the state. In the effort to advance its "law and order" agenda, the Canadian government has poured considerable monies into shoring up its penitentiary system. The annual budget of the Correctional Service of Canada increased by 86.6 percent after 2005–6. Expenditures in this area were projected to rise to $3.178 billion by 2012–13 (Piche 2011).

Another powerful rationale for reframing the problem is the human and social capital that is at stake. In the Manitoba context, Michael Mendelson (2004: 8) argued that "the increasing importance of the Aboriginal workforce to Manitoba ... cannot be exaggerated. There is likely no single more critical economic factor for [the Prairie] provinces." Manitoba's Aboriginal population is predicted to grow from about 159,000 in 2001 to 231,000 by 2017 (Loxley 2010). These figures suggest that Aboriginal youth will be an important resource for the province — but only if current conditions of racialized poverty and social exclusion are addressed. In this respect, inner-city communities where Aboriginal peoples are to be found in large proportions are the site of a growing number of community-based organizations whose mandate is to attend to the complex material, cultural and emotional needs of the residents (see, for example, Silver 2006; CCPA-MB 2007).

By and large these community-based organizations — many of which are Aboriginal-driven — adopt a community development approach that involves strategies by which people participate directly or through organizations that they control in bottom-up planning and community action (Wharf and Clague 1997). Community development, in other words, is geared towards enabling communities to overcome poverty and social exclusion in ways of their choosing. As Jim Silver and his colleagues (2006: 134) explain:

> Community development involves the continuous process of capacity-building: building upon and strengthening local resources to generate well-being among community members ... Community development is based on the premise that community members need to gain control of resources to generate economic well-being. The general goal of community development is to benefit those who have been marginalized from the current economic system.

Aboriginal community development is even more comprehensive. It is aimed at decolonization, or the process of undoing colonialism by attending to the devastating effects that it has wreaked on Aboriginal peoples, in terms not only of their material circumstances but also their identity. In contrast to criminal justice strategies that focus on punishment, discipline and control, Aboriginal community development focuses on healing, wellness and capacity building. Honouring Aboriginal traditions, values and cultures becomes an important part of this healing process. So too does reclaiming a sense of self-worth and pride that has been systematically stripped from Aboriginal peoples by colonial strategies manifested in the residential schools, the reserve system and the Indian Act and dominant discourses that "other" them as "welfare recipients" and "criminals." By adopting a holistic approach that focuses on strengthening the individual, the family and the community, Aboriginal community-based organizations aim to move Aboriginal peoples out of and beyond colonialism's straitjacket (see Silver et al. 2006).

Non-Aboriginal people are also implicated in this process of decolonization. Similar to the strategies adopted by the women's movement, Aboriginal community development is constituted as being carried out "by" and "with" Aboriginal peoples because Aboriginal peoples (as in women's struggles for equality) ultimately need to claim their entitlements through their own organizations. But just as men are not absolved of their responsibility in making change to realize substantive equality for women, non-Aboriginal people have a role to play as allies, walking beside and not in front of or behind Aboriginal peoples in their quest for change (Silver et al. 2006: 156). The police too could play a role in this project of decolonization and community development, albeit a very different role than has traditionally been designed for them.

COMMUNITY MOBILIZATION

Given that police have occupied a central role in the reproduction of order — more specifically, in the dreadful task of policing the conflict and abuses that arise from the particular forms of poverty and social exclusion that our society has created — reframing the problem and re-envisioning the strategies for resolving it open up new possibilities for the role of the police in the form of community mobilization.

Although most modern police forces tend to adopt a blended approach in which a variety of policing models are employed, typically the core strategy involves the traditional crime-fighting model of policing, with other initiatives (community policing, specialized units and the like) positioned as a supplementary or secondary consideration. The traditional model of policing sets the police up as an outside force sent into troubled and troublesome communities to quell disorder. Rather than being an outside force, police need to be a more integral part of the communities they are mandated to serve. One way of doing so is to shift their organizational focus from crime-fighting to community mobilization.

Community mobilization involves working in close partnership with community-based organizations and social service agencies engaged in a wide variety of neighbourhood revitalization initiatives. It involves police officers walking the beat, getting to know people and the community, developing relationships, using conflict resolution and problem-solving skills, earning the trust of people. It involves the police working *with* the community to collectively build safer and healthier neighbourhoods (Comack and Silver 2006). Clearly, the role of police as crime fighters would not disappear within this model of policing, but it would be a subsidiary to the refashioned core strategy of community mobilization.

Working in close contact with community members would enable police to know where the problems are, and to intervene, at least in some cases, before problems occur. In these terms, police would become part of a process of "asset-based community development" (Kretzmann and McKnight 1993). While the traditional approach to inner-city communities is to see them through a "deficit lens" — that is, solely in terms of their problems — an "asset-based" approach identifies and builds upon the strengths of a neighbourhood. In this way, the role of police as "reproducers of order" would be transformed. Rather than reproducing the status quo, police could participate in the fashioning of a new form of social order; one not founded on race and racism — and racialized policing.

A common response to the argument that race and racism invade the practice of policing is that the presence of racism in a police force merely reflects the racism in the wider society and is therefore not a special matter of concern. AJI commissioners Hamilton and Sinclair (1991b: 111) disagree:

> Police officers occupy a unique and powerful position in our society. They have the ability to interfere with the freedom of citizens and are called upon to protect society from the misdeeds of its members. The position of police officers provides them with opportunities to intrude into our lives — a right denied to all others. We have every right to expect and demand from them that they fulfill their responsibilities fully, fairly and in a manner that does not discriminate against anyone on account of race. It is not acceptable for any member of society to do that, but it is even more unacceptable for a police officer to do so.

Police alone cannot solve the problems that trouble Aboriginal communities and their residents. But policing *can* be part of a long-term solution that involves decolonization and community mobilization and revitalization. At the very least, making such change requires political will. But it starts with the recognition that a fundamental problem exists in Aboriginal–police relations — a problem rooted in colonialism, poverty and social exclusion.

References

Bayley, D.H. 2005. "What Do the Police Do?" In T. Newburn (ed.), *Policing: Key Readings*. Portland: Willan Publishing.
Bittner, E. 2005. "Florence Nightingale in Pursuit of Willie Sutton: A Theory of the Police." In T. Newburn (ed.), *Policing: Key Readings*. Portland: Willan Publishing.
cbc News. 2007. "No Jail Time for Ex-Cop who Killed Woman in Car Crash." October 29. <cbc.ca/news/canada/manitoba/story/2007/10/29/harveymordenzenk.html>.
____. 2008a. "Winnipeg Police Apologize to Rapper for Gunpoint Pullover." June 7. <cbc.ca/news/arts/music/story/2008/06/07/winnipeg-rapper-apology.html>.
ccpa-mb (Canadian Centre for Policy Alternatives–Manitoba). 2007. *Step by Step: Stories of Change in Winnipeg's Inner City*. <policyalternatives.ca/sites/default/files/uploads/publications/Manitoba_Pubs/2007/State_of_the_Inner_City2007.pdf>.
Chaco, J., and S. Nanco (eds.). 1993. *Community Policing in Canada*. Toronto: Canadian Scholars' Press.
Chan, J. 1996. "Changing Police Culture." *British Journal of Criminology,* 36, 1.
Closs, W.J., and P.F. McKenna. 2006. "Profiling a Problem in Canadian Police Leadership: The Kingston Police Data Collection Project." *Canadian Public Administration,* 49, 2.
Comack, E., and E. Bowness. 2010. "Dealing the Race Card: Public Discourse on the Policing of Winnipeg's Inner-City Communities." *Canadian Journal of Urban Research,* 19, 1.
Comack, E., and J. Silver. 2006. *Safety and Security in Winnipeg's Inner-City Communities: Bridging the Community-Police Divide*. Winnipeg: ccpa-mb.
____. 2008. "A Canadian Exception to the Punitive Turn? Community Reponses to Policing Practices in Winnipeg's Inner City." *Canadian Journal of Sociology,* 33, 4.
Commission on Systemic Racism in the Ontario Criminal Justice System. 1998. "Racism in Justice: Perceptions." In V. Satzewich (ed.), *Racism and Social Inequality in Canada: Concepts, Controversies and Strategies of Resistance*. Toronto: Thompson Educational Publishing.
ctv Winnipeg. 2011. "Police Helicopter Used More Than 50 times During First Week." February 10. <winnipeg.ctv.ca/servlet/an/plocal/ctvNews/20110210/wpg_helicopter_110210/20110210/?hub=WinnipegHome>.
Davies, W.H. (Commissioner). 2008. *Alone and Cold: The Davies Commission Inquiry into the Death of Frank Paul*. Interim Report (February 12). Vancouver, British Columbia. <frankpaulinquiry.ca/report/>.
Davis, A. 2000. *The Prison Industrial Complex and Its Impact on Communities of Color*. Videocassette. Madison: University of Wisconsin.
Ericson, R. 1982. *Reproducing Order: A Study of Police Patrol Work*. Toronto: University of Toronto Press.
Fielding, N. 1995. *Community Policing*. Oxford: Clarendon Press.
____. 2005. "Concepts and Theory in Community Policing." *Howard Journal,* 44, 5.
Fridell, L., R. Lunney, D. Diamond, and B. Kobu. 2001. *Racially Biased Policing: A Principled*

Response. Washington, DC: Police Executive Research Forum.

Gabor, T. 2004. "Inflammatory Rhetoric on Racial Profiling Can Undermine Police Services." *Canadian Journal of Criminology and Criminal Justice,* 46, 4.

Gilroy, P. 1991. *There Ain't No Black in the Union Jack: The Cultural Politics of Race and Nation.* Chicago: University of Chicago Press.

Gold, A. 2003. "Media Hype, Racial Profiling, and Good Science." *Canadian Journal of Criminology and Criminal Justice,* 45, 3.

Greene, Jack. 2000. "Community Policing in America: Changing the Nature, Structure, and Function of the Police." *Criminal Justice,* 3.

____. 2006. "From *Stonechild* to Social Cohesion: Anti-Racist Challenges for Saskatchewan." *Canadian Journal of Political Science,* 39, 3.

Hamilton, A.C., and C.M. Sinclair (Commissioners). 1991a. *Report of the Aboriginal Justice Inquiry of Manitoba. Volume 1. The Justice System and Aboriginal People.* Winnipeg: Queen's Printer.

____. 1991b. *Report of the Aboriginal Justice Inquiry of Manitoba. Volume 2. The Deaths of Helen Betty Osborne and John Joseph Harper.* Winnipeg: Queen's Printer.

Harris, D. 2002. *Profiles in Injustice: Why Racial Profiling Cannot Work.* New York: New Press.

Herbert, S. 2001. "Policing the Contemporary City: Fixing Broken Windows or Shoring up Neo-liberalism?" *Theoretical Criminology,* 5, 4.

Holdaway, S. 2003. "Police Relations in England and Wales: Theory, Policy, and Practice." *Police and Society,* 7, 1.

James, C. 1998. "'Up to No Good': Blacks on the Streets and Encountering Police." In V. Satzewich (ed.), *Racism & Social Inequality in Canada: Concepts, Controversies & Strategies of Resistance.* Toronto: Thompson Educational Publishing.

King, T. 2003. *The Truth about Stories: A Native Narrative.* Toronto: House of Anansi Press.

Kretzmann, J.P., and J.L. McKnight. 1993. *Building Communities from the Inside Out: A Path toward Finding and Mobilizing a Community's Assets.* Evanston, IL: The Asset Based Community Development Institute, Institute for Policy Research.

LERA (Law Enforcement Review Agency). n.d. *Annual Report 2010.* Winnipeg: Manitoba Justice. <gov.mb.ca/justice/lera/annual_report/pdf/2010/2010-annual_report.pdf>.

Linden, R., D. Clairmont, and C. Murphy. 2000. "Aboriginal Policing in Manitoba: A Report to the Aboriginal Justice Implementation Commission." Winnipeg: Manitoba Justice. <ajic.mb.ca/consult.html>.

Loxley, J. 2010. *Aboriginal, Northern, and Community Economic Development: Papers and Retrospectives.* Winnipeg: Arbeiter Ring.

Lugosi, N. 2011. "'Truth-Telling' and Legal Discourse: A Critical Analysis of the Neil Stonechild Inquiry." *Canadian Journal of Political Science,* 44, 2.

MacAlister, D. 2010. *Police-Involved Deaths: The Failure of Self-Investigation. Final Report.* Vancouver: British Columbia Civil Liberties Association. <bccla.org/othercontent/Police_involved_deaths.pdf>.

Makin, K. 2003. "Police Use Racial Profiling, Appeal Court Concludes." *Globe and Mail,* April 17.

Manning, P. 1989. "Occupational Culture." In W.G. Bailey (ed.), *The Encyclopedia of Police Science.* New York: Garland.

Marin, A. 2008. "Oversight Unseen: Investigation into the Special Investigation

Unit's Operational Effectiveness and Credibility." Toronto: Ombudsman Ontario. <ombudsman.on.ca/Ombudsman/files/8a/8acb8114-b212-42b5-8221-3d5e4e95a3f1.pdf>.
McLean, C. 2006. *When Police Become Prey: What Lies Behind Starlight Tours*. Silver Harvest Productions.
Mendelson, M. 2004. *Aboriginal People in Canada's Labour Market: Work and Unemployment, Today and Tomorrow*. Ottawa: Caledon Institute of Social Policy.
Morrow, A. 2011. "What Price for Law and Order?" *Globe and Mail*, January 8.
Nova Scotia. 1989. *Royal Commission on the Donald Marshall, Jr., Prosecution: Digest of Findings and Recommendations* (Chief Justice T. Alexander Hickman, Chairman). <gov.ns.ca/just/marshall_inquiry/_docs/Royal%20Commission%20on%20the%20Donald%20Marshall%20Jr%20Prosecution_findings.pdf>.
OHRC (Ontario Human Rights Commission). 2003. *Paying the Price: The Human Cost of Racial Profiling*. Inquiry Report. Toronto: Ontario Human Rights Commission.
Omni, M., and H. Winant. 1994. *Racial Formation in the United States*. New York: Routledge.
Ontario. 1989. *The Report of the Race Relations and Policing Task Force* (Clare Lewis, Chair). Toronto: Task Force on Race Relations and Policing.
____. 1992. *Report of the Advisor on Race Relations to the Premier of Ontario* (Advisor: Hon. S. Lewis). Toronto: Advisor on Race Relations.
Owen, B. 2009. "Police Act Tears Down 'Blue Wall.'" *Winnipeg Free Press*, April 15.
____. 2011. "Police Inspector Changes His Hat." *Winnipeg Free Press*, August 13.
Paoline, E.A. 2003. "Taking Stock: Toward a Richer Understanding of Police Culture." *Journal of Criminal Justice*, 31.
Piche, J. 2011. "Tracking the Politics of 'Crime' and Punishment in Canada." <tpcp-canada.blogspot.com/2011/06/what-austerity-and-small-government.html>.
Rankin, J., J. Quinn, M. Shephard, J. Duncanson, and S. Simmie. 2002. "Singled Out." *Toronto Star*, October 19.
Razack, S. 2000. "Gendered Racialized Violence and Spatialized Justice: The Murder of Pamela George." *Canadian Journal of Law and Society*, 15, 2.
____. (ed.). 2002. *Race, Space and the Law: Unmapping the White Settler Society*. Toronto: Between the Lines.
____. 2007. "When Place Becomes Race." In T. Das Gupta, C.E. James, R. Maaka, G-E. Galabuzi and C. Andersen (eds.), *Race and Racialization: Essential Readings*. Toronto: Canadian Scholars' Press.
Reiner, R. 1992. *The Politics of the Police*, 2nd edition. London: Harvester Wheatsheaf.
Rosenbaum, D. (ed.) 1994. *The Challenge of Community Policing: Testing the Promises*. London: Sage.
Salhany, The Honourable R. (Commissioner). 2008. *Report of the Taman Inquiry*. Manitoba: Taman Inquiry into the Investigation and Prosecution of Derek Harvey-Zenk. <tamaninquiry.ca/pdf/taman_inquiry_A.pdf>.
Sewell, J. 2010. *Police in Canada: The Real Story*. Toronto: James Lorimer.
Shearing, C., and R. Ericson. 1991. "Culture as Figurative Action." *British Journal of Sociology*, 42, 4.
Silver, J. (ed.). 2006. *In Their Own Voices: Building Urban Aboriginal Communities*. Halifax and Winnipeg: Fernwood Publishing.

Silver, J., P. Ghorayshi, J. Hay, and D. Klyne. 2006. "Sharing, Community and Decolonization." In J. Silver (ed.), *In Their Own Voices: Building Urban Aboriginal Communities*. Halifax and Winnipeg: Fernwood Publishing.

Skolnick, J. 1975. *Justice without Trial: Law Enforcement in a Democratic Society*, 2nd edition. New York: John Wiley.

Solomos, J. 1988. *Black Youth, Racism and the State: The Politics of Ideology and Policy*. Cambridge: Cambridge University Press.

Stenning, P., C. Birkbeck, O. Adang, D. Baker, T. Feltes, L. Gerardo Gabaldón, M. Haberfeld, E. Paes Machado, and P. Waddington. 2009. "Researching the Use of Force: The Background to the International Project." *Crime, Law and Social Change*, 52.

Stroud, C. 1983. *The Blue Wall: Street Cops in Canada*. Toronto: McClelland and Stewart.

Tanovich, D. 2003–2004. "E-Racing Racial Profiling." *Alberta Law Review*, 41.

____. 2006. *The Colour of Justice: Policing Race in Canada*. Toronto: Irwin law.

Tator, C., and F. Henry. 2006. *Racial Profiling in Canada: Challenging the Myth of 'A Few Bad Apples.'* Toronto: University of Toronto Press.

Wharf, B., and M. Clague (eds.). 1997. *Community Organizing: Canadian Experiences*. Toronto: Oxford University Press.

Williams, T. 2001. "Racism in Justice: The Report of the Commission on Systemic Racism in the Ontario Criminal Justice System." In Susan C. Boyd, Dorothy E. Chunn, and Robert Menzies (eds.), *(Ab)using Power: The Canadian Experience*. Halifax: Fernwood Publishing.

WPS (Winnipeg Police Service). 2009. *Annual Report*. <winnipeg.ca/police/annualreports/2009/2009_wps_annual_report_english.pdf>.

Wright, Justice D.H. (Commissioner). 2004. Report of the Commission of Inquiry into Matters Relating to the Death of Neil Stonechild. <justice.gov.sk.ca/stonechild/finalreport/Stonechild.pdf>.

Chapter 10

TOWARDS A THEORY OF TERRORISM

Gary Teeple

From: *Anti-Terrorism: Security and Insecurity after 9/11*, Chapter 2 (reprinted with permission of the author).

Throughout the twentieth century, Western governments have applied the epithet "terrorist" to actions or groups that challenged the established order. The term was often used after the 1918 Russian Revolution as synonymous with "communist" or "socialist" and implying an association with the Soviet Union. During World War II, the Nazis branded internal resistance to occupation as "terrorist"; and after the War, the allied nations gave the same label to national liberation movements in colonial countries. Following the disintegration of the Soviet Bloc and the events of September 11, 2001, use of the word acquired a new importance. In 2002, Washington made "terrorism" the defining characteristic of the present era and the foreseeable future. "The enemy is terrorism," it declared, and the "war" against it would be indefinite (White House 2002).

Enormous political pressure was applied and massive military resources were marshalled to prosecute this war. In the United States, new security laws were pushed through Congress or promulgated by executive fiat, and government departments were reorganized to reflect these new priorities. Under U.N. Security Council Resolution 1373, Washington promoted "counter-terrorist" emergency laws for every member country, undermining the rule of law everywhere. The invasion of

Afghanistan in 2001 and then Iraq in 2003 took place with fabricated justifications and little regard for international law (Parry 2006; Corn 2003; Rampton and Stauber 2003). In other countries, such as Canada and the U.K., anti-terrorist laws were passed quickly and without significant public debate. The world order, as reflected in the U.N. Charter and Universal Declaration of Human Rights and other international agreements, was turned on its head.

THE ANTILOGIES OF THE "WAR ON TERRORISM"

The rationale for such a transformation, however, has been less than convincing. Statistical data on terrorist acts reveal a striking discord between the purported threat, on the one hand, and the resources marshalled and extraordinary legislative changes made, on the other, to fight terrorism. According to the U.S. State Department's (2000) annual survey of terror, the number of reported deaths from terrorist acts show an irregular but steady decline from the late 1980s. Although the year 2001 was anomalous, with an estimated 3,000 fatalities on 9/11, the loss of life appears to rise after the U.S. declared its "war" (Enders and Sandler 2002; Tilly 2005). In 2002 the report listed 725 people killed and 625 in 2003 — both higher than in 2000 or throughout the 1990s.

There are other seeming disjunctions. Former U.S. Secretary of Defense Donald Rumsfeld, for instance, admitted that "we lack the metrics to see if we are winning or losing the war on terror" (Krueger and Laitin 2004). If data on the nature of the "enemy" appear unimportant, so too do data on how many innocents have been killed and injured by U.S. military and allied forces. Whatever their faults, reasoned estimates of the number of deaths in Iraq do exist. Within the first two years of the invasion, they ranged from about 30,000 to over 100,000 (Iraq Body Count; BBC News 2004, 2006). In the fall of 2007, the highest estimate had risen to over one million and the lowest to about 75,000 (*LA Times* 2007; Iraq Body Count 2007; Media Lens 2007). This is not to mention the civilian casualties caused by the U.S. military attack on Afghanistan, or the loss of life caused by years of sanctions in Iraq before the invasion, during which the death toll is estimated to be between 500,000 and 1.8 million (Gordon 2002; Rubin 2001; Campaign Against Sanctions on Iraq 1999). In short, U.S., British and other military forces have killed vastly more innocent people in the "war on terrorism" than have officially designated terrorist acts.

Some argue that the threat of terrorism is not to be found so much in property damage and the number of victims as in the destabilization of democratic politics or a "way of life" (Laqueur 1986). It can safely be said, however, that since 9/11, the "war on terrorism" has dramatically undermined the principles of liberal democracy, overridden the rule of law, expanded the use of executive fiat, held thousands in secret detention without the right of *habeas corpus* or representation or trial, opened the door to torture as acceptable despite its status as *jus cogens* in international law and killed tens of thousands of civilians. The principles of the U.N. Charter and the Universal Declaration of Human Rights and associated covenants and conventions, moreover, have all been trumped by declarations of unilateralism and pre-emptive intervention. As for Western freedoms, the anti-terrorist laws passed by the majority of states since 9/11 allow for more executive arbitrariness.

Compared to other causes of death and property damage around the world, the losses due to terrorist acts make the enormous "counter-terror" efforts seem patently illogical. The annual murder rate in the U.S. over the past few decades, for example, exceeds the cumulative death total due to terrorism over the whole decade preceding 9/11. In the U.S., each year since 2000, the number of road deaths has exceeded forty thousand, while fatalities related to smoking and alcohol consumption number well over 100,000 annually. Globally, since 1981 over 25 million people have died from the HIV/AIDS (UNAIDS 2008; Avert 2008). The effects of HIV/AIDS and other diseases, such as tuberculosis, malaria, measles, dysentery and cholera, are so great that the economies of some developing countries are "crippled by these diseases" (BBC 1999; WHO 1996). Such a list could easily be extended, but it suffices to indicate that, in light of all the issues that threaten humankind and actually destabilize social systems, the threat of terror is insignificant.

Even the official explanation for the "war on terrorism" does not correspond well with what we actually know. Despite U.S. assertions about al Qaeda, for example, knowledge of the supposed architects of September 11 remains indefinite (Griffin 2004; Tarpley 2005; Ahmed 2002, 2005; Marrs 2004). The nature, size and significance of al Qaeda remain unknown, although we do know it was created by intelligence services, mainly the CIA and the Pakistani ISI, to confront the Soviet military in Afghanistan (Ahmed 2002).

A major part of the "war," moreover, was launched in Afghanistan in 2001 and Iraq in 2003 without any evidence that either government was involved in the terror of 9/11. U.S. and British government officials repeatedly blamed al Qaeda for the bombings in Madrid in March 2004 and London in July 2005, but these pronouncements have been difficult to prove in subsequent investigations and trials (Porteous 2006; Ahmed 2007).

There is, furthermore, no evidence that all the military actions and expenditures since 9/11 have increased the security of the world. The loss of life and property in Afghanistan and Iraq has had little effect other than to destabilize the region. The war on Iraq has led to much death and destruction and has left the country without the infrastructure, food and industrial production and security that it had under the dictatorship of Saddam Hussein. There is no evidence that the anti-terrorist measures introduced throughout the Western world have prevented any terrorist attacks. We know very little, moreover, of the alleged terrorists who have been incarcerated, interrogated and tortured, because their detention and treatment have been carried out outside national and international law. Across three U.S. prisons in Iraq, for instance, there were about 18,000 detainees in 2007, with an expected 20,000 by the end of 2008. Few have been formally charged; arrests and detentions have been arbitrary and beyond the reach of international law. The question of guilt or innocence has appeared to be irrelevant, and the effect is to create terror in the subject population and, by extension, across the world (*Washington Post* 2007; *Guardian* 2005).

The military and economic power of the industrial states, it cannot be overstated, greatly outweighs all the officially designated terrorist groups and "state sponsors" put together. Any one of the industrial states has repressive apparatus vastly more powerful than even the largest sub-state organizations accused of terrorism. The industrial nations have extensive police and military forces and bureaucratic machinery at their disposal, access to a vast global surveillance system and the use of global institutions.

All these points suggest that the threat of terror is not as significant as the authorities claim. Even this cursory examination of the evidence makes it clear that the reaction to the declared threat is far out of proportion to what we know of "terrorist" activities and their effects. If the rationale for the "war on terrorism" appears to be wanting, it is not immediately clear what would explain the monumental commitment of state resources to fighting it and the systematic undermining of the political principles of liberal democracy.

WHAT IS TERRORISM?

Definitions

In order to fathom this disconnection between the declared purpose of the "war" and the nature of the enemy, it is necessary to establish what is meant by terrorism. As is widely noted, there is no single meaning that is generally accepted — suggesting that the referent is elusive and that definitions have partisan implications. There is much to be gained by accepting and using one definition. Even more may be gained, perhaps, by leaving the term undefined, just a label to be deployed.

Definitions delimit a phenomenon, but depending on how the limits are cast, the phenomenon can be quite different. Most official definitions, for instance, preclude the state as perpetrator, yet there is no self-evident reason to suggest that the state cannot commit acts of terrorism. States have a definite interest in defining terrorism strictly as opposition by organized non-state forces to legitimate authorities, especially when such states use terror themselves to defend or advance their own particular or hegemonic interests.

The lack of definitional consensus has not stopped governments from legislating anti-terrorist laws or implementing counter-terrorist measures. In many cases, however, the definition employed is vague enough to encompass many kinds of protest and dissent that were once considered normal and legitimate, producing a chilling effect on the exercise of liberal democratic liberties and, more particularly, on the activities of dissident or critical journalists, teachers, academics, environmentalists, trade unionists and political or other groups (*USA Today* 2004; American Civil Liberties Union "Don't Spy on Me").

Even the absence of a definition has not hampered the development of counter-terrorist measures and activities. At the urging of the United States in 2001, the U.N. Security Council established the Counter-Terrorism Committee, bureaucratic machinery for mounting counter-terrorist measures and overseeing the new anti-terrorist legislation of U.N. member states. Here we find the absurdity of an administrative organization with a sizeable budget dedicated to coordinating global state-based executive powers and machinery for counter-terrorism — without defining the object of their work. On a practical level, the problem is self-evident: what passes for terrorist acts or actors becomes subject to the arbitrary designations of state-appointed administrators (Rosand 2003). The spectacle of the United Nations gearing up to do battle with an undefined phenomenon, however, points to questions about the nature of the phenomenon and the motives of the Security Council.

Despite the absence of agreement, most official definitions of terrorism contain two common elements. One is that perpetrators are always non-state actors. In the definition most widely employed by the U.S. government, for instance, only "subnational groups or clandestine agents" are considered to be terrorists.[1] The underlying argument is that the legitimacy of governments and their constitutionality put them beyond acts that are not also legitimate, or that, if the state does commit such acts, it does so ostensibly to protect the legality of the system threatened by alien forces. Such views can be employed to justify the circumscription of a range of human rights. Labelled as terrorist and seen as a threat to purported democracy and human rights, critics or opposition can be dealt with by means outside the normal law and procedures. There is nothing, however, to say the state is not capable of terrorism. Indeed, it could be argued that the history of state terrorism to thwart insurrection or simply maintain power coincides with the history of the state, and there are many instances where the loss of state legitimacy becomes a reign of terror (Blum 1998; Chomsky and Herman 1979).

The U.S. State Department does allow that a state can be a "sponsor" of terrorism, but it reserves to itself the task of identifying those states[2] and subjects them to forms of U.S.-sanctioned censure. The partisan nature of this proscription is obvious. Because few governments or their agents can claim never to use terror, maintaining a monopoly on the making of such designations is a useful foreign policy instrument, while avoiding the risk of including the state that is doing the defining.

The other common practice in official definitions is to label terrorism as unlawful or criminal.[3] By implication, such an attribute not only precludes the state as terrorist, but also makes terrorism into an offence against due process and formal authority. The problem here is two-fold. First, the law itself is not sacrosanct. It has often been employed as a means of terror, and history is replete with examples of laws aimed at certain sectors of a population with the intent to intimidate and coerce their behaviour in a particular direction. We need only mention women, slaves, Jews, Catholics (Myers 1960), Indigenous peoples, trade unions and vagrants, among many other groups, to make the case. In a class-divided society, moreover, the legal system itself — the law, police, courts, prisons — may be employed as forms of terror against certain classes or strata. The police and other state agencies, moreover, do commit criminal acts for purposes of intimidation with official approval (Dion 1982; Sawatsky 1980; Sallot 1979; Palango 1998, 1994). By extension, even the principle of the rule of law, where the law is profoundly iniquitous, can also be a form of terrorism; within the law, class or religious bias can parade as principle. Second, non-state terrorism may well be criminal in that it breaks laws, but it is never merely criminal; it always has a political dimension that calls into question the status quo and that mere criminal acts possess only implicitly.

Although a world of conflicting interests has prevented general agreement on a definition, this does not mean that no definition is possible. There is nothing to prevent us from sifting through the discord and partiality to argue a workable definition of terrorism. It goes without saying that if a phenomenon of terrorism exists, then it must be definable, and the classification defensible. A dictionary definition will suffice as a starting point: terrorism is "the practice of exercising intimidation [through violence or the threat of it] to coerce people toward a certain course." The key elements found in most definitions of terrorism are included or implied here: it is purposive or calculated behaviour, not accidental; it involves a threat or act of violence; it is intended to influence a larger population than those directly affected; and its goal is to alter certain expectations, patterns of behaviour, or government policy.

Perhaps the most obvious, if least discussed, aspect of this definition is that terrorism is a practice, a tactic or strategy. It is not a phenomenon in and of itself; it is not a creed, philosophy, utopian ideal, or political goal; there is no terrorism for its own sake; it is always only a means to an end. It is defined not by who does it, but by the sort of practice it is. As a tactic it can and has been employed by diverse social entities, including individuals, social movements, political parties, dissident groups, criminal organizations, religious and ethnic factions, vigilantes and governments. The goals, of course, are entirely different, as is the kind of terror used and the reason for the choice of this tactic and not others, but all this is immaterial to the definition. It follows that it is pointless to search for a common element in terrorist acts, other than the practice itself, to define it.

If we accept that this is correct if obvious reasoning, it does raise a question not often asked: if terror is a tactic and not a goal, what does a "war on terrorism" mean? What does it mean to have a war on a tactic, especially one that has been used so pervasively? The answer lies in who uses the label and why. Employed by the state, it can embrace all those who oppose or resist the status quo or its expansion. It can serve as an umbrella slogan for opportunistic use, justifying repression against whomever or whatever may stand in the way of foreign or domestic policy, including other governments, political parties, separatists, nationalists, critics of any sort and religious factions. This instrumentality can even extend to the use of terror by a government against its own citizens in the form of "demonstration terror" — acts deceitfully attributed to a group or state and intended to justify morally questionable or illegal counter-terrorist actions by those waging the "war" or carrying out repression (Ganser 2005; Blackstock 1975; Gelbspan 1991; Goldstein 1978; Davis 1997).

However incomplete, this brief examination of definitions reveals terrorism to be in essence a tactic, not a thing in itself, open to use by states, organizations and individuals alike, for a variety of ends. All are terrorists if they commit acts of terror; what they have in common, their motives being different, is the nature of the act they have committed. The explanations of why this kind of attack is employed and by whom remains to be examined.

Explanations

Among the most common theories of terrorism are psychological explanations or behavioural hypotheses that reduce its causes to individual pathologies (Hudson et al. 1999). Such an approach discovers the source of terrorism in the distempered individual or in defective group dynamics, without reference to the broader system, which is left as the unexamined assumption in the analysis. To be sure, the advocacy or execution of terrorist acts may well attract some people who for personal or monetary and not political reasons are willing to commit terror. Individual idiosyncrasies, then, may help to explain some of the actions of certain perpetrators, but for this to be a sufficient explanation we would have to assume that the historical era and the current conflicts in the world were irrelevant to individual behaviour, and that the origin of social problems lay with aberrant and asocial individuals.

In mainstream political science (McCamant 1984), most theories of terrorism ignore the state as perpetrator (unless it is "socialist" or defined as a "sponsor") because the discipline assumes liberal democracy to be legitimate and to possess formal mechanisms for expressing dissent and achieving change. No political system, in any event, willingly admits that its principles are open to challenge that is simultaneously justifiable *and* unlawful. If liberal democratic states commit terrorist acts at home or abroad, conventional political science sees them as committed in the defence of the realm or for the worthy spread of its principles, and therefore as legitimate acts (Ignatieff 2004). For this reason, most theories in political science see terrorism as strictly a non-state form of illegal opposition to rightful principles. In general, the opposition — whether based on class conflict, political conviction, or religious belief — is seen as arising not from the system itself but from alien systems, beliefs, or personal pathologies. There is little appreciation that contradictions, conflicts and inequalities in the system itself may give rise to resistance from sectors of civil society, not to mention that these sectors or the state may use terrorism in repressing opposition (Stohl and Lopez 1986).

In many of these theories, insurgencies and guerrilla armies are often conflated with or reduced to terrorist groups. Although such opposition forces may employ terror, there is no necessary link between the two. A cursory knowledge of U.S. interventions around the world makes it clear that there are many countries in which opposition is spawned by the brutality, amorality and illegality of these and other state interventions (Blum 1998; Chomsky 1992). Resistance in itself has nothing to do with terrorism.

There are also socio-economic theories that focus on the grievances of certain sub-national entities (the poverty, chronic unemployment, political frustration, hopelessness, or humiliation of strata, classes, aspiring "nations," or occupied peoples) that are said to provide the rationale for terrorism as a means of countering an oppressive system. While these factors may well underlie some non-state terror, how they transform their victims into terrorists is left unexplained. The weakness of such theories becomes evident in light of the many hundreds of millions who suffer such conditions and do not turn to terror. These grievances may point to a partial rationale, but they are insufficient to explain why some turn to terrorism and others not, and they completely ignore the issue of state terrorism and the terror embedded in the system itself.

None of the conventional theories of terrorism should be dismissed out of hand; where they do focus on one or other proximate cause, they offer partial explanations. They are not, however, sufficient accounts.

Another approach to explain the origins of terrorism, rarely mentioned in these discussions, takes the nature of the system itself as the cause. This approach is difficult to grasp and admit if one is part and product of the system and a believer in it. Terror, it is argued, is employed by all power holders to uphold the status quo and counter oppositional tendencies within the body politic. It is a mechanism of political control whose function is "not only to punish acts of disobedience and resistance but also to sap the potential for disobedience in advance and to break the nature of the power to resist" (Walter 1969: 10). In this theory, terrorism is culturally relative in form, but the content is "a universal process" in social systems ruled by a state or quasi-state. It is not a process used only in emergency situations but a regular "option" in a range of political choices, and it is rationalized by "collective fantasies" about threats to the system (Walter 1969: 340).

In general, the notion that terror is a strategy exercised by all states at times to maintain power and to contain opposition is not difficult to demonstrate, and in fact it is easy to find earlier arguments along these lines about dictatorships (Neumann 1965; Neumann 1957). But what may appear self-evident still provides little by way of explanation. If the rule is legitimate, the need for terror and the reason for the opposition must be explained.

Many studies (George 1991, Sluka 2000; Stohl and Lopez 1986, 1988; Blackstock 1975; Chester 1985; Davis 1997; Gelbspan 1991; Nutter 2000) provide an abundance of empirical evidence and argumentation pointing to the state as terrorist. Nevertheless, the explanations remain tied to a proximate cause — the need to maintain the conditions for capital accumulation and to create quiescent intellectual and working classes. These causes might well be considered sufficient if the argument is that state terrorism is a policy instrument of ruling that can be changed or corrected with a change of government, increased legitimacy, or pacification of opposition, as often these studies assume. They constitute demonstrable explanations for state terror, but they do not address the underlying cause. If the position is that the use of terrorism is inherent in the state, moreover, the question remains about the nature of a system that makes terrorism intrinsic to its operation.

SYSTEMIC TERROR

The argument here is that all state-dominated social formations inherently reflect and generate the conditions that require terror against their own members, to varying degrees given the circumstances, and that the state engages in terrorist activities as a matter of course while defending the dominant interests at home and abroad. Terrorism, it is suggested, is endemic to all class-based social systems; it is both implicit and explicit in the normal systemic processes of these social formations. To reiterate, terror is but a tactic, and while its use varies, it is always a significant means of maintaining social control in a system characterized by chronic antagonisms. While the state is its most visible perpetrator, the state merely represents and defends the root of terror that lies in the nature of the prevailing property relations and in the social structures that embody them.

Contemporary capitalist society is characterized by the separation of state and civil society. Here civil society includes the classes, groups, religions, clubs, individuals and, most importantly, corporations and trade unions, among other organized interests. Relations between these components of civil society are based on possession of private property — individual, but mainly corporate — and are exclusive, competitive and conflictual. These relations constitute capital and labour markets and are the principal means of allocating resources in a capitalist society. The state is the institutional representative of the prevailing property relations and associated conflicts that define civil society. It is the mechanism by which the dominant relations of private property are formally delineated, maintained, defended and advanced, and the related conflicts contained. The state, however, can also be made, wholly or partially, an alternative mechanism for allocating resources.

To maintain the market as the key mechanism for distributing goods and services (that is, through prices), and therefore to maintain its separation from the state, civil society must be kept divided against itself. Neither the capitalist nor working classes can be allowed to become a coherent whole lest it challenge the operation of the market or the role of the state.

Capitalism is dynamic, however, and the logic of competition that marks its development leads inexorably to its opposite, that is, forms of monopoly. It evolves progressively, diminishing the differences between the various and often-competitive strata of the working class and concentrating and centralizing the aggregations of capital. The two principal components of civil society move according to the logic of the system itself, each in the direction of greater coherence. Both sides become over time more monolithic in their interests.

While the state makes efforts to maintain the divisiveness on both sides — anti-trust/combination laws for corporations and anti-union laws for the working class — it is a capitalist system that it oversees. To inhibit the tendency toward monopolization restrains the development of the system itself. Mergers and acquisitions, cartelization, oligopolies, market sharing, price fixing and so on cannot be significantly curtailed without affecting the process of capital accumulation. As the unity of capitalists grows and expands globally, the role of the state becomes less concerned with managing inter-capitalist relations and more with restraining the growth of a monolithic power and interest in the working class, the main systemic challenge to the capitalist class. A system defined by class contradictions and exploitation in civil society, a system overseen and maintained by a not-disinterested state, is also defined by terror — of the market and the state.[4]

Terrorism of the Markets
It is difficult to grasp marketplace society as intrinsically terrorist because it is the normal state of affairs. For the citizens of modern industrial societies, the markets in capital and labour create a chronic but implicit state of intimidation that coerces them to act and think in certain defined ways. Because this fear is immanent and

systemic, it is experienced as ordinary and natural. To understand this terrorism, then, one has to "problematize" normalcy.

In civil society, terror is an inherent characteristic of the labour and capital markets. As competitive mechanisms, they are defined by supply and demand, over which there is only limited control, and they allocate social resources while providing the main avenue for the accumulation of wealth, always unequally. Markets are by definition "imperfect," that is, they always present unequal access and offer unequal advantages for some over others; there is no such thing as a market of equal competitors, and there are always winners and losers. Conceptualizing the market as terrorist means recognizing that participation in society for workers and corporations is through competitive processes over jobs and other contracts, more or less outside individual or political control. The uncertain outcome for workers translates into greater or lesser access to the means of life, and for corporations more or less accumulation of capital. Failure in the market can mean bankruptcy or mergers for corporations, and for workers the denial of the very means of life. It can mean the end of participation in society as marketplace with all the implications of unemployment. To avoid these fates, both workers and corporations often feel obliged to compete without morality, compelled to advance the accumulation process at any cost.

Terrorism is implied not only in the very operation of a market, but also in the fact that markets follow cyclical patterns. They are always in flux, developing through periodic economic booms and slumps that provide a backdrop of intimidation to the system as a whole. The inevitability of recurring economic crises in a market system, with the attendant bankruptcies and unemployment, creates a permanent sense of insecurity and uncertainty about sources of revenue and future prospects. The terror of the possible loss of livelihood on all sides hangs over the whole system. Again, the effect is compulsion to work harder to accumulate and to act unscrupulously in an effort to avoid becoming a victim of economic crisis.

The labour market, moreover, has never provided full employment; it has always precluded a certain percentage of the labour force from work, whatever the trend in the business cycle. The terrorism here lies in the chronic failure to provide for some, and the periodic inability to provide for many, that stand as warnings for all. The one constant in the labour market is the possibility of being excluded from access to the means of life. For the worker the threat of joining the unemployed is always present, and the effect of this threat is to modify behaviour, producing compliance with the goals of the system.

Because it is defined in part by competition between workers, the labour market becomes the breeding ground for all sorts of attempts to establish preferential treatment. The working class turns on itself, or is turned on itself, with individuals, groups, strata, unions or regions, searching for means to gain advantages over another. Racism, bigotry, sexism, ethnocentrism, nationalism and individual disparagement all become instruments to create a privileged status in the market. They all result in increased market terror for the targets of discrimination who, by virtue of skin colour, religion, gender, ethnicity, strata and so on face a socially constructed disadvantage in competition, a disadvantage often confirmed in discriminatory laws (Vann Woodward 1974; Allen 1994; Myers 1960).

The corporation alone, moreover, possesses the right to work in that it owns the means of production and distribution. Management controls who works and when and at what. The worker has some control at the point of production, through knowledge, skill and experience, but these characteristics are not generally peculiar to an individual or group, and only when controlled by a union of some sort do they usually become an advantage to labour. If the right to work is a prerogative of capital, the worker has the right *not* to work, but this is less a right than a prescription for poverty and deprivation. The terrorism implicit in corporate control over the right to work lies in the consequent managerial power to dismiss individuals, control pensions, impose mass layoffs and plant closures, and the threat to the worker of unemployment, potential social death and impoverishment.

If subordinating access to the means of life to markets is intrinsically a framework of terror, then any use of the market carries similar implications. Access to the justice system in capitalist nations, for example, is for the most part dependent on legal representation as private property. This places access beyond the reach of many and always subject to one's financial status, which also subverts the purported equity of the legal system itself. Similarly, a medical system that is subordinated to private property makes access to health care dependent on individual financial resources, with the attendant fear of personal bankruptcy and impoverishment as a result of a medical condition. Without state assistance, moreover, old age, illness, accidents, pregnancy, handicaps and so on, all can subject individuals to the terror of the markets.

After World War II, both the effects of markets and the conflict at the point of production in industrial nations were somewhat mitigated. In these countries, the realization of trade union rights and degrees of state intervention ensured that the worst of these market effects were not so severe as to undermine the legitimacy of the system. Trade union reduction of labour competition, state regulation of markets and a set of social security policies and programs, however, are contradictions in a capitalist system where unmitigated economic relations allow for maximization of profits and in theory are supposed to have positive results for all. In reality, the alleviation of market terror for workers came only with unionization and state intervention.

Increasingly, global labour markets operate without the restrictions of trade union representation or the protection of enforced social reforms. The terrorism implicit in labour markets is being given new life in the era of global accumulation (Giroux 2004).

Terrorism by the State
From the sixteenth to the eighteenth centuries, before modern industrial capitalism, European mercantilist states played a significant economic role in providing the foundation of the capitalist mode of production. Acts of violence on a colossal scale were perpetrated in order to transform the wealth of "national" as well as "foreign" lands into capital and the inhabitants into workers. From the domestic enclosure movements or "clearances" and related work and vagrancy laws to the violence of the colonization process and its forced labour, the state played a largely terrorist role (Polanyi 1944; Rodney 1981; Davis 2001; Elkins 2005; Hochschild 1999). Such activities of the state continue today wherever the capitalist mode of production has not yet been fully established.

Once industrial capitalism and the modern liberal democratic state had been established, different forms of state terror were developed. These states are defined by the principle of the rule of law. It not only guards market relations and so perpetuates the instability of competition, but it also has brought a degree of security from state arbitrariness. All such states, however, possess the constitutional right of exception to this principle in the form of so-called "official secrets," "reasons of state," "state of emergency," "national interests," forms of "constitutional dictatorship" (Rossiter 1963; Galnoor 1977) and, more recently, "anti-terrorist laws" (Cole and Dempsey 2002; Chang 2002; Brown 2003). State arbitrariness is itself intimidating, but in the form of legal exceptions, police impunity, or emergency statutes, it carries the element of fear to the whole system.

Even the normal functioning of the law has a terrorizing effect. Criminal law, for instance, by and large stands as a bulwark for the economic inequalities that result from a system of private property. In fact, the legal system as a whole presents itself as a coercive force in defence of unequal access to the necessities of life. Many other laws are intended to keep the working classes from combining to challenge the system. The existence of such constraining laws intimidates those who would seek to organize or protest even within the constraints set out within the law (Panitch and Swartz 1993; Moody 1999).

Besides the law itself, there is the legal and illegal use of police in harassment, assassinations, beatings, unwarranted searches, arrests and incarcerations, espionage, sabotage, infiltration, blackmail and so on. Most groups or individuals who have dared to offer a serious critique of the status quo or worked to unite parts of civil society and possibly challenge the prevailing property relations have met with various levels of intimidation by law enforcement officials striving to maintain the divisiveness of civil society (Mackenzie 1997; Blackstock 1975; Chester 1985; Gelbspan 1991; Goldstein 1978; Davis 1997; Johnson 1989; Nutter 2000; Wise and Ross 1964; Wise 1976).

The conscious non-enforcement of law or the non-prosecution of certain criminals also serves as a means to keep civil society divided against itself, allowing its component parts to sort themselves out according to what might be termed "the law of the jungle" (Jacobs 2006; Fitch 2006; Chavez and Gray 2004). Some laws promote the divisiveness of civil society, most obviously the gun ownership laws of the United States, which constitute one of the foundations of pervasive fear in U.S. civil society and a powerful mechanism by itself to control the working class. On a global scale, the vast sales of small military weapons perform a similar role.

The state can also manipulate the degree to which the markets affect the working class. By increasing or decreasing the extent of social reforms, the state can raise or lower the disciplinary impact of the market on the working class. In other words, the state can manipulate the degree of terrorism of the market in order to achieve certain desired effects. The limits on unemployment insurance, for instance, are managed for this purpose; immigration policy can be manipulated to increase competition and lower wages; and the promotion of a private medical system, subordinating health care to the market, to the demands of profit maximization, creates employee passivity where medical insurance is attached to a job and chronic fear where it is not affordable (Moynihan and Cassels 2005; Griffith, Iliffe and Rayner 1987; Andrews 1995; Doyal 1979).

The Great Depression of the 1930s plunged capitalist nations into one of the longest and most serious periods of market terror yet experienced. To contain social unrest, all the industrial states attempted to further institutionalize class conflict, to restrict civil liberties, to introduce extra-market reforms, to launch anti-communist fear campaigns and to employ the police and the courts in more systematic oppression. In Italy and Germany, where the effects of World War I created social upheaval, the growing power of the socialist and communist parties was kept in check by the corporate financing of political parties and leaders that employed terrorism as their stock in trade (Guerin 1973; Salvemini 1973; Brady 1937).

No controlling agency or institution can ignore the importance of ideas in maintaining power — and in instilling terror. The state must promote a set of ideas that fashions a common understanding and acceptance of the prevailing form of property relations, their reproduction and consequences. Unquestioning obedience to secular authority, a belief in a spiritual power, the notion of predestination, the idea of meritocracy and the belief in a genetic basis to ethnic differences are some of the ideas that support the hierarchical and authoritarian relations necessary to maintain the status quo. Implicit in these ideas are elements of intimidation; they are beliefs that constrain behaviour by means of real or imagined fears of one sort or another or acceptance of what is deemed to be ordained.

The ideas of socialism and communism have always been a threat to the ideas that complement capitalism. After World War II, the Cold War, in part a war of ideas, was employed to challenge the promise of socialism and its reality abroad. In the U.S., a wave of anti-communism was given free rein by Congress and the courts in the late 1940s and 1950s. This propaganda was aimed at bringing critical intellectuals and the working classes, living with the terror of an unpredictable labour market and the memory of its failure in the 1930s, into line with U.S. post-war ambitions. Anti-communist sophistry had several purposes: to demonize the U.S.S.R. and the Peoples' Republic of China as possible alternative economic models, to mask U.S. interventions around the world (countering either struggles for socialism or liberal democratic governments espousing nationalism or reformism), to provide the rationale for the military-industrial complex, and to undermine state intervention designed to regulate or de-commodify the markets.[5] For their ideas and principles, scores of U.S. citizens were sent to jail, some committed suicide, thousands lost their jobs and were socially ostracized and harassed, and many more thousands lived in fear of arbitrary dismissal and ostracism. More than a decade of anti-communist witch-hunts went a long way to instilling fear over one's beliefs and undermining the credibility of socialism, not to mention associated organizations (Caute 1978; Schrecher 1986, 1998; Price 2004).[6]

Terrorism has not been confined to systems of market capitalism. The coming of the first socialist state in 1918 expanded the necessity for using terror. The Bolsheviks employed revolutionary terror in their first couple of years of existence to ensure their survival in the face of civil war and intervening Western armies (Trotsky 1961; Isitt 2011). They also used terror to consolidate their rule and collectivize property over the first decade, and from the late 1920s until his death in 1953, Stalin used terror as a means of maintaining his personal power over the regime. A state capitalist system, parading as socialist, without the chronic pervasive terror of the markets, must lean towards other mechanisms for social control. Given the lack of workers' control and the monopoly of capital by the state, the police state is one of the few answers to questions of legitimacy.

During World War II, the use of terror was widespread, in particular by the Nazis and Japanese military. Slave labour, concentration (and death) camps, widespread indiscriminate summary executions, collective punishment, "medical" experiments, systematic rape and prostitution of women and massive bombing of civilian targets were all part of their rule and methods of war. In certain measure, the Allied forces replied in kind with the bombing of non-military targets, particularly Dresden, Hamburg, Tokyo and then Hiroshima and Nagasaki (Garrett 2004; Lackey 2004). Historical comparisons are always problematic, but it is probably accurate to say that there were more innocent victims systematically annihilated in the six years of this war for the purpose of terrorizing one or the other side into capitulation than any comparable period in history.

Part of the explanation lies in the unprecedented degree to which science and technology were applied to the production of weaponry in this war. Applied science and technology also made possible the colossal acts of terror that ended the war — two bombs that leveled two cities and killed tens of thousands of civilians in an instant. The threat of atomic and later nuclear bombing with ballistic missiles became a terrorist tactic employed many times over by the United States — in Eastern Europe, Korea, Vietnam and Cuba — and a significant part of the general backdrop to the Cold War (Morgan 1996). It was one of the main pillars of the policy to contain socialism. The strategy of nuclear deterrence soon led to a nuclear arms' race, culminating in the policy of "mutually assured destruction" — MAD. The whole world was held in the grip of the possibility of nuclear annihilation; the civilian populations of the Soviet Union and the West were the stakes in this exercise in terror. Fear was palpable throughout the industrial world and systematically maintained lest any doubts be raised about the need for military expenditures (Prins 1983; Cox 1981; Lifton and Falk 1982).

Another significant use of terrorism after World War II was in the building of the "new world order," which included the process of de-colonization. In 1945, the largest part of humanity lived in European or American colonies or spheres of influence, but such nation-based structures had to be dismantled to accommodate U.S. designs for expansion and the globalization of capital (Fann and Hodges 1971; Magdoff 1969). The problem was how to allow for independence from colonial or imperial rule while keeping the newly independent countries within the orbit of global capital. This dilemma was addressed with military coups, fomented civil wars, mass arrests, assassinations, the outlawing of socialist, communist and even nationalist parties, the suppression of human rights even as they were being declared by the U.N., the development of counterinsurgency warfare, coercive diplomacy, the expansion of torture, the creation of death squads, the promotion of arms sales and Western-created secret police forces and sponsored military and police training programs throughout the non-industrial world. In little more than two decades after World War II, many millions were killed throughout Asia, Africa and Latin America by the United States and European colonial powers in an attempt to forestall the struggle for independent national development or socialism in these countries (Blum 1998, 2000).

More indirect means were also applied to keep these nations tied to the emerging global capitalist system, in the form of economic terrorism. Although many forms of coercion fall into this category, the main instruments have been the policies of the IMF and World Bank. Through a variety of mechanisms, dependent countries were indebted to these institutions and quickly found that increasing indebtedness carried obligations that led, in effect, to the near-suspension of their capacity to determine economic development independently. The policies imposed called for the reduction of state activities, including subsidized health care, education, social reforms, assistance to agriculture and national industries, and the building of infrastructure for civilian benefit. All the policies implied a set of broader objectives: the use of the national state to prevent national or "mixed-economy" policies, to reduce wages, to provide open access to foreign investment and to promote commodity exports. No longer were there colonial or imperial administrations; now global institutions, the IMF and World Bank, GATT and then the World Trade Organization, were to enforce the rules of a skewed market in the new world order. The consequences included a reduction in standards of living, food riots, the loss of a self-sufficient national agricultural base, the denial of national aspirations, the perpetuation of illiteracy and poor health, the destruction of pre-capitalist modes of production and the consequent displacement of millions, and a constant "brain drain" to the metropolitan countries (Perkins 2004; Payer 1974; Hayter 1971; Walton and Seddon 1994). The terror of a highly skewed global market was imposed by the IMF and World Bank.

Liberal Democracy and Terrorism

Liberal democracy as a political system is rarely if ever understood as related to terrorism, but there is a relation. Above all, liberal democracy legitimizes the state that oversees the framework for market terror. Because the state is understood as democratically elected, it is seen as beyond the use of terror, indeed as the embodiment of the very opposite method for achieving political goals. This legitimacy suggests it is a defender — not a violator — of rights and the rule of law. Liberal democracy, however, is a form of governance restricted to alternations in power of a small range of parties, within a framework of corporate private property; it is not direct democracy by and for the working majority. The democracy in question does not countenance parties or movements that advocate the abolition, or seriously challenge the operation, of the market as the chief means of allocating social resources.

What parades as the rule of the people is a mechanism for changing political parties through periodic elections, which merely alternates the management of the relations of corporate private property. Its form allows it to appear to be a process of mass decision-making, and so it serves to placate opposition to the system, while providing the framework for rule by market forces. For this reason, the forms of liberal democracy have been used to replace, and then excuse and paper over, the terrorism of bankrupt dictatorships *and* to provide the apparent voluntary acceptance of the unseen and less contentious terrorism of the market (Herman and Brodhead 1984).

When advancing corporate interests abroad, these same industrial states defined as liberal democratic are, and have been, by far the leading practitioners of terrorism. In the postwar era, moreover, most of the dictatorships and authoritarian governments throughout the Third World have been largely a product of economic or military interventions by the industrial liberal democratic states (Blum 1998, 2000; Fann and Hodges 1971; Chomsky 1992; McGowan 2000).

Liberal democracy also obscures the terror of the market and state in that it makes it possible to exercise a limited popular leverage over public policy to exact modest social reforms. These reforms, promulgated under pressure to secure the political support of working people, provide a certain relief from the terror of the marketplace by "de-commodifying" aspects of life. Publicly funded medical care, old age pensions, unemployment insurance, disability pensions, education, utilities and so on, go far to bolster the legitimacy of the system if only because they counter some of the effects of the market and attest to a limited influence of the working class within the system via liberal democracy.

A system that gains its legitimacy by appearing to give popular control over corporate capitalism, and by allowing for certain policies that contradict its very principles, is a system whose legitimacy exists but is illusory. Indeed, it is respected by the powers that be only as long as it provides social control and conditions conducive to capital accumulation. When it no longer performs these functions, the corporate sector does not hesitate to take arbitrary, brutal authoritarian measures.

THE AGE OF TERRORISM

When Washington declared in 2002 that, with its "unequalled … strength and influence in the world" (White House 2002), the "war on terrorism" would be fought unilaterally if necessary and would be of "uncertain duration" against an "elusive enemy," the vision was not that of one particular administration. The evidence suggests that this declaration announced the coming end of the age of liberal democracy and national capitalism.

Globalization

As long as the state and civil society remained national, unemployment limited and material betterment a hope, the legitimacy of national governments could be maintained. As the site of capital accumulation shifted progressively to regional and global levels, however, national markets have been increasingly subordinated to the transnational. As a consequence, the role of the national state has been subverted by the creation of supranational quasi-state structures and agencies designed to regulate larger markets. Not only do these markets operate largely beyond the jurisdiction of national governments, but they also require policies to facilitate the increasingly supranational accumulation of capital.

These neo-liberal policies have an impact on the legitimacy of liberal democracy, which is invariably national. If the traditional powers and roles of the national state are increasingly usurped or overshadowed by these supranational policies and institutions, it gradually becomes evident to the citizenry that the electoral process is losing its meaning. When national policies are broadly determined at other levels, national officials find it ever more difficult to pretend that government policies are representative of popular or national interests. Legitimacy, grounded in the supposed consent of the governed, begins to wane.

Legitimacy also begins to falter for another reason. Neo-liberal policies are designed to maximize corporate control of social reproduction, in part through the process of privatization and de-regulation of the public sector. The expansion of the market, a euphemism for increased control by private corporations, is made the principle and practice of state policy, and thus pressure builds to retrench social reforms, to undermine the policies and programs that alleviate the worst consequences of the market. The terror of the market and of corporate monopoly over the right to work is promoted vigorously in practice and as ideal. Legitimacy, based on social reforms, increasingly comes into question.

End of the Cold War (or Peace as a Problem)
Criticism of market terror has been countered by suppressing the idea and promotion of possible alternatives to a market-based economy, in theory and practice. In part, portraying markets as the bastion of civil and political freedoms has obfuscated their inherent terror, while their antithesis, socialism or communism, has been painted as the epitome of evil. Anti-communism has been widely used to attack even capitalist national development projects in the developing world. In domestic politics, it has served as a means to denounce state provision of socialized services and interventions into the economy. Cold War anti-communism was also the principal means for legitimating the postwar arms' race, helping to convince the populations of the West to support massive expenditures for arms. The vilification of the Soviet Union and its connection to ever-greater arms production reached a nadir in the 1980s with U.S. President Reagan's campaign against the "evil empire."

Anti-socialist propaganda was made easier by the fact that most examples of socialism as it actually existed had been perverted into forms of dictatorial rule that allowed little if any workers' control. Revelations about the prison gulags, political trials, suppression of rights and political dissent, cultural conformity, mass deaths and pervasive surveillance went a long way to undermine popular interest in the idea of socialism. Nevertheless, struggles against the status quo in the West continued to grow during and after these revelations, along with interest in alternative modes of production — all testaments to the negative effects of global capitalism and desire for people's control over the market (Miliband, Saville and Liebman 1984).

The use of anti-communist rhetoric, of course, came more or less to an end with the 1991 demise of the U.S.S.R. and the earlier Chinese policy shift to the "capitalist road." This moment in history engendered hope for what was widely called the "peace dividend," the idea that with the end of the ostensible reason for vast military expenditures, these funds could be shifted to programs intended to improve the lot of humankind.

Discussion of the "peace dividend" was short lived, however. Even with the demise of state capitalism, world peace was impossible. Global capital creates and depends on inequality, and the iniquitous relations produced by capitalism the world over continue to motivate resistance and critical analysis. To maintain and expand these global relations, military spending had to be sustained and even increased.

Now, however, one of the main ideological weapons for social control was lost. Globalization, moreover, was calling into question the legitimacy and viability of national liberal democracy. Because of this loss and the emerging global economy, in an era when peace remained impossible, a new rationale was needed to obfuscate growing global inequity and justify increased military spending. The threat of terrorism — a sort of generic source of fear, a threat whose content is discretionary — presented itself as the only option available to Washington, not to mention the other industrial powers.

Anti-communism and anti-terrorism are very similar in many ways; indeed, they have often been employed interchangeably. Both have been used to instill fear in a population in order to galvanize it and suppress criticism, to support continued military spending and to rationalize the defence of corporate private property. Both have also been used to undermine the rule of law and constitutional practices in support of the primacy of corporate right.

The difference between the anti-communism of the Cold War era and the "war on terrorism" today is that the Cold War was an attempt to defend one system from encroachments by another, to maintain — albeit by fear — the loyalty of a citizenry to a liberal democratic system that was still viable and that reflected the interests of national capital. The anti-terrorism of post-9/11 is an attempt to maintain social order in an era in which liberal democracy has no future, at least not as a national political system overseeing a national economy. As a generic undifferentiated label, moreover, anti-terrorism points to a grander emerging struggle: one between the representatives of global capital on the one hand, and the working people of the world on the other — a struggle that has yet to be completely distilled from the lingering existence of national systems.

CONCLUSIONS

In all social formations resting on systemic inequality, terror is an integral part of the system. In a capitalist society, the main source of terror lies in the operation of the markets. Here, terror is by and large implicit, an entrenched and largely unseen aspect of everyday life. Similarly, private corporate ownership of the means of production and distribution places the power of terror in the hands of those who manage and control the system. Terror, it follows, is not a deviation from the norm, but an inherent part of society as marketplace.

In order to maintain these market relations, the state works to facilitate their operation and to promulgate the laws, attitudes and practices conducive to a hierarchy of subordination. It must also guarantee the ongoing reproduction and subordination of the working class and enable the creation of a working class where it is, as yet, inchoate. These tasks are part of its necessary role in sustaining the conditions of capital accumulation, legitimizing the system, containing contested iniquitous relations and preventing subordinate classes and strata from coalescing. Global and regional quasi-states must perform similar functions to create the conditions for global capital accumulation.

The terrorism inherent in the system also derives from other sources. While non-state political, ethnic and religious organizations are often portrayed as the chief grounds of terror, they are far less significant than the market or the state. This is because they command far fewer resources, and because their influence, organization and power are invariably much smaller than those of the state or markets. Some of this terrorism may be a form of resistance to oppression, political exclusion, or intolerable conditions of various sorts, and spawned out of desperation. But any assessment of non-state terror as acts of resistance must be approached with skepticism because such groups have often been created and employed to discredit those in whose name the terror is done, because it is rare that such terror produces significant political change, and because that terror can easily be made the excuse for state repression and counter-terror.

Patriarchy, that pervasive assumption and practice of the primacy of male right, is also a significant source of terror, a terror experienced particularly by one-half of the population. Its terror for women lies in the arbitrariness of its assertion, its wide unconscious acceptance by both genders, and the relative powerlessness of its victims to respond in the face of a system framed by its assumptions.

The instrumental use of religion and ethnicity today and historically is also well known and needs no review here (Dreyfuss 2005; Grant 1960). With respect to contemporary terror, religion and ethnicity have been employed to obscure state violence and terror, to undermine the rule of law by the establishment of religious courts and decrees, to justify the occupation of territory and the displacement of millions, to perpetuate the subordination of women and a general hierarchy of obedience, and to rationalize the so-called "war on terrorism." Religious and ethnic terror are usually adjuncts to state and market terror.

The corporate-controlled media also plays a significant role. It provides views of the world and entertainment that conform to and endorse the values of capitalism. Its programming presents views of life through the lenses of violence, horror, suspense, war, misogyny and misanthropy. All contribute to a generalized sense of fear, a worldview that suggests humans are largely malevolent, self-interested, competitive, untrustworthy and dangerous. Much of what the media covers as news concentrates on the disastrous: fires, deaths, accidents, tragedies and natural catastrophes. It is a portrayal of uncertainty, lack of control, acts of gods, abandonment to the fates and generic violence — a world to be feared in which relief, if it can be found, lies in religion or the state. It does not portray these effects as those of government policies, priorities, omissions, or the ordinary workings of a system.

Terrorism cannot be the subject of a war because it is merely the generic term for a particular sort of practice that employs intimidation to achieve certain ends. It is not a belief or a phenomenon or an ideal or a goal that can be identified and fought for or against. Unlike the Cold War, this "war" has no identifiable enemy, except those defined by the powers that be. Here lies its usefulness and power; as a rhetorical device, it can be employed to embrace whatever groups or acts (including staged acts) a government decides to include, and made into the reason for state repression. A war on a certain practice without a specific goal can plausibly be seen as a mechanism for generating fear to disguise the imperatives of a new era.

The "war on terrorism" can credibly be understood as a "war *of* terrorism" (Herman 2004), a pretext to justify the undermining of national liberal democracy in a world that can no longer pretend to operate according to its former principles and practices. It can be seen as a "war" to help transform governance so that the limited control of a liberal democratic state is subordinated to the principles and practices of global markets. It can also be taken as the terrorism of a system needing to parade as if under threat, a perpetrator disguised as victim, in order to advance its interests. It can be understood as the terror of the global markets in search of an excuse to coerce the world into giving up what limited democratic controls exist in favour of submission to one freedom alone, the freedom of corporate private property.

Since 9/11, almost all the actions of the U.S. administration point to such a conclusion. In its domestic policies, it has systematically moved to protect corporations from prosecution, to grant them increased tax benefits, to boost military spending, to dismantle health and safety regulations, to reduce state welfare benefits, and to encourage market principles and practice wherever possible. In order to police the world, Washington has proclaimed a unilateral foreign policy, threatened pre-emptive strikes against countries or groups it deems a threat, intimidated the world with nuclear weapons, and declared its opposition to international rule of law by rejecting many international treaties and agreements. It has set up prisons around the world out of the reach of international law for the purposes of holding unknown numbers of unnamed detainees for indefinite periods and for undisclosed reasons — a fate beyond the rule of law and a warning to us all (Van Bergen 2005; *Washington Post* 2005).

Capital has moved beyond the stage of development that required governance in the form of liberal democracy; there can be no return to the twentieth century and the nation-state as the political shell of national capital. Increasingly, global and regional markets and their regulatory agencies prevail, without civil legitimacy. In their defence, Washington has declared a "global war" without an apparent end — a "long war" whose objectives and enemies are not identified. It is difficult to imagine a clearer example of global state terrorism to establish and maintain the hegemony of global markets.

Notes

1. The U.S. State Department uses the definition in Title 22 of the U.S. Code: "The term terrorism means premeditated, politically motivated violence perpetrated against noncombatant targets by sub-national groups or clandestine agents usually intended to influence an audience."
2. "Notably, 2004 was marked by progress in decreasing the threat from states that sponsor terrorism. Iraq's designation as a state sponsor of terrorism was formally rescinded in October 2004. Libya and Sudan took significant steps to cooperate in the global war on terrorism. Unfortunately, Cuba, North Korea, Syria, and, in particular, Iran continue to embrace terrorism as an instrument of policy" (U.S. State Department 2004, chapter 2).
3. The U.S. federal statutes define terrorism as "the unlawful use of force and violence against persons or property to intimidate or coerce a government, the civilian population, or any segment thereof, in furtherance of political or social objectives."
4. Under state capitalism (the former U.S.S.R. and Peoples Republic of China), the state maintained control of civil society by monopolizing its representation under the guise of an identity of interests — the state and party purportedly representing the interests of the workers. All the organizations and associations of civil society, then, were state or party controlled, denying the existence of civil society as distinct from the state. Terrorism in the U.S.S.R. and the PRC was employed to prevent a reality for civil society separate from the state, to maintain a monopoly of power for the state and ruling party, thereby maintaining the illusion of socialism, which was really socialized capital centrally controlled. They comprised forms of state capitalism premised on state ownership of the main means of production; the state and party controlled capital, and the workers continued as workers. The principal contradiction remained between labour and capital, although here the state as capitalist. Legitimacy was based on the provision of social

reforms and the pretence of democracy — both camouflaging a *de facto* class divide. This illusion of socialism, with the state as capitalist parading as representative of labour and workers without control of their own destiny could only be held together in the end as a police state, marked by pervasive terror.
5. None of this is to say that the U.S.S.R. and China should not be criticized for their repressive regimes that passed for socialism and the terror employed to maintain them. If socialism implies the subordination of the state to society, then these regimes are more appropriately seen as state capitalist. They did, however, represent significant social advancement for tens of millions of people. They never had the resources to spend on the military that the West did, and they never had the hundreds of military bases with tens of thousands of active military personnel around the world. For the West, the real danger they represented was two-fold. Their economic model as socialized and not private corporate capital was a threat but not nearly as much if it had been a genuinely worker-run economy; that is, state capitalism still left all the fundamental capitalist relations intact. The other main issue was the exclusion of their populations and resources from the global markets.
6. The anti-communism of the West met with an unwitting "confirmation" from the socialist states themselves. Among other issues, revelations about the crimes of Stalin in the mid-1950s, Russian troops in Hungary in 1956 and Czechoslovakia in 1968, the excesses of the "cultural revolution" in China roughly between 1966 and 1976, and the tyranny in North Korea were significant blows to the credibility of the idea of socialism, compounded by China's turn to capitalism in the 1970s and the collapse of the Soviet Bloc in the late 1980s. That "actually existing socialism" proved not to be genuine socialism does not negate the hope that the working classes saw in it as freedom from the insecurity and unfreedom of the market, from a system that did not embody their interests.

References

ACLU (American Civil Liberties Union). "Don't Spy on Me." <www.aclu.org/safefree/spyfiles/index.html>.
Ahmed, N.M. 2002. *The War on Freedom.* Joshua Tree: Tree of Life Publications.
____. 2005 *The War on Truth: 9/11, Disinformation, and the Anatomy of Terrorism.* Northampton, MA: Olive Branch Press.
____. 2007. *The London Bombings, An Independent Inquiry.* London: Duckworth.
Allen, T.W. 1994. *The Invention of the White Race, Volume One: Racial Oppression and Social Control* and *Volume Two: The Origins of Racial Oppression in Anglo-America.* London: Verso.
Andrews, C. 1995. *Profit Fever.* Monroe: Common Courage Press.
AVERT. 2008. "Wolrdwide HIV and AIDS Statistics." <avert.org/worldstats.htm>.
BBC News. 1999. "Health: Six Diseases Threaten the World." June 18. <news.bbc.co.uk/2/hi/health/371522.stm>.
____. 2004 "Iraq Death Toll 'Soared Post-war.'" October 29. <http://news.bbc.co.uk/go/pr/fr/-/2/hi/middle_east/3962969.stm>.
____. 2006. "Iraqi Civilian Deaths Shrouded in Secrecy." March 22. <news.bbc.co.uk/2/

hi/middle_east/4830782.stm>.
Blackstock, N. 1975. COINTELPRO: *The FBI's Secret War on Political Freedom*. New York: Vintage.
Blum, Wm. 1998. *Killing Hope, U.S. Military and CIA Interventions Since World War II*. Montreal: Black Rose Books.
____. 2000. *Rogue State*. Munroe: Common Courage Press.
Brady, R.A. 1937. *The Spirit and Structure of German Fascism*. London: Victor Gollancz.
Brown, C. (ed.). 2003. *Lost Liberties, Ashcroft and the Assault on Personal Freedom*. New York: The New Press.
Campaign Against Sanctions on Iraq. 1999. "Starving Iraq: One Humanitarian Disaster We Can Stop." March.
____. 2001. "U.N. Agency Reports on the Humanitarian Situation in Iraq." November.
Caute, D. 1978. *The Great Fear: The Anti-Communist Purge under Truman and Eisenhower*. New York: Simon and Schuster.
Chang, N. 2002. *Silencing Political Dissent*. New York: Seven Stories.
Chavez, L., and D. Gray. 2004. *Betrayal: How Union Bosses Shake Down Their Members and Corrupt American Politics*. New York: Crown Forum.
Chester, E.T. 1985. *Cover Network*. Armonk: M.E. Sharpe.
Chomsky, N. 1992. *Deterring Democracy*. New York: Hill and Wang.
Chomsky, N., and E.S. Herman. 1979. *The Washington Connection and Third World Fascism*. Boston: South End Press.
Cole, D., and J. Dempsey. 2002. *Terrorism and the Constitution: Sacrificing Civil Liberties in the Name of National Security*. New York: The New Press.
Corn, D. 2003. *The Lies of George Bush*. New York: Crown Publishing.
Cox, J. 1981. *Overkill*. Harmondsworth: Penguin.
Davis, J.K. 1997. *Assault on the Left*. Westport: Praeger.
Davis, M. 2001. *Late Victorian Holocausts: El Nino Farmers and the Making of the Third World*. London: Verso.
Dion, R. 1982. *Crimes of the Secret Police*. Montreal: Black Rose.
Doyal, L. 1979 *The Political Economy of Health*. Boston: South End Press.
Dreyfuss, R. 2005. *Devil's Game: How the United States Helped Unleash Fundamentalist Islam*. New York: Metropolitan Books.
Elkins, C. 2005. *Imperial Reckoning: The Untold Story of Britain's Gulag in Kenya*. New York: Holt.
Enders, W., and T. Sandler. 2002. "Patterns of Transnational Terrorism, 1970–1999: Alternative Time-Series. Estimates." *International Studies Quarterly*, 46.
Fann, K.T., and D.C. Hodges (eds.). 1971. *Readings in U.S. Imperialism*. Boston: Porter Sargent.
Fitch, R. 2006. *Solidarity for Sale: How Corruption Destroyed the Labor Movement*. New York: Public Affairs.
Galnoor, I. (ed.). 1977. *Government Secrecy in Democracies*. New York: Harper and Row.
Ganser, D. 2005. *NATO's Secret Armies: Operation Gladio and Terrorism in Western Europe*. London: Frank Cass.
Garrett, S.A. 2004. "Terror Bombing of German Cities in World War II." In I. Primoratz (ed.), *Terrorism: The Philosophical Issues*. London: Palgrave/Macmillan.

Gelbspan, R. 1991. *Break-ins, Death Threats and the FBI.* Boston: South End Press.
George, A. (ed.). 1991. *Western State Terrorism.* Oxford: Polity Press.
Giroux, H.A. 2004. *The Terror of Neoliberalism.* Aurora: Garamond.
Goldstein, R.J. 1978. *Political Repression in Modern America.* New York: Schenkman.
Gordon, J. 2002. "Cool War: Economic Sanctions as a Weapon of Mass Destruction." *Harper's Magazine,* November.
Grant, M. 1960. *The World of Rome.* London: Cardinal.
Griffin, D.R. 2004. *The New Pearl Harbor: Disturbing Questions about the Bush Administration and 9/11.* Norhampton, MA: Olive Branch Press.
Griffith, B., S. Iliffe, and G. Rayner. 1987. *Banking on Sickness.* London: Lawrence and Wishart.
Guardian. 2005. "One Huge US Jail." March 19.
Guerin, D. 1973. *Fascism and Big Business.* New York: Pathfinder.
Hayter, T. 1971. *Aid as Imperialism.* Harmondsworth: Penguin Books.
Herman, E.S. 2004. "The War of Terrorism." *Znet Commentary,* 11 (September).
Herman, E.S., and F. Brodhead. 1984. *Demonstration Elections: U.S.-staged Elections in Dominican Republic, Vietnam and El Salvador.* Boston: South End Press.
Hochschild, A. 1999. *King Leopold's Ghost.* London: Pan Macmillan.
Hudson, R., and Staff of the Federal Research Division, Library of Congress. 1999. *Who Becomes a Terrorist and Why: The 1999 Government Report on Profiling Terrorists.* Guildford, CT: Lyons Press.
Ignatieff, M. 2004. *The Lesser Evil: Political Ethics in an Age of Terror.* Toronto: Penguin.
Isitt, B. 2011. "Siberian Intervention." In Gordon Martel (ed.), *The Encyclopedia of War.* New Jersey: Wiley and Sons.
Jacobs, J.B. 2006. *Mobsters, Unions, and Feds: The Mafia and the American Labor Movement.* New York: New York University Press.
Johnson, L.K. 1989. *America's Secret Power: The CIA in a Democratic Society.* New York: Oxford University Press.
Krueger, A.B., and D.D. Laitin. 2004. "'Misunderestimating' Terrorism, The State Department's Big Mistake." *Foreign Affairs,* September/October.
LA Times. 2007. "Poll: Civilian Toll in Iraq May Top 1m." September 14.
Lackey, D. 2004. "The Evolution of the Modern Terrorist State: Area Bombing and Nuclear Deterrence." In I. Primoratz (ed.), *Terrorism: The Philosophical Issues.* London: Palgrave/Macmillan.
Laqueur, W. 1986. "Reflections on Terrorism." *Foreign Affairs,* Fall.
Lifton, R.J., and R. Falk. 1982. *Indefensible Weapons.* Toronto: CBC.
Mackenzie, A. 1997. *Secrets: The CIA's War at Home.* Berkeley: University of California Press.
Magdoff, H. 1969. *The Age of Imperialism.* New York: Monthly Review.
Marrs, J. 2004. *Inside Job, Unmasking the 9/11 Conspiracies.* San Rafael: Origin Press.
McCamant, J.F. 1984. "Governance Without Blood: Social Science's Antiseptic View of Rule; or, The Neglect of Political Repression." In M. Stohl and G.A. Lopez (eds.), *The State as Terrorist.* Westport: Greenwood Press.
McGowan, D. 2000. *Derailing Democracy.* Munroe: Common Courage Press.
Media Lens. 2007. October 3. <www.medialens.org>.
Miliband, R., J. Saville and M. Liebman. 1984. *Socialist Register 1984: The Uses of*

Anti-Communism. London: Merlin Press.
Moody, K. 1999. *Workers in a Lean World: Unions in the International Economy*. London: Verso.
Morgan, D. 1996. "Threats to Use Nuclear Weapons: The Sixteen Known Nuclear Crises of the Cold War, 1946–1985." <www.vana.ca/articles/threatsofwar.html>.
Moynihan, R., and A. Cassels. 2005. *Selling Sickness*. Vancouver: Douglas and McIntyre.
Murtha, J. 2006. "Iran and al-Qaeda Benefit from U.S. in Iraq." *Reuters*, March 5.
Myers, G. 1960. *History of Bigotry in the United States*. New York: Capricorn Books.
Neumann, F. 1957. *The Democratic and Authoritarian State*. London: Free Press.
Neumann, S. 1965 *Permanent Revolution*. New York: F.A. Praeger.
Nutter, J.J. 2000 *The CIA's Black Ops*. Amherst: Prometheus.
Palango, P. 1994. *Above the Law*. Toronto: McClelland and Stewart.
____. 1998. *The Last Guardians: The Crisis in the RCMP*. Toronto: McClelland and Stewart.
Panitch, L., and D. Swartz. 1993. *The Assault on Trade Union Freedoms*. Toronto: Garamond Press.
Parry, R. 2006. "George W. Bush Is a Liar." April 14. <http://www.consortiumnews.com/2006/041306.html>.
Payer, C. 1974. *The Debt Trap, The IMF and the Third World*. Harmondsworth: Penguin Books.
Perkins, J. 2004. *Confessions of an Economic Hit Man*. San Francisco: Berrett-Koehler.
Polanyi, K. 1944. *The Great Transformation*. Boston: Beacon Press.
Porteous, T. 2006. "The Al Qaeda Myth." April 12. <http://www.tompaine.com/articles/2006/04/12/the_al_qaeda_myth.php>.
Price, D.H. 2004. *Threatening Anthropology: McCarthyism and the FBI's Surveillance of Activist Anthropologists*. Durham: Duke University Press.
Prins, G. (ed.). 1983. *Defended to Death*. Harmondsworth: Penguin.
Radosh, R. 1968. *American Labor and U.S. Foreign Policy*. New York: Random House.
Rampton, S., and J. Stauber. 2003. *Weapons of Mass Deception*. New York: Penguin.
Rodney, W. 1981. *How Europe Underdeveloped Africa*. Washington, D.C.: Howard University Press.
Rollings-Magnusson, Sandra. 2009. *Anti-Terrorism: Security and Insecurity after 9/11*. Halifax and Winnipeg: Fernwood Publishing.
Rosand, E. 2003. "Security Council Resolution 1373, the Counter-Terrorism Committee, and the Fight Against Terrorism." *The American Journal of International Law*, 97, 2.
Rossiter, C. 1963. *Constitutional Dictatorship, Crisis Government in the Modern Democracies*. New York: Harcourt, Brace and World.
Rubin, M. 2001 "Sanctions on Iraq: A Valid Anti-American Grievance?" *Meria Journal*, 5, 4 (December).
Sallot, J. 1979. *Nobody Said No.* Toronto: James Lorimer.
Salvemini, G. 1973. *The Origins of Fascism in Italy*. New York: Harper and Row.
Sawatsky, J. 1980. *Men in the Shadows*. Toronto: Totem Books.
Schrecher, E. 1986. *No Ivory Tower: McCarthyism and the Universities*. New York: Oxford University Press.
____. 1998. *Many Are the Crimes: McCarthyism in America*. New York: Little, Brown.
Sluka, J.A. 2000. "Introduction: State Terror and Anthropology." In J.A. Sluka (ed.), *Death Squad: The Anthropology of State Terror*. Philadelphia: University of Pennsylvania Press.

Stohl, M., and G.A. Lopez (eds.). 1984. *The State as Terrorist*. Westport: Greenwood Press.

____. (eds.). 1986. *Government Violence and Repression*. New York: Greenwood Press.

____. (eds.). 1988. *Terrible Beyond Endurance? The Foreign Policy of State Terrorism*. New York: Greenwood Press.

Tarpley, W.G. 2005. *9/11: Synthetic Terror — Made in the USA*. Joshua Tree: Progressive Press.

Tilly, C. 2005. "Terror as Strategy and Relational Process." *International Journal of Comparative Sociology*, 46, 1–2.

Trotsky, L. 1961. *Terrorism and Communism: A Reply to Karl Kautsky*. Ann Arbor: University of Michigan Press.

UNAIDS. 2008. "2008 Report in the Global AIDS Epidemic." <unaids.org/en/KnowledgeCentre/HIVData/GlobalReport/2008>.

U.S. State Department, Office of the Coordinator for Counterterrorism. 2000. *Patterns of Global Terrorism*. <www.state.gov/s/ct/ris/crt/>.

____. 2004. *Country Reports on Terrorism*. Ch. 2 and ch 4. <http://www.state.gov/documents/organization/45313.pdf>.

Van Bergen, J. 2005. *The New CIA Gulag of Secret Foreign Prisons: Why it Violates both Domestic and International Law*. <http://writ.news.findlaw.com/commentary/20051107_bergen.html>.

Vann Woodward, C. 1974. *The Strange Career of Jim Crow*. New York: Oxford University Press.

Walter, E.V. 1969. *Terror and Resistance*. New York: Oxford University Press.

Walton, J., and D. Seddon. 1994. *Free Markets and Food Riots: The Politics of Global Adjustment*. Cambridge: Blackwell.

Washington Post. 2005. "CIA Holds Terror Suspects in Secret Prisons." November 2.

____. 2007. "U.S. Holds 18,000 Suspects in Secret Prisons." April 15.

White House. 2002. *The National Security Strategy*. <http://whitehouse.gov/nsc/nss>.

WHO (World Health Organization). 1996. "The World Health Report 1996 — Fighting Disease, Fostering Development." <who.int/whr/1996/en>. <www.who.org/int>.

Wise, D. 1976. *The American Police State*. New York: Random House.

Wise, D., and T.P. Ross. 1964 *The Invisible Government*. New York: Random House.

Custom Textbooks from Fernwood Publishing

Custom textbooks are for instructors and professors who want to hand-select material for their students from every Fernwood Publishing title. Teaching a course on Indigenous social work? Labour unions in Canada? Racism and the law? We have content on a huge range of topics in the social sciences and humanities that can be combined to fit your course.

HOW IT WORKS

We will compile individual chapters from any title we've previously published and deliver a professionally printed and bound book to be used in your course. No photocopies, and no coiled binding. You need only provide us with the titles of the chapters from our books that you want to use. Because the material is already published by us, we can create these custom texts quickly and cost effectively.

You can browse our full title list on our website (www.fernwoodpublishing.ca) for more detailed information as well as the tables of contents, and we're happy to provide examination copies if you need a closer look.

If you have a course but you need some help with choosing material, please contact us at editorial@fernpub.ca.

THE FINE PRINT

We need at least six months notice prior to the course start date to create your custom textbook. The minimum number of students enrolled is 40. Retail price is based on the number of students enrolled in the course and length of the book.

For more information, please contact editorial@fernpub.ca.